D1285465

Science and the Arts

A Study in Relationships
from 1600-1900

Science and the Arts

A Study in Relationships
from 1600-1900

Jacob Opper

Rutherford • Madison • Teaneck
Fairleigh Dickinson University Press

Associated University Presses, Inc.
Cranbury, New Jersey 08512

Library of Congress Cataloging in Publication Data
Opper, Jacob, 1935–
    Science and the arts.

    Bibliography: p.
    1. Science and the arts. 2. Music—Philosophy and aesthetics.
NX180.S3066   700   70-178042
ISBN 0-8386-1054-4

*To John F. Spratt, my teacher and
friend, and to my mother and father,
without whose support and patience over
the years this work would not have been
completed.*

Printed in the United States of America

The author wishes to thank Walker and Company, New York, for
permission to quote from *A History of Biology* by Maurice Caullery.
Copyright © by Walker and Company. Reprinted by Permission of the
Publisher, Walker and Company, New York.

Contents

7

Preface

The following remarks are concerned with the current state of musicology, its methodological premises, and with epistemology in general.

Musicology, conceived as an autonomous, self-contained discipline, arose in the nineteenth century. Adopting the then-current positivistic methodology, with its exclusive attention on factual accuracy, objectivity, and descriptive fidelity, musicology made great strides in the reconstruction of the musical past. Indeed, the very refusal of most musicologists at this time to place music in a broader, historical-ideational context guaranteed the immense success of this discipline. This had to be so. Musicology, before proceeding to examine the relationship of music to other cultural phenomena, and before attempting to understand music in terms of a larger, integrated whole, had to acquire a sufficient amount of factual content in order to render this whole meaningful. It had to go through what Northrop terms "the natural history stage of inquiry," a stage which "begins with immediately apprehended fact and ends with described fact."[1]

It is with these epistemological premises that musicology has entered the twentieth century, dominating scholarly research even today, in the 1970s. There are signs, however, from recently written articles on method in musicology, and on epistemology in general, that the age of description has come to an end, and that a more comprehensive method of musical scholarship must be formulated. Or, more properly speaking, positivism, which regards music "as an almost isolated artistic world *per se*," must at least be complemented by an approach which views music as

---

1. F. S. C. Northrop, *The Logic of the Sciences and the Humanities* (New York: The Macmillan Company, 1947. Reprinted by The World Publishing Company, Meridian Books, New York, 1959), p. 35.

a manifestation of a larger mentality rooted in the world view of a given historical style-period. This is the express opinion found in a recent article by Ivo Supičić.

Supičić asserts that "the positive exploring of musical facts according to the most rigorous methods ought to be linked to a breadth of perspective and analysis that should also embrace extramusical facts associated with purely musical facts." This, however, it is pointed out, is hardly a novel approach, for the relationship between music and the other creative arts has been studied by such musicologists as Paul H. Lang, Curt Sachs, and Friedrich Blume, to mention the most prominent names. The weakness in the writings of these authors however, is the one-sided attention "to extramusical facts in neighboring arts, to the exclusion of science," a weakness traceable to the time-honored separation and opposition between the sciences and the humanities. In contrast to this, Edward E. Lowinsky, more than a quarter of a century ago, hoped to place music in a more comprehensive totality which would include science, or at least the philosophical implications of science. Music would then be considered

as one province in the vast realm of the human mind, which cannot be fully understood in isolation but only in constant comparison with the growth of human thought, seen as one single process though expressed in various media. . . . Also—and this is a more essential shortcoming— studies of this kind indulge too often in vague generalities. What we need, are studies dealing with specific problems of musical style and structure . . . and that examine with the same care and penetration *the basic trends of contemporary thought in their exact correspondence and relationship*. This procedure would lead us to a method that would reconcile technical analysis and interpretation instead of setting them up in opposition.[2] [Italics added.]

It is unimaginable, at least to this writer, for "the basic trends of contemporary thought" to be divorced from the philosophical implications of pure science, i.e., science as a theory of nature. The Report of the Harvard Committee on General Education in a Free Society, published in 1945, also holds the view that through the history and philosophy of science we gain "not only specific knowledge and skill, but conceptual interrelations, a world view, a view of man and knowledge, which together constitute the philosophy of science; a history which forms a continuous

---

2. Ivo Supičić, "Science on Music and Values in Music," *The Journal of Aesthetics and Art Criticism* 28 (Fall 1969):72; Lowinsky's statement quoted in *ibid.*: 72–73.

and important segment of all human history."[3] Unfortunately, observes Supičić with respect to Lowinsky's statement, recent trends in musicology have moved in the opposite direction in their quest for more "historical details." He continues, "the value of such research is unquestionable. What is questionable is the naïveté which believes that so much complex musical phenomena would be satisfactorily, sufficiently, and completely explained and understood exclusively in this manner."

The inadequacy of an exclusively positivisitic approach to musicology has also been noted by Robert E. Wolf. According to this writer,

> well-furnished as it is with knowledge of the techniques of the past, musicology still largely ignores past attitudes, *the psycho-philosophical climate* which made use of those techniques for an aesthetic end. Neither literary nor art historians are so indifferent to this significant tool; musicologists lag far behind their colleagues in parallel disciplines, and while the latter have . . . the advantage of dealing with—apparently—more "concrete" materials, musicologists need not abandon the quest because of the more "abstract" nature of their art.[4] [Italics added.]

The similarity between Lowinsky's "basic trends of contemporary thought" and Wolf's "psycho-philosophical climate" will be noticed here.

The method of musicology, in these terms, parallels in principle the epistemology of science, in the sense that science deals chiefly with causal explanation. In this respect, writes Treitler, to understand music "is to be able to *explain* it, and to *explain* a thing is to give its *causes*. Briefly, *understanding* is knowledge of *causes*."[5] (Treitler's italics.) In addition to such understanding, Supičić would also add an explanation of musical value and quality, features conspicuously absent in current musicological practice. What is needed is a continual interaction between the positivistic specialism of musicology and musicology conceived in terms of a broader historical and interdisciplinary context. Above all, musicologists, like any researcher, must be constantly vigilant in matters of basic epistemology if their work is to have

3. Quoted by Dorothy Stimson, "The Place of the History of Science in a Liberal Arts Curriculum," in Marshall Clagett, ed., *Critical Problems in the History of Science* (Madison, Wis.: The University of Wisconsin Press, 1959), p. 224.

4. Supičić, "Science on Music," p. 73; Wolf's statement, appearing in his "The Aesthetic Problem of the Renaissance," *Revue belge de Musicologie* 9 (1955): 3–4, quoted in *ibid.*, p. 84.

5. Leo Treitler, "On Historical Criticism," *The Musical Quarterly* 53 (April 1967): 190.

any relevance and viability. As Supičić declares, "it is necessary for the health of their work that historians of music and musicologists in general be more concerned with methodology."[6]

That an intolerable state has been reached in the narrow positivistic confines within which musicology has been operating until the present day may be gathered from the recently published "Guidelines for The Doctor of Philosophy Degree in Musicology," as prepared by the American Musicological Society. In the section entitled "Motivation and Objectives," Alexander Ringer describes musicology as "a field that has by and large been characterized by an unusually large degree of esotericism." To counteract this predicament, writes Ringer further, "the ultimate *objective* of musicology, as of all other humanistic fields of inquiry, must be a better understanding of man," i.e., it might be added, man as a culturally conditioned and as a natural animal.

> This is why auxiliary fields of inquiry . . . are often basic to the musicologist's concerns. In that same regard, the specialist in fifteenth-century secular music unfamiliar with the art, literature, philosophy, and general history of his period is ultimately as helpless as one approaching Polynesian music without the necessary anthropological and geo-historical preparation. While either may be able to discern to some extent what happened, and possibly how, these results manifestly fall short of the task. For it is understanding we seek; facts alone will not do.[7]

To the list of subjects which Ringer enumerates may be added such additional areas as neurophysiology, physical biology, studies in perception, gestalt psychology, cybernetics, and information theory; in short all those studies which deal with man as a natural being, studies which transcend man's particular cultural conditioning.[8]

The predicament in historiography in general is similar to the predicament in music history and musicology. Here also, it is noted by the French historian Marrou, an unmitigated positivism constitutes one of the dangers to human civilization. Marrou writes,

---

6. Supičić, "Science on Music," pp. 73–74.

7. First ed. (December 1969); prepared by the Committee on Curriculum and Accreditation by Alexander Ringer, Denis Stevens, and George J. Buelow, Chairman, p. 2.

8. For the incorporation of these areas in a recent investigation dealing with ethnomusicology and with Western music, see Gene F. Taylor, "Culturally Transcendent Factors in Musical Perception" (Ph.D. diss. The Florida State University, Tallahassee, 1969).

Our profession is burdensome, overwhelming us with technical servi-
tudes. It tends eventually to produce the mentality of the specialized
insect in those who are its practitioners. Instead of helping the scholar
to react against professional deformation, positivism gave him a quiet
conscience. . . . The scholar who makes use of a method when he knows
nothing of its logical structure, or who applies rules without knowing
how to gauge their efficacy, becomes like a worker who has charge of a
factory machine, controlling its operation but quite incapable of making
repairs—and even less able to construct it. We must sternly repudiate
any such attitude of mind because it constitutes one of the gravest dangers threatening the future of our Western civilization, already on the
verge of foundering in an atrocious technological barbarism.[9]

I have noted the inadequacy of an exclusively positivistic
method in musicology, music history, and historiography. What
has been said with respect to these provinces of knowledge may
be extrapolated to the humanities in general. Positivism *alone*
severely restricts our vision of the world and man's place in it.
That this is the case in cognitive processes in general, i.e., processes which also embrace scientific knowledge, has been disclosed
by such thinkers as A. N. Whitehead and, more recently, Michael
Polanyi. Polanyi's basic thesis is that knowledge, whether it be
in the humanities or in the sciences, must transcend mere factual
data in order to be meaningful. This transcendence he terms the
"tacit dimension" of knowing, meaning thereby that in any cognitive experience one always knows more than is expressible by
language or logical analysis. As Polanyi writes, *"we can know
more than we can tell."* An exclusive attention to purely factual
knowledge, or the mere "specification of particulars," on the
other hand, "may obscure beyond recall" the meaning of such
subjects as literature, history, or philosophy. And, generally
speaking, continues Polanyi, "the belief that since particulars are
more tangible, their knowledge offers a true conception of things
is fundamentally mistaken." That these observations are relevant
to both the humanities and the sciences is made clear by Polanyi's
criticism of nineteenth-century aestheticians Wilhelm Dilthey
and Theodor Lipps. Dilthey and Lipps made a distinction between the sciences and the humanities by declaring that only the
humanities can be properly understood by indwelling, or empathy
(a form of tacit knowing), whereas Polanyi's "analysis of tacit

9. Henri-Irénée Marrou, *The Meaning of History,* trans. Robert J. Olsen from
the originally entitled *De la connaissance historique* (Baltimore and Dublin:
Helicon Press, Inc., 1966), pp. 10–11.

knowing shows that they were mistaken in asserting that this sharply distinguished the humanities from the natural sciences. Indwelling, as derived from the structure of tacit knowing, . . . underlies all observation."[10]

Perhaps the clearest and most comprehensive critique of positivism is found in the writings of A. N. Whitehead. Such works as *Science and the Modern World, Adventures of Ideas,* and *Modes of Thought* are scattered with penetrating observations which disclose the fundamental weakness of this method. In *Modes of Thought,* for example, we find the following analysis of cognitive experience:

> Concentration of attention on sheer qualitative detail can result in consciousness of mere succession of such detail. For example, we record a red-and-green pattern succeeded by a blue-and-grey pattern, the experience being closed by a clear bell-like sound. There is a qualitative *subjective* experience. That and nothing more. The whole meaningless. This is the result of obtaining a clear-cut experience by concentrating on the *abstractions* of consciousness. [Italics added.]
>
> But we are conscious of more than clarity. The importance of clarity does not arise until we have interpreted it in terms of the vast issues vaguely haunting the fullness of existence.
>
> It is here that the prominent epistemology of the modern centuries has been so weak. It has interpreted the totality of experience as a mere reaction to an initial clarity of sensa. The result is that the reaction is limited to the data provided by the sensa.[11]

It is striking and ironic that what the positivists consider to be objective and concrete facts of experience, in their distinct clarity, are conversely regarded by Whitehead as mere subjective "abstractions of consciousness." On the contrary, the concrete objectivity for Whitehead is the totality of experience in terms of which the clear and distinct facts are to be interpreted.

The fatal weakness of positivistic epistemology has also been revealed in *Adventures of Ideas.* Here, in describing the transition from the Hellenic to the Hellenistic age, i.e., from the comprehensive type of knowledge cultivated by Plato and his Academy in Athens, to the departmental specializations at the university in Alexandria, Whitehead remarks, "the untroubled faith in lucidity within the depths of things, to be captured by some happy

10. Michael Polanyi, *The Tacit Dimension* (Garden City, N. Y.: Doubleday & Company, Inc., Anchor Books, 1967), pp. 4, 19, 17.

11. Alfred N. Whitehead, *Modes of Thought* (New York: The Macmillan Company, 1938. Reprinted by G. P. Putnam's Sons, Capricorn Books, New York, 1958), pp. 147–48.

glance of speculation, was lost forever. Duller men were content with limited accuracy and constructed special sciences." By no means does this imply that Whitehead advocates armchair speculation divorced from empirical evidence. On the contrary, he stands for the type of epistemology where "theories are built upon facts; and conversely the reports upon facts are shot through and through with theoretical interpretation."[12]

It is hoped that in the following pages Whitehead's demands, and the demands of authors noted previously, will, at least to some extent, be met.

12. Alfred N. Whitehead, *Adventures of Ideas* (New York: The Macmillan Company, 1933. Reprinted by The New American Library, Mentor Books, New York, 1959), pp. 103, 11.

Acknowledgments

I wish to express my gratitude to my friends and colleagues whose inquiring minds have provided the necessary stimulus in the completion of this work; to Albert C. Yoder for his numerous and invaluable bibliographic suggestions; to the Interlibrary Loan personnel of The Florida State University Library for their untiring assistance; to Mary L. Long for typing the final copy of the manuscript; to Rose Barber for rendering the music examples; and to Mathilde E. Finch, Editor-in-Chief, Scholarly Books, Associated University Presses, Inc., for introducing the final refinements into the manuscript, thus making the work more readable.

I am also deeply indebted to Dr. Sarah Herndon, to Dr. Victor R. B. Oelschlager, and to Mr. Owen F. Sellers, for their interest in the study and their perusal of the text.

Finally, my profound gratitude is extended to Dr. John F. Spratt, who is the ultimate source of the ideas and methods represented herein. It is hoped that his world view and his view of knowledge have been at least partially realized in the following pages.

The author wishes to express his gratitude to the following authors, publishers, and literary executors for their kind permission to reprint extracts from the copyrighted works listed below:

George Allen & Unwin Ltd., for extracts from *A History of Western Philosophy*, by Bertrand Russell, 1945; for an extract from *Number: the Language of Science,* by Tobias Dantzig, 1930; and from *Brahms: His Life and Works,* by Karl Geiringer, 1936.

The American Musicological Society, for extracts from: "The Concepts of Physical and Musicological Space in the Renaissance," by Edward E. Lowinsky, *Papers of The American Musicological Society—1941;* from "Principles of Form in Use From the Middle Ages to the Present Day," by Hans David, *Bulletin of The American Musicological Society* (1947); from the Review of Rudolph Reti's *The Thematic Process in Music,* by Alvin Bauman, *Journal of The American Musicological Society* (Summer 1951); and from "Guidelines for The Doctor of Philosophy Degree in Musicology," by Alexander Ringer, Denis Stevens, and George J. Buelow, 1st ed. (December 1969).

Appleton-Century-Crofts, New York, for an extract from *Faust,* Part I, by Johann W. von Goethe. Translated by Bayard Taylor, edited by B. G. Morgan. A Crofts Classic, reprinted by permission of Appleton-Century-Crofts, 1946.

The Architectural Record, New York, for extracts from "Organic Architecture," by Frank Lloyd Wright, March 1908. The extracts are taken from *The Humanities in Contemporary Life,* by Robert F. Davidson *et al.,* published by Holt, Rinehart and Winston, New York, 1965.

Bärenreiter-Verlag, Kassel, for extracts from *Das Werk Arnold Schönbergs,* by Josef Rufer, 1959; and for extracts from "Rameau, Jean-Phillipe," by Erwin R. Jacobi, and "Descartes, René," by Rudolf Stephan, in *Die Musik in Geschichte und Gegenwart,* edited by Friedrich Blume, 1949-1968.

Barrie & Rockliff Ltd., London, for extracts from *Constable Oil Sketches,* by John Baskett, 1966; and from *Composition with Twelve Tones,* by Josef Rufer, 1954.

Basic Books, Inc., Publishers, New York, for extracts from *The Beginnings of Modern Science,* vol. 2 of *The History of Science,* edited by René Taton, translated by A. J. Pomerans, 1964; and from "Scientific Background of Evolutionary Theory in Biology," by Maurice Mandelbaum, in *Roots of Scientific Thought,* edited by Philip P. Wiener and Aaron Noland, 1957.

Belmont Music Publishers, Los Angeles, for extracts from *Style and Idea,* by Arnold Schoenberg, 1950. Used by permission of Belmont Music Publishers, Los Angeles, California 90049. Originally published by The Philosophical Library, New York, 1950.

Breitkopf & Härtel, Wiesbaden, for extracts from *Clara Schumann—Johannes Brahms, Briefe aus den Jahren 1853-1896,* edited by Berthold Litzmann, 1927. With permission of Breitkopf & Härtel, Wiesbaden.

Curtis Brown, Ltd., New York, for extracts from *The Age of Ideology,* by Henry Aiken, 1956. By permission of Curtis Brown, Ltd.; Copyright © 1956 by Henry D. Aiken; and for an extract from *The Age of Reason,* by Stuart Hampshire, 1956. By permission of Curtis Brown, Ltd.; Copyright © by Stuart Hampshire.

The Bruckner Society of America, and its publication, *Chord and Discord,* for extracts from "The Cyclic Principle in Musical Design, and the Use of it by Bruckner and Mahler," by Warren S. Smith; *Chord and Discord,* vol. 2, no. 9 (1960).

Cambridge University Press, New York, for extracts from *Adventures of Ideas,* 1933 (reprinted by The New American Library, 1955), *Science and the Modern World,* 1925 (reprinted by The New American Library, 1959), and *Modes of Thought,* 1938 (reprinted by G. P. Putnam's Sons, 1958), by A. N. Whitehead; from *A History of Science and Its Relations with Philosophy and Religion,* 1943, and *A Shorter History of Science,* 1944, by Sir William C. Dampier; and from *The Philosophical Works of Descartes,* translated by E. S. Haldane and G. R. T. Ross, n.d. (reprinted by the Encyclopaedia Britannica in *Great Books of the Western World).*

Professor Jane P. Camp, for extracts from her "Temporal Proportion: A Study of Sonata Forms in the Piano Sonatas of Mozart." Doctoral dissertation, School of Music, The Florida State University, Tallahassee, 1968.

Professor Roy E. Carter, for extracts from his "Barock, by Friedrich Blume: a Translation." Master's thesis, The Florida State University, Tallahassee, 1961.

Chatto & Windus Ltd., London, for extracts from *The Seventeenth Century Background,* 1934, *The Eighteenth Century Background,* 1940 (reprinted by the Beacon Press, 1961), and *More Nineteenth Century Studies,* 1956 (reprinted by Harper & Row, 1966), by Basil Willey.

L. Herbert, 1964; from *From the Classicists to the Impressionists: A Documentary History of Art and Architecture in the 19th Century*, by Elizabeth G. Holt, 1966; from *The Tacit Dimension*, by Michael Polanyi, 1966; and from *Darwin's Century*, by Loren Eiseley, 1958.

Dover Publications, Inc., New York, for an extract from *A History of European Thought in the Nineteenth Century*, by John T. Merz, 1965; for an extract from *Liszt*, by Sacheverell Sitwell, 1967; and for extracts from *The History of Orchestration*, by Adam Carse, 1964.

Professor John M. Eddins, for extracts from his "A Study of Cartesian Musical Thought, with a Complete Translation of the Compendium musicae." Master's thesis, School of Music, The Florida State University, Tallahassee, 1959.

Encyclopaedia Britannica, Chicago, for extracts from the following Articles: "Goethe, Johann Wolfgang von," by Elizabeth M. Wilkinson; "Poussin, Nicolas," by Michael W. L. Kitson; "Novel," by Ian Watt; "French Literature," by Pierre-Georges Castex; and "Metamorphosis," by Ernest W. Mac-Bride and Vincent B. Wigglesworth, all from the 1964 edition.

The English Association, London, for an extract from "Tennyson and the Theory of Evolution," by William R. Rutland, in *Essays and Studies by Members of the English Association*, vol. 26, 1940.

Faber and Faber Ltd., London, for extracts from *The Thematic Process in Music*, by Rudolph Reti, 1968.

Farrar, Straus & Giroux, Inc., New York, for an extract from *Brahms*, by Peter Latham, 1949.

Victor Gollancz, Ltd., London, for extracts from *Darwin's Century*, by Loren Eiseley, 1958.

John Grant, Ltd., Edinburgh, for an extract from *Contingencies and Other Essays*, by Cecil Gray, 1947.

Harcourt Brace Jovanovich, Inc., New York, for extracts from *A General History of Music*, by Charles Burney, n.d.; from *Aesthetics: Problems in the Philosophy of Criticism*, by Monroe C. Beardsley, 1958; from *A History of Music and Musical Style*, by Homer Ulrich and Paul A. Pisk, 1963; and from *Modern Science and the Nature of Life*, by William Beck, 1961.

Harper & Row, Publishers, New York, for extracts from *Physics and Philosophy,* by Werner Heisenberg, 1962; from *Understanding Music,* by William S. Newman, 1961; and from *Realism and Nationalism,* by Robert C. Binkley, 1935.

Harvard University Press, Cambridge, for extracts from *Musical Form,* 1951, and from *Music, History, and Ideas,* 1964, by Hugo Leichtentritt; also from the *Harvard Dictionary of Music,* by Willi Apel, 1958.

Helicon Press, Inc., Baltimore, for an extract from *The Meaning of History,* by Henri-Irénée Marrou, 1966.

Holt, Rinehart and Winston, Inc., New York, for extracts from *Arts and Ideas,* 3d ed., by William Fleming, n.d.; from *The Humanities in Contemporary Life,* by Robert F. Davidson, et al., 1960; and from *The Prelude with Other Poems, and Three Essays on the Art of Poetry,* by William Wordsworth, edited by Carlos Baker, 1965.

Horizon Press, New York, for extracts from *The Future of Architecture,* by Frank Lloyd Wright, 1958; and from *Writings & Buildings,* by Frank Lloyd Wright, edited by Edgar Kaufmann and Ben Raeburn, 1960 (reprinted by Meridian Books, Inc., New York, 1960).

Houghton Mifflin Company, New York, for extracts from *The Human Use of Human Beings: Cybernetics and Society,* by Norbert Wiener, 1950; and from *The Making of the Modern Mind,* by John H. Randall, 1926.

Mrs. Humphry House, for an extract from "Man and Nature: Some Artists' Views," by Humphry House, in *Ideas and Beliefs of the Victorians,* E. P. Dutton & Co., Inc., New York, 1966.

Henry E. Huntington Library and Art Gallery, San Marino, Calif., for extracts from *Discourses on Art,* by Sir Joshua Reynolds, edited by Robert R. Wark, 1959. Reprinted with the permission of the Henry E. Huntington Library and Art Gallery.

Iowa State University Press, Ames, for extracts from *The Musical Symbol,* by Gordon Epperson. © 1967 by The Iowa State University Press; and from *The Death of Adam: Evolution and Its Impact on Western Thought,* by John C. Greene. © 1959 by The Iowa State University Press. Reprinted by permission.

Johnson Reprint Corporation, New York, for an extract from *Memoirs of the Life, Writings, and Discoveries of Sir Isaac Newton,* by Sir David Brewster, 1965. Reprinted by courtesy of Johnson Reprint Corporation, New York, New York.

ACKNOWLEDGMENTS   23

Journal of Aesthetics and Art Criticism, Detroit, for extracts
from "The Aesthetic Relevance of Belief," by Henry D.
Aiken, vol. 9 (1950); and from "Science on Music and
Values in Music," by Ivo Supičić, vol. 28 (1969).

Journal of Music Theory, New Haven, for extracts from "New
Theories of Form and the Problem of Thematic Identities,"
by Jan Nordmark, vol. 4 (1960).

Alfred A. Knopf, Inc., New York, for an extract from *Gustave
Courbet,* by Gerstle Mack, 1951.

Little, Brown and Company, Boston, for extracts from *Classic,
Romantic, and Modern,* 1963, and *Darwin, Marx, Wagner,*
1958, by Jacques Barzun.

Longman Group Limited, Harlow, for an extract from *History
and Philosophy of Science,* by Lewis W. H. Hull, 1959.

Louisiana State University Press, Baton Rouge, for extracts from
The Sacred River: Coleridge's Theory of the Imagination,
by James V. Baker, 1957; and from *Darwin and the Modern World View,* by John C. Greene, 1961.

Macdonald & Co. (Publishers) Ltd., London, for an extract
from *Brahms: The Man and His Music,* by E. Markham
Lee, 1916.

The Macmillan Company, New York, for extracts from *Number:
The Language of Science,* by Tobias Dantzig, 1930 (reprinted by Doubleday & Company, Inc., New York); from
Adventures of Ideas, 1933, *Science and the Modern World,*
1925 (Copyright renewed 1953 by Evelyn Whitehead; both
reprinted by The New American Library, New York), and
Modes of Thought, 1938 (reprinted by G. P. Putnam's
Sons, New York), by A. N. Whitehead; from *A History
of Science and Its Relations with Philosophy and Religion,*
1943, and *A Shorter History of Science,* 1944, by Sir William C. Dampier; also from *The Meeting of East and West,*
1946, and *The Logic of the Sciences and the Humanities,*
1947, by F. S. C. Northrop; from *The Musical Idea,* by
Walter Nallin, 1968; from *The Idea of Progress,* by J. B.
Bury, 1920; from *The Origins of Modern Science,* by H.
Butterfield, 1951; from *Body, Man, and Citizen,* by Thomas
Hobbes, Introduction by Richard S. Peters (© The Crowell-Collier Publishing Company, 1963); from *The Thematic
Process in Music,* by Rudolph Reti, 1968.

Macmillan & Company, Ltd., London, for an extract from *A
History of Melody,* by Bence Szabolcsi, 1965.

Professor Stephen F. Mason, for extracts from his "The Ideal of

Music in the Baroque Era, by Manfred F. Bukofzer, 1947; from *Music in the Renaissance,* 1954, and from *Music in the Middle Ages,* 1940, by Gustave Reese; from *Music in the Romantic Era,* by Alfred Einstein, 1947; from *A History of Western Music,* by Donald J. Grout, 1960; and from *Louis Sullivan: Prophet of Modern Architecture,* by Hugh Morrison, 1935.

Oxford University Press, New York, for extracts from *The Idea of History,* 1946, and from *The Idea of Nature,* 1945, by R. G. Collingwood; from *Mathematics in Western Culture,* by Morris Kline, 1953; from *A Study of History,* by Arnold J. Toynbee, abridged by D. C. Somervell; from *The Mozart Companion,* edited by H. C. Robbins Landon and Donald Mitchell, 1956; from *The Mirror and the Lamp: Romantic Theory and the Critical Tradition,* by M. H. Abrams, 1953; and from *Brahms: His Life and Works,* by Karl Geiringer, 1936.

Penguin Books, Ltd., Harmondsworth, for extracts from *Discourse on Method,* by René Descartes, translated by Arthur Wollaston, 1960; from *The Pelican Guide to English Literature IV: From Dryden to Johnson,* edited by Boris Ford, 1963; from *A Dictionary of Art and Artists,* by Peter and Linda Murray, 1963; and from *An Outline of European Architecture,* by Nikolaus Pevsner, 1961.

Praeger Publishers, Inc., New York, for extracts from *Color in Turner,* by John Gage, 1969.

Prentice-Hall, Inc., Englewood Cliffs, for extracts from *Music in the Classic Period,* by Reinhard G. Pauly, © 1965; and from *Our Musical Heritage: A Short History of Music,* by Curt Sachs, Second Edition © 1955. Reprinted by permission of Prentice-Hall, Inc., Englewood Cliffs, N. J.

Theodore Presser Company, Bryn Mawr, for extracts from Paul Badura-Skoda's Preface to the Fantasy in C Major ("Wanderer"), by Franz Schubert; Universal Edition (Vienna), 1965.

Princeton University Press, Princeton, for extracts from *The Philosophy of the Enlightenment,* by Ernst Cassirer, translated by Fritz A. Koelln and James P. Pettegrove (copyright 1951 by Princeton University Press; Princeton Paperback, 1968); reprinted by permission of Princeton University Press; from *Rousseau, Kant and Goethe,* by Ernst Cassirer, translated from the German by James Gut-

sented at the American Musicological Society Convention, South Central Chapter, March, 1968.

St. Martin's Press, Inc., New York, for an extract from *A History of Melody,* by Bence Szabolcsi, 1965.

Studio Vista Ltd., London, for extracts from *Color in Turner,* by John Gage, 1969.

Professor Gene F. Taylor, for extracts from his "Culturally Transcendent Factors in Musical Perception." Doctoral dissertation, The Florida State University, Tallahassee, 1969.

University of California Press, Berkeley, for an extract from *Theories of Modern Art: A Source Book by Artists and Critics,* edited by Herschel B. Chipp, 1968. Originally published by the University of California Press; reprinted by permission of The Regents of the University of California.

The University of Chicago Press, for extracts from *Emotion and Meaning in Music,* by Leonard B. Meyer (© 1956 by The University of Chicago); from *Harmony,* by Heinrich Schenker, edited and annotated by Oswald Jonas, translated by Elizabeth Mann Borgese (© 1954 by The University of Chicago); from *The Structure of Scientific Revolutions,* by Thomas S. Kuhn (© 1962 by The University of Chicago Press); and from *Movements of Thought in the Nineteenth Century,* by George H. Mead, edited by Merritt H. Moore (copyright 1936 by The University of Chicago).

University of Minnesota Press, Minneapolis, for an extract from Joseph W. Beach, *A Romantic View of Poetry.* University of Minnesota Press, Minneapolis © 1944 University of Minnesota.

University of North Carolina Press, Chapel Hill, for extracts from *The Sonata in the Classical Era,* 1963, and from *The Sonata in the Baroque Era,* 1959, by William S. Newman.

The University of Oklahoma Press, Norman, for an extract from *Johannes Brahms and Theodor Billroth: Letters from a Musical Friendship,* translated and edited by Hans Barkan. Copyright 1957 by The University of Oklahoma Press.

The University of Wisconsin Press, Madison, for extracts from "Biology and Social Theory in the Nineteenth Century: Auguste Comte and Herbert Spencer," by John C. Greene, and from "The Place of the History of Science in a Liberal Arts Curriculum," by Dorothy Stimson, both in *Critical*

Problems in the History of Science, edited by Marshall Clagett, 1959; also from *William Wordsworth: His Doctrine and Art in Their Historical Relations,* by Arthur Beatty (First Edition, 1922, and Second Edition, 1927, were published as Number 17 and Number 24 in the University of Wisconsin Studies in Language and Literature), 1960, 1962.

Professor Abraham Veinus, for an extract from his *The Concerto* (Doubleday, Doran & Co., Inc., 1945).

Walker and Company, New York, for an extract from *A History of Biology,* by Maurice Caullery. Copyright © 1966 by Walker and Company. Reprinted by Permission of the Publisher, Walker and Company, New York.

Professor J. W. N. Watkins, for extracts from his "Philosophy and Politics in Hobbes," in *Hobbes Studies,* edited by K. C. Brown (Basil Blackwell, Oxford, 1965).

Watson-Guptill Publications, New York, for extracts from *Constable Oil Sketches,* by John Baskett, 1966.

George Wittenborn, Inc., New York, for extracts from *Kindergarten Chats and Other Writings,* by Louis H. Sullivan, 1965.

The World Publishing Company, New York, for an extract from *A Treatise of Human Nature, Book I: Of the Understanding,* by David Hume, 1962.

Yale University Press, New Haven, for extracts from "The Rise and Impact of Evolutionary Ideas," by Robert Scoon, from "Naturalism in American Literature," by Malcolm Cowley, from "The Idea of Organic Expression and American Architecture," by Donald Egbert, and from "Evolution in its Relation to the Philosophy of Nature and the Philosophy of Culture," by F. S. C. Northrop, all in *Evolutionary Thought in America,* edited by Stow Persons, 1950; also for extracts from *A History of Modern Criticism: 1750-1950,* vol. 1, 1955, and from *Concepts of Criticism,* 1963, both by René Wellek.

The Yale Journal of Biology and Medicine, New Haven, for an extract from "The History of Modern Physics in Its Bearing Upon Biology and Medicine," by F. S. C. Northrop, vol. 10 (January 1938).

Introduction

The principal task of this study is, broadly speaking, to explore the relation between the natural sciences and the humanities during the eighteenth and nineteenth centuries. It is guided by the conviction that science as theory of nature plays a dominant role in determining the character of culture. More specifically it is argued that mathematical physics and its attendant epistemology infected all sectors of civilized thought in the eighteenth century, while the mental bent of the nineteenth century is derivative more from the life sciences and their peculiar methodology. The difference in subject matter between physics and biology is of obvious importance, accounting for the distinction between the root metaphor of the fixed clock, relevant to eighteenth-century cosmology, and the root metaphor of the evolving organism, pertinent to the nineteenth-century world view. More important and less obvious is the epistemological distinction, for it is the chiefly deductive method of the physical sciences which manifests itself in the mentality of the Enlightenment in such areas as philosophy, literature, music, and the visual arts. The same domains in the Romantic era, on the other hand, exhibit a mentality rooted in the immediate apprehension of fact and traceable to the primarily inductive method of biology.

Although the investigation is largely centered on the eighteenth and nineteenth centuries, temporal boundaries are of necessity not adhered to in a rigid manner. For example, reference is frequently made to Galileo and Descartes, whose mechanistic conception of nature in the seventeenth century was made more explicit in the same and succeeding centuries by Newton, Lagrange, and Laplace. In similar fashion the organismically oriented thought of the nineteenth century was most completely formulated in the following century by such men as Bergson and Whitehead.

29

Chapter 1 deals with the shift in the theory of nature from the eighteenth to the nineteenth centuries as reflected in the emergence of the biological sciences and as disclosed by the thought of Goethe, Herder, and Coleridge. This chapter thus constitutes the nucleus out of which the remainder of the study evolves. Chapters 2 and 6 are concerned with the development of the physical and biological sciences in the eighteenth and nineteenth centuries respectively. Here are also traced the cosmologies relevant to each period and its scientific preoccupation. The nonmusical components of culture derivative from the logocentric eighteenth-century world view and from that of the biocentrically oriented nineteenth-century are analyzed in chapters 3 and 7 respectively.

Chapters 4, 5, and 8 are devoted to music of the two centuries, chapters 4 and 5 being concerned with the Baroque era and with Classicism, chapter 8 dealing with Romanticism. The large proportion of space and effort devoted to music is explained by the fact that this province is the author's area of concentration.

Fundamental to the investigation, in matters of epistemology and in the study of culture, are the writings of A. N. Whitehead, F. S. C. Northrop, and J. F. Spratt. Without such works as Whitehead's *Science and the Modern World,* Northrop's *The Meeting of East and West,* and various published and unpublished papers of Professor Spratt, this study would not have been possible.

Science and the Arts

A Study in Relationships
from 1600-1900

1

The Shift in Theory of Nature from the Eighteenth to the Nineteenth Centuries

The change in theory of nature from the eighteenth to the nineteenth century is one of inanimate to animate, from inorganic to organic, from static to developmental. The change is most clearly characterized by the contrast between Newtonian science and its derivative, logico-mathematical cosmology dominating the so-called Enlightenment, and Darwinian science and its derivative biologico-evolutionary world view dominating the Romantic era. The change is from the logical abstractions of mathematical physics to the concrete phenomena of natural-history biology. Admittedly, the physical sciences, still largely based on the Newtonian model, continued to proliferate at an unprecedented rate during the nineteenth century. The names of Dalton, Maxwell, and Mach give eloquent testimony to this expansion. Still, when we consider the nineteenth century as a whole, it is the life sciences, associated with such names as Lamarck, Cuvier, and Darwin, that give the dominant tenor to the century. Testimony to this, given by writers on science and culture, is copious:

> In the great advance which marked the nineteenth century, it was not the vast development of physical knowledge . . . which most effectually widened man's mental horizon and led to one more revolution in his ways of thought. The point of real interest shifted from astronomy to geology, and from physics to biology and the phenomena of life. The hypothesis of natural selection . . . carried the human mind over the next long stage of its endless journey, with Darwin as the Newton of biology—the central figure of nineteenth-century thought.[1]

1. Sir William C. Dampier, *A History of Science and Its Relations with Philosophy and Religion* (New York: The Macmillan Co., 1943), p. 269.

The thought of the nineteenth century was dominated by the concept of evolution.[2]

It is significant that the term *biology* was coined in 1802, on the very threshold of the century. One of the main features of the nineteenth century was, in fact, the unification of the sciences of life.[3]

. . . In the second half of the nineteenth century . . . the fragments of the great doctrine of development, have been united together . . . and that what was once vague, fanciful, and legendary has become a leading idea of the natural sciences.[4]

Anyone who assesses the history of 19th-century science is likely to regard the growth of evolutionary ideas as the movement of greatest importance. The technical and intellectual developments in physical science had far-reaching effects: but it was biology, in its evolutionary aspect, that really shook the 19th century as astronomy shook the 17th.[5]

This is only a brief sampling; the list of authors expressing this opinion could go on almost *ad infinitum*.

The tendency toward the phenomenal, intrinsic to the biological sciences, is equally evident in the more abstract physical sciences of the century. It is this predicament which warrants A. N. Whitehead's statement that "the greatest invention of the nineteenth century was the invention of the method of invention," understanding thereby the technological, and hence phenomenal by-products of pure, abstract science. Such interpretation of this statement is further confirmed when Whitehead, in the next paragraph, states that science in the nineteenth century was "conceived not so much in its principles as in its results," thus fulfilling "the prophecy of Francis Bacon."[6] In view of this it can hardly be mere coincidence that the famous German physicist Ernst Mach, at the close of the century, employs the phrase "phenomenological physics"[7] to describe his approach to thermodynamics,

2. F. S. C. Northrop, "Evolution in its Relation to the Philosophy of Nature and the Philosophy of Culture," in *Evolutionary Thought in America,* ed. Stow Persons (New Haven: Yale University Press, 1950), p. 44.

3. Maurice Caullery, *A History of Biology* (New York: Walker and Company, 1966), p. 132.

4. John T. Merz, *A History of European Thought in the Nineteenth Century* (New York: Dover Publications, Inc., 1965), 2 : 278.

5. Lewis W. H. Hull, *History and Philosophy of Science* (London: Longmans, Green and Co., 1959), p. 281.

6. Alfred North Whitehead, *Science and the Modern World* (New York: The Macmillan Company, 1925. Reprinted by The New American Library, Mentor Books, New York, 1959), p. 91.

7. Stephen F. Mason, *A History of the Sciences* (New York: Crowell-Collier Publishing Company, 1962; previously published as *Main Currents of Scientific Thought,* by Abelard-Schuman Limited, New York, 1956), p. 500.

while William James has his final writings published under the title *Essays in Radical Empiricism* (1912). What is common to both Mach and James is the desire to eliminate from knowledge all hypothetical or theoretical *a priori* models which are not directly justified by the empirical data. It is striking, and likewise hardly mere coincidence, that the contemporaneous movement in the arts known as Impressionism exhibits a similar concern for bare empirical data, "pure fact"[8] as Northrop calls it, apart from any inferential factors in knowledge. In music this concern constitutes the almost total rejection of formal elements by Debussy.

The conspicuous feature of the change in theory of nature from the eighteenth to the nineteenth centuries is thus seen to involve a shift from mathematical physics to natural-history biology, from the noumenon to the phenomenon, from the " 'logo-centrism' of traditional epistemology" to " 'biocentrically oriented' romantic thought."[9]

A similar change can be observed in culture. Already in the second half of the eighteenth century, in such domains as philosophy, historiography, literature, and the arts in general, the metaphor of the living, evolving organism begins to replace the metaphor of the mechanical, nonevolving clock. Whitehead refers to this period as the "romantic reaction," meaning thereby a general disaffection with a cosmology reduced to a mechanistic scheme of mathematical abstractions. The error of assuming that this scheme exhausts our concrete experience of nature is referred to by Whitehead as "the fallacy of misplaced concreteness."[10]

The key figures in this period are Herder, Goethe, and Coleridge. Herder, a prolific German writer in such realms as philosophy, history, and aesthetics, exerted an immense influence on the habits of mind now emerging and increasingly becoming dominant during the nineteenth century. Although not a systematic thinker, his numerous suggestions about, and insights into, the nature of art, literature, language, and history greatly stimulated his contemporaries and followers. The main feature of Herder's philosophy of nature and culture is the idea of genesis, growth, and development. This idea is especially evident in his

---

8. F. S. C. Northrop, *The Logic of the Sciences and the Humanities* (New York: The Macmillan Company, 1947; reprinted by Meridian Books, Inc., New York, 1959), pp. 39–49.

9. Alexander Gode-von Aesch, *Natural Science in German Romanticism* (New York: Columbia University Press, 1941; reprinted by the AMS Press, New York, 1966), pp. 7–8.

10. *Science,* pp. 72–90, 58.

philosophy of history where historical process and evolution are depicted in terms of the evolving organism as it undergoes various stages of growth.

> Has there not been progress and development in a higher sense? The growing tree, the struggling man, must pass through various stages always progressing. . . . The past and present are the bases of the future. This the analysis of nature . . . in general shows. Thus it is also with the human race. The Egyptian could not be without the Oriental; the Greek built on both; the Roman rose upon the shoulders of the entire world. Genuine progress, constant development, even if no individual gain anything thereby, this is the purpose of God in history.[11]

There is a radical difference between this biocentrically oriented historical epistemology and the Enlightenment view of history. The Enlightenment, rather than regarding itself as the product of the evolving past, saw itself as a drastic departure from the "unenlightened," barbaric Middle Ages deemed unworthy of historical investigation. It found no value in the creative products of former ages, and sought chiefly to propagandize its own ideas. Thus, observes R. G. Collingwood, ". . . the historical outlook of the Enlightenment was not genuinely historical; in its main motive it was polemical and anti-historical." Undoubtedly, the almost exclusive attention on "the conception of human nature as something uniform and unchanging"[12] further intensified this predicament.

Herder's attitude to aesthetics, literature, and, implicitly, to all art is likewise symptomatic of biologically centered thought. Here too it is the historical evolution of an art and its origins which are of cardinal importance in its comprehension. For example, he is convinced that "it is absolutely impossible to have a philosophical theory of the beautiful in all arts and sciences without history." And, "if we want ever to achieve a philosophical poetics or a history of poetry, then we must begin with the individual genres and trace them back to their origins." Still further, again reverting to the biological metaphor, he says that as the "tree from the root, so must the progress and the flowering of an art be deduced from its origin. It contains the whole being of its product just as a whole plant is hidden with all its parts in a grain of seed." René Wellek, who cites the above excerpts,

---

11. *Philosophy of History* (1774), as quoted by John H. Randall in *The Making of the Modern Mind* (New York: Houghton Mifflin Co., 1926), p. 456.

12. *The Idea of History* (New York: Oxford University Press, 1946. Reprinted by Oxford Galaxy Books, 1959), pp. 77, 86.

comments that the "evolution of literature is conceived of by Herder as literal evolution, as the growing of a germ, on a completely biological analogy,"[13] thus confirming our assertion that biology, as we approach the nineteenth century, is progressively becoming the implicit and explicit paradigm for human thought and creative activity. Herder therefore

> heralds the age of biologism: the area of the most exciting and seminal discoveries having shifted from physical science to the science of life, biology has begun to replace Cartesian and Newtonian mechanics as the great source of concepts which, migrating into other provinces, were modifying the general character of ideation.[14]

The archetypal protagonist of the biological and evolutionary ideas emerging during the second half of the eighteenth century was Goethe. Throughout his long life, embracing the second half of the eighteenth and the first three decades of the nineteenth centuries, Goethe devoted himself to establishing a view of reality where life, growth, metamorphosis, and the vivid experience of the phenomenal world were central. In this sense he virtually created his own environment. The Newtonian theory of nature in terms of mathematical physics was anathema to him. Consequently, his own world view

> was one continued attack on Newton and Newtonian physics. During the course of his life this attack grew sharper and sharper, and it finally led to a tragic climax. Everywhere—among philosophers, physicists, biologists—he looked for allies in this contest, but he was able to convince scarcely anyone. Here he stood alone, and this isolation filled him with a growing bitterness.[15]

"Gray are all theories, and green alone Life's golden tree" says Mephistopheles to the Student[16] in his devastating parody of a view of nature reduced to a mechanistic, linear, cause-and-effect explanation. Nevertheless, it would be erroneous to conclude from the above that Goethe was opposed, at least in principle, to all theoretical knowledge, and that he depended solely on intuitive

13. *Vom Erkennen und Empfinden der menschlichen Seele,* as quoted by René Wellek, *A History of Modern Criticism: 1750–1950.* 4 vols. (New Haven: Yale University Press, 1955), 1 : 188–89.
14. M. H. Abrams, *The Mirror and the Lamp: Romantic Theory and the Critical Tradition* (New York: Oxford University Press, 1953; reprinted by W. W. Norton & Co., Inc., New York, 1958), p. 204.
15. Ernst Cassirer, *Rousseau, Kant and Goethe* (Princeton, N.J.: Princeton University Press, 1945; reprinted by Harper & Row, New York, 1963), p. 62.
16. Johann W. von Goethe, *Faust,* pt. 1, trans. Bayard Taylor (New York: Appleton-Century-Crofts, Inc., 1946), p. 53.

insight. Rather, his approach to knowledge, as to the world, is holistic in the sense that it incorporates both theory and intuition.

> Goethe recognized no sharp boundary between intuition and theory; for such a boundary would have contradicted his own experience as scientific investigator. For him the two realms were not separated. The foreword to the *Theory of Color* already expresses this idea. "Merely looking at a thing," says Goethe, "can tell us nothing. Each look leads to an inspection, each inspection to a reflection, each reflection to a synthesis; and hence we can say that in every attentive glance at the world we are already theorizing."[17]

In other words, the world is known largely by inference. Still, Goethe's overall epistemology "was of the inductive, sensuous, natural history type,"[18] as opposed to the more deductive method of the physical sciences. His, just like Herder's world view, is mirrored in organic nature and such biological processes as metamorphosis and evolution.

Goethe's scientific activity is not widely known. During the course of his long life he was constantly engaged in a wide range of scientific pursuits, among which we find botany, geology, comparative anatomy, physiology, mineralogy, optics, and theory of color. He in fact "devoted more time to scientific investigation . . . than to all his poetry and prose combined."[19] In comparative anatomy he independently discovered the intermaxillary bone in man, thus demonstrating man's relatedness to the higher animals, and anticipating evolutionary principle. This, according to one writer, "caused Darwin to hail him as a forerunner."[20] Furthermore, Goethe's publication of his discovery (1784) is regarded as "the first treatise ever written that can be properly described as lying in the field of comparative anatomy, and thus it is a milestone in the history of this science."[21] He founded and named the science of morphology. However, morphology, "as he understood it, was the systematic study of formation and transformation—whether of rocks, clouds, colours, plants, animals or the cultural phenomena of human society—as these present themselves to sentient experience."[22] The same notion of

---

17. Cassirer, *Rousseau*, p. 82.

18. F. S. C. Northrop, *Man, Nature and God* (New York: Pocket Books, Inc., 1963), p. 153.

19. Will and Ariel Durant, *The Story of Civilization*, Part 10: *Rousseau and Revolution* (New York: Simon and Schuster, 1967), p. 615.

20. Elizabeth M. Wilkinson, "Goethe, Johann Wolfgang von," *Encyclopaedia Britannica* (1964), 10 : 527.

21. Rudolf Magnus, *Goethe as a Scientist* (New York: H. Schuman, 1949), p. 42.

22. Wilkinson, "Goethe," p. 528.

"formation and transformation" is fundamental in his botanical studies, which were published under the title *Metamorphosis of Plants* (1790). Here he postulated the theory that all parts of the plant are transformations of a basic leaf archetype. This theory was later generalized to include the animal kingdom. Writing to Herder in 1787, he said, " 'The same law . . . will be applicable to all that lives'—i.e., to animals as well as plants; they too are variations on one structural theme."[23]

It is clear from the above that the idea of metamorphosis, change, and transformation—all properties of growth which begin with the potential seed or germ—is regarded by Goethe as a primordial process in the nature of things. This leads writers like Alexander Gode-von Aesch to describe his thought, and the thought of his era, as "biotic." The idea of metamorphosis "is of generally biotic significance and represents the key to all of Goethe's thought." And if we are to "conceive of him as the summary and fullest representative of his entire era," then we mean "by implication that a basic assertion found to be valid with respect to the individual Goethe cannot be entirely devoid of meaning when applied to the age to which he gave his name."[24] It is not surprising, therefore, that we further read, "Goethe is metamorphosis. Beethoven finds metamorphosis." (*"Goethe ist Metamorphose. Beethoven findet Metamorphose."*)[25] The meaning of these aphoristic expressions is to be found in the fact that beginning with Beethoven (after 1800), who had personal contact with Goethe, the musical technique of the metamorphosis of themes, customarily conjoined to cyclical form, progressively becomes the dominant mode of musical composition in multi-movement instrumental works. Stated in different terms, with the year 1800 and forward, the number of works employing cyclical form and the metamorphosis of themes is directly proportional to the increasing influence of the biologico-evolutionary sciences and the organic world view they engendered, and inversely proportional to the decreasing influence of the mathematico-physical sciences and their concomitant logico-mathematical cosmology. Hence what is implicit in Beethoven becomes explicit in Brahms, Berlioz, Liszt, and Wagner with respect to culture (in this case music), the assumption being that meta-

---

23. Quoted by Durant in *Civilization*, p. 617.
24. Gode-von Aesch, *Natural Science*, p. 3.
25. Fritz Cassirer, *Beethoven und die Gestalt* (Stuttgart: Deutsche Verlags-Anstalt, 1925), p. ix.

morphosis of themes and cyclical form are biological or organic metaphors of musical process and unity.

It is significant that, unlike later nineteenth-century thinkers, Goethe did not divorce science from art, but saw the latter as an inference from the former. Above all he was a holistic thinker, and his dual role as a scientist and as a poet eloquently illustrates this.

> He deliberately pursued these as mutually illuminating kinds of activity, each new hypothesis or discovery he made in biology duly reappearing in the form of new organizing principles or insights in the field of his criticism. "As I have looked upon nature," he wrote to Frau von Stein from Italy, "so do I now look upon art, and I am now achieving what I have striven after for so long, a more perfect conception of the highest things which men have made."[26]

The same epistemological environment which produced men like Herder and Goethe in Germany (and, conversely, their creation of this environment) also produced Coleridge in England. Thus, predictably, Coleridge shares Herder's and Goethe's predilection for the phenomenal world of biology and derivative notions therefrom, and their general antipathy to anything tainted with Cartesian and Newtonian deductive epistemology. This is particularly evident in Coleridge's theory of literary invention, where extensive use is made of the biological metaphor as it relates to the origin, growth, and evolution of a work of art. Accordingly, Coleridge frequently has recourse to such words and phrases as "vital," "powers of growth and production," and "assimilative power."

> "Productivity or Growth," Coleridge said, is "the first power" of all living things, and it exhibits itself as "evolution and extension in the Plant." No less is this a power of the greatest poets. In Shakespeare, for example, we find "*Growth* as in a plant." "All is growth, evolution, *genesis*—each line, each word almost, begets the following."[27] [Coleridge's italics]

The similarity of Coleridge's and Goethe's thought as exhibited in the above passage is striking. For both, the concepts of life, growth, and evolution are elemental processes in nature and culture. To a large extent, however, this similarity may be explained by the general intellectual climate existing in Europe at this time, and by the direct and indirect influence on Coleridge

---

26. Abrams, *Mirror*, p. 206.
27. *Ibid.*, pp. 320–21, 171.

of such German organismic thinkers as A. W. Schlegel, Schelling, Herder, and Goethe. Most writers on early romantic literature note this influence.

Coleridge's famous distinction between the so-called mechanical "fancy" and organic "imagination" in the creative process likewise partakes of the biological metaphor of growth and transformation. For example, with respect to the organic imagination he says,

> They and they only can acquire the philosophic imagination, the sacred power of self-intuition, who within themselves can interpret and understand the symbol, that the wings of the air-sylph are forming within the skin of the caterpillar; those only, who feel within their own spirits the same instinct, which compels the chrysalis of the horned fly to leave room in its involucrum for antennae yet to come.[28]

The fancy, on the other hand, is mechanical by virtue of its "fixities and definites."[29] It

> knows only of distance and nearness, composition (or rather juxtaposition) and decomposition, in short the relations of unproductive particles to each other; so that in every instance the result is the exact sum of the component quantities, as in arithmetical addition.

Implicit here are two things: 1) Coleridge's rejection of the mechanistic, logico-mathematical world view engendered by Descartes and Newton, and, 2) his vitalistic and teleological conception of the universe, with regard to both nature and culture. Concerning 1) J. V. Baker writes,

> Every serious student of Coleridge soon becomes aware of his hostility to the mechanistic psychology and to the materialistic or matter-and-motion theory of the universe of which it formed a part. But the extent and depth of that hostility do not become apparent until the whole corpus of Coleridge's published work is examined; when the evidence is all in, when the poems, the letters, . . . *Biographia,* . . . the *Aids to Reflection,* the *Shakespearean Lectures,* the *Philosophical Lectures* are sifted, it is extraordinary how all this sizable body of work is unified by that hostility and how large a percentage of Coleridge's total output and energy as a writer is directed to that lifelong campaign.[30]

With respect to 2), i.e., his vitalistic and teleological conception

28. *Biographia Literaria,* 1 : 167, as quoted by James V. Baker, *The Sacred River: Coleridge's Theory of the Imagination* (Baton Rouge: Louisiana State University Press, 1957), p. 108.

29. Abrams, *Mirror,* p. 168.

30. Baker, *Sacred River,* pp. 110, 99.

of the universe, Coleridge maintained the position that nature and art are vitalistic in the sense that they are generated innately, spontaneously, like the growth of a plant from the potential seed, their wholeness always being greater than the sum of their parts. Hence, just as the living thing in its wondrous incomprehensibility ultimately lies beyond explanation in terms of physical and chemical law alone, so the work of art in its wholeness and unity lies beyond mere logical analysis. Needless to say, this is, generally speaking, Goethe's position.

It is noteworthy that the centuries-long dispute between the vitalists and mechanists concerning organic nature is not a dead issue even today. Writers like Walter M. Elsasser and Norbert Wiener, however, seem to have bridged the gap between the two camps, Elsasser[31] by upholding the essentially Leibnizian postulate that "organism is mechanism ad infinitum,"[32] Wiener[33] by noting the anti-entropic and homeostatic nature of organisms and self-regulating automata, both of which maintain their homeostasis through feedback mechanisms. It is likewise noteworthy that the paradigm of the cosmos patterned on the living organism as opposed to the lifeless machine is not new with Coleridge, Goethe, or Herder. As far back as the fourth century B.C. Plato, in describing the origin and creation of the universe says, ". . . intending to make this world like the fairest and most perfect of intelligible beings [the Deity] framed one visible animal comprehending within itself all other animals of a kindred nature."[34] And Aristotle, arguing from his concept of motion remarks,

> if an animal is ever in a state of absolute rest, we have a motionless thing in which motion can be produced from the thing itself, and not from without. Now if this can occur in an animal, why should not the same be true also of the universe as a whole? If it can occur in a small world it could also occur in a great one.[35]

---

31. *Atom and Organism; A New Approach to Theoretical Biology* (Princeton: Princeton University Press, 1966), pp. 16, 81.
32. Paraphrased by James Benziger in "Organic Unity: Leibniz to Coleridge," *Publications of the Modern Language Association* 66 (March 1951):46.
33. *The Human Use of Human Beings; Cybernetics and Society* (New York: Houghton Mifflin Company, 1950; reprinted by Avon Books, New York, 1967), pp. 47, 130.
34. "Timaeus," *The Dialogues of Plato,* trans. Benjamin Jowett, *Great Books of the Western World,* vol. 7. (Chicago: Encyclopaedia Britannica, Inc., 1952), p. 448.
35. Aristotle, *Physics, Great Books of the Western World,* vol. 8. (Chicago: Encyclopaedia Britannica, Inc., 1952), p. 336.

The primacy of the phenomenal, immediately experienced fact associated with a biologically oriented cosmology is equally a feature of Coleridge's epistemology, as it is of Goethe's and Herder's. Furthermore, it makes little difference whether this experience is in the form of external *sensa* or internal feelings. Thus, in commenting on "The Rime of the Ancient Mariner," Joseph W. Beach says,

> The extraordinary power of [this poem] results from a combination of several elements very seldom brought together. The one I wish to stress is this of sensory appeal on the level of primary physical experience. And, along with Coleridge, I shall refer to his fellow romantics as they make their notations of things seen, heard, felt, tasted, and smelt.[36]

The purpose of this chapter has been threefold: 1) to show a change in theory of nature from the eighteenth to the nineteenth centuries involving a shift from the physical to the biological sciences; 2) to show a corresponding change in epistemology, from an abstract, deductive, to a natural-history type of inductive, method; and 3) to show that symptomatic of the above two is a change in humanistic activities embracing such biological metaphors as growth, metamorphosis, and evolution. In the following chapter the eighteenth century will be examined with respect to the connections between culture and the prevalent theory of nature.

---

36. *A Romantic View of Poetry* (Minneapolis: The University of Minnesota Press, 1944), pp. 8–9.

2

The Logocentric World View
of the Enlightenment

It is indisputable that the dominant figure of the eighteenth century, the so-called Enlightenment, is Isaac Newton. Not only does his work form the basis of physical science and technology for the ensuing two centuries, but his influence in matters of fundamental assumptions and general epistemology concerning theory of nature and various components of culture permeates the fabric of eighteenth-century mentality. Newton's theory of nature is variously referred to as mechanism, materialism, mechanistic materialism, and so on. Perhaps the most appropriate term is logico-mechanism because 1) Newtonian cosmology is based on that branch of physics commonly known as theoretical mechanics, i.e., the science which deals with the properties of bodies in motion and at rest; 2) theoretical mechanics, as formulated by Newton, rests on purely abstract *logical* relations expressed in mathematical form. An example of these relations is Newton's three laws of motion from which the remainder of mechanics is deduced and experimentally confirmed, the first three laws or postulates being unverifiable and hence assumed to be true under ideal, empirically nonexistent conditions. Hence, the fundamental premise of Newton's cosmology is that nature is at bottom simple, rational, and reducible to logically quantitative abstraction. Methodologically its essence consists of direct and inverse ratio equations, as in the famous law of universal gravitation, which simultaneously accounted for the legendary fall of the apple on Newton, the moon's rotation around the earth, and the movements of the stars. Such universality of

44

natural law, explained by a relatively simple equation, had an incalculable effect on the eighteenth-century mind. It was in fact assumed that, with the proper use of reason and given enough time, similar laws could be discovered in the entire spectrum of human endeavor, from social institutions to artistic creations, thus bringing society to a state of perfection. This was the principal aspiration of the Enlightenment.

The mechanistic theory of nature manifest in Newton's *Principia Mathematica* (three editions: 1687, 1713, 1726) stands at midpoint in time between two hundred years of formulation and two hundred years of application. The period of formulation, from *ca.* 1500 to *ca.* 1700 may be divided into two parts, the speculative stage and the stage of confirmation. The speculative stage is represented by Copernicus and his heliocentric hypothesis; the stage of confirmation by Galileo and his quantitative interpretation of observational and experimental data. Newton, who was born in the year Galileo died (1642), generalized the findings of Galileo into a comprehensive system of nature which was not seriously threatened (outside of biology) until the close of the nineteenth century. He thus embodies the first great cosmological synthesis since the time of Plato. So elemental and abstract were the postulates of this synthesis "that the impetus to overhaul them could only spring from the demands of empirical fact,"[1] i.e., when the accumulating empirical evidence began to create insuperable discrepancies with the system. Albert Einstein's observation is corroborated by Whitehead, who states that "the world was given . . . two centuries which it required in order to digest Newton's laws of motion."[2] These two centuries, from *ca.* 1700 to *ca.* 1900, constitute the period of application, meaning thereby the rendering explicit of technological innovations implicit in Newton's theory of nature.

The above has been a deliberate oversimplification with respect to temporal boundaries and the exclusion of such names as Kepler, Huygens, and Descartes, thus allowing us to survey the Renaissance-Modern world in perspective as it witnessed the development of mathematical physics and its attendant logocentric cosmology. The attainment of these men has been charac-

---

1. Albert Einstein, "The Mechanics of Newton and Their Influence on the Development of Theoretical Physics," *Ideas and Opinions*, ed. Carl Seelig (New York: Crown Publishers, Inc., 1954), p. 257.
2. A. N. Whitehead, *Science and the Modern World* (New York: The Macmillan Company, 1925; reprinted by The New American Library, Mentor Books, New York, 1959), p. 50.

terized by Whitehead "as the greatest single intellectual success which mankind has achieved."[3] Similarly, the emergence of the life sciences during the second half of the eighteenth and during the nineteenth centuries has here been ignored. The biocentric and evolutionary world view engendered by these sciences in the nineteenth century profoundly challenged the strictly mechanistic cosmology and actually superseded it in terms of influence on various domains of culture. This is discussed elsewhere in the study (see chapters 7 and 8).

Before proceeding with an analysis of the causal connections between the prevailing theory of nature and various components of culture during the eighteenth century, let us trace the antecedents of this theory, which have their beginnings on the threshold of the Renaissance-Modern world. According to R. G. Collingwood, the mechanistic cosmology had its inception with the Copernican heliocentric hypothesis. As expounded in the *De revolutionibus orbium coelestium* (published posthumously in 1543), the heliocentric hypothesis accounted in much simpler and more elegant fashion for the accumulated observations of planetary movements and for the prediction of the positions of the various planets than did the established Ptolemaic system with its intricate maze of epicycles. It proceeded on the assumption that the order of nature is basically simple, intelligible, and ultimately capable of reduction to the mathematical uniformity of a rational scheme. The profound consequence of this notion was that the hylozoic or organic view of nature, derivative from Greek philosophy and still extant in Renaissance thought, was gradually superseded by the idea of nature as mechanism. In different terms, nature as *natura naturans,* i.e., as something "divine and self-creative," was being replaced by nature as *natura naturata,* meaning thereby a complex of "changes and processes" ultimately traceable to mathematical pattern. The affinity of the latter view to Plato's deductive epistemology founded in the more abstract mathematico-physical sciences, as opposed to Aristotle's inductive method of natural-history biology, is noted by Collingwood.

> This conception was much closer to Plato than to Aristotle, for the tendency of Plato's Pythagorean cosmology was to explain the behaviour of natural things as an effect of their mathematical structure, a tendency quite in harmony with the work of the new physical science; whereas

---

3. *Ibid.*

Aristotle's cosmology tended to explain it through an elaborate chain of imitations of imitations of the divine nature. Hence the Renaissance philosophers enrolled themselves under the banner of Plato against the Aristotelians, until Galileo, the true father of modern science, restated the Pythagorean-Platonic standpoint in his own words by proclaiming that the book of nature is a book written by God in the language of mathematics. For the Aristotelian doctrine that change is an expression of tendency, the sixteenth century substituted the Platonic doctrine . . . that change is a function of structure.[4]

Thus Plato's doctrine of the primacy of mathematics in our comprehension of the external world and in our realization of the idea of the good for man[5] was being fulfilled by Galileo and his followers.

Galileo's statement, referred to by Collingwood above, is so striking in its modernity and in its resemblance to Plato's theory of nature that it bears full quotation here.

Philosophy is written in this grand book, the universe, which stands continually open to our gaze. But the book cannot be understood unless one first learns to comprehend the language and read the letters in which it is composed. It is written in the language of mathematics, and its characters are triangles, circles, and other geometric figures without which it is humanly impossible to understand a single word of it; without these, one wanders about in a dark labyrinth.

Implicit in this passage is the fully developed cosmology made explicit in Newton's *Principia*, the consequent philosophy of John Locke with his distinction between primary and secondary qualities, and the romantic reaction against this distinction, a distinction which relegated the phenomenal, sensed world to the second-rate status of mere appearance. In fact the differentiation between primary and secondary qualities, basic in Locke, is already explicitly present in Galileo when he writes,

tastes, odors, colors, and so on are no more than mere names so far as the object in which we place them is concerned, and . . . they reside only in the consciousness. Hence if the living creature were removed, all these qualities would be wiped away and annihilated. But since we have imposed upon them special names, distinct from those of the other

4. *The Idea of Nature* (New York: Oxford University Press, 1945; reprinted by Oxford Galaxy Books, 1960), p. 94.
5. See further "Republic," in *Great Dialogues of Plato,* trans. W. H. D. Rouse, ed. Eric H. Warmington and Philip G. Rouse (New York: The New American Library, Mentor Books, 1956), bk. 7, pp. 312–31, and summary thereof, pp. 122–23.

and real qualities mentioned previously, we wish to believe that they really exist as actually different from those.[6]

Here we have, in Northrop's analysis, the three-termed epistemology of traditional Renaissance-Modern theory of nature, the terms being 1) the real material substances with their abstract, deductively formulated primary qualities existing in a postulated, universally valid space-time, 2) mental substances or minds apprehending the material substances in the form of 3) the seemingly real but only apparent secondary qualities which are ever changing and singularly unique for every individual. In short, "the whole of reality is nothing but material substances to cause the latter to project sensed qualities in sensed space and time as appearances."[7] The logical consequences of this view, as elucidated in the following passage by A. N. Whitehead, have the character of a *reductio ad absurdum*.

> Thus nature gets credit which should in truth be reserved for ourselves; the rose for its scent: the nightingale for his song: and the sun for his radiance. The poets are entirely mistaken. They should address their lyrics to themselves, and should turn them into odes of self-congratulation on the excellency of the human mind. Nature is a dull affair, soundless, scentless, colorless; merely the hurrying of material, endlessly, meaninglessly.[8]

The mechanistic theory of nature is perhaps most clearly articulated by Descartes in the seventeenth century. To this extent he clearly represents an index to the thought of his era. In his cosmology mechanism was a feature not only of the inanimate, but also of the animate, world. Undoubtedly William Harvey's contemporaneous discovery that the human heart serves the mechanical function of a pump further reinforced this view. According to Northrop,

> Harvey in his lectures on the motion of the heart and blood makes the first application of the mechanical ideas of Galilei to a gross physiological process. What Descartes had indicated for biology in general, Harvey demonstrated in particular for a specific physiological system.[9]

6. Galileo Galilei, "The Assayer," *Discoveries and Opinions of Galileo*, trans. Stillman Drake (Garden City, N. Y.: Doubleday & Company, Inc., Anchor Books, 1957), pp. 237–38, 274.
7. F. S. C. Northrop, *The Meeting of East and West* (New York: The Macmillan Co., 1946), p. 83.
8. *Science*, p. 55.
9. "The History of Modern Physics in Its Bearing Upon Biology and Medicine," *Yale Journal of Biology and Medicine* 10 (1937–38):212.

It has been observed above that Leibniz regarded the living organism as mechanism *ad infinitum*. Descartes's position in this respect is similar, since he admits that "different *automata* or moving machines can be made by the industry of man, without employing in so doing more than a very few parts," but living organisms are above all distinguished by a "great multitude of bones, muscles, nerves, arteries, veins, or other parts that are found in the body of each animal. From this aspect the body is regarded as a machine," but one "incomparably better arranged, and . . . more admirable, than any of those which can be invented by man."[10]

The basis of the Cartesian mechanistic world view is an epistemology which is in certain respects similar to, and in others different from, Galileo's method. The similarity resides in Descartes's almost exclusive attention on those cognitive entities which lend themselves to quantitative expression, while the difference lies in his systematic avoidance of empirical considerations. It is for this reason that the Cartesian physics of vortices, having no empirical concomitants, found no productive followers, whereas Galileo's investigations, exhibiting a greater epistemological balance of rational and empirical factors, led directly to Newton and beyond. Descartes's methodology is well known. After a period of thoroughgoing doubt with respect to things which can or cannot be known with absolute certainty, he begins with the residue of indubitable "clear and distinct ideas" (first principles) arrived at intuitively and proceeds henceforth by pure deduction to structure his epistemological edifice. "Give me motion and extension, and I will construct the world,"[11] writes Descartes, illustrating thereby that the first principles, such as motion and extension, must be susceptible of purely abstract, quantitative formulation. The world of sense experience, as with Galileo, is for Descartes only a source of confusion. It is deceptive by virtue of its constant variability and the constant variability of man. Thus he writes,

> various experiences ruined all my faith in the senses. For I often observed that towers that looked round from a distance seemed square when I approached them, and the huge statues, erected on the summits of these towers, looked very small when I gazed up at them from below; and

10. *Discourse on Method, Great Books of the Western World,* vol. 31 (Chicago: Encyclopaedia Britannica, Inc., 1952), p. 59.
11. Quoted by Stephen F. Mason, *A History of the Sciences* (New York: Collier Books, 1962), p. 169.

so, in innumerable other instances, I found that judgements based on the outer senses were erroneous.

He writes further, "But what I understand clearly and distinctly, all, that is to say, that in general constitutes the object of mathematical science, this at least is what it purports to be."[12] Therefore, Descartes's system of knowledge and his theory of nature constitute a *"mathesis universalis"* by means of which the external world, from distant galaxies to the lowly worm, was sought to be understood in solely rational terms. This *mathesis universalis* would implicitly subsume a theory of the arts, even though such theory was not explicitly postulated by Descartes, for "the absolute unity in which . . . the nature of knowledge consists, and which is to overcome all its arbitrary and conventional divisions, is extended in the Cartesian system to include also the realm of art."[13]

It has been mentioned earlier in this chapter that Newton represents a synthesis of the mechanistic world view which had its inception with the speculative phase of Copernicus in the sixteenth century and which went through the phase of confirmation with Galileo, Kepler, and to a lesser extent Descartes, in the seventeenth century. This century, with respect to science "achieved its most spectacular triumphs," according to Bertrand Russell, thus separating the "modern world from earlier centuries."[14] It is curious that although over 280 years have elapsed since the first publication of the *Principia,* divergence of opinion still exists regarding Newton's method, some writers maintaining that he was primarily an empiricist, others that he was first and foremost a deductive thinker. The general impression one gets from reading Cassirer is that Newton was above all an empiricist. For example, Cassirer asserts that Newtonian physics proceeds "not from concepts and axioms to phenomena, but *vice versa."* He further writes that "physics can never consist in proceeding from . . . [an] *a priori* starting point, from a hypothesis."[15] Bertrand Russell, on the other hand, appears to take the opposite stand by stating that "the form of Newton's *Principia,* in spite of its admittedly empirical material, is entirely dominated by

12. "Meditations," *Discourse on Method and Other Writings,* trans. Arthur Woolaston (Baltimore: Penguin Books, 1960), pp. 157, 160.
13. Ernst Cassirer, *The Philosophy of the Enlightenment,* trans. F. C. A. Koelln and J. P. Pettegrove (Princeton, N. J.: Princeton University Press, 1951; reprinted by the Beacon Press, Boston, 1964), p. 27.
14. *A History of Philosophy* (New York: Simon and Schuster, Inc., 1965), p. 525.
15. Cassirer, *Philosophy,* pp. 8, 7.

Euclid."[16] Although the present writer would tend to agree with Russell, the true nature of the scientific method appropriate to Newton's mathematical physics seems to elude both Cassirer and Russell, since the one places undue emphasis on the empirical, the other on the deductive, side of the epistemological scale. Assuming the essential identity of Galileo's and Newton's methodology, and this is believed to be a reasonable assumption, the reader is here referred to the first two chapters of F. S. C. Northrop's *The Logic of the Sciences and the Humanities* for a painstaking analysis of the epistemological stages relevant to the method of Galileo and Newton.

The dominance of the mathematico-physical sciences, their deductive, abstract epistemology, and their consequent mechanistic cosmology continues from the seventeenth into the eighteenth centuries. Here "progress was in the form of direct developments of the main ideas of the previous epoch,"[17] thus supporting our earlier contention that the eighteenth century constitutes the first stage of application generated in the preceding century by the discoveries of Galileo, Kepler, and Newton. Above all, the idea of mechanism, with its corollary, determinism, was firmly consolidated by a series of great mathematical physicists beginning with Maupertuis, who occupies the first half of the century, and ending with Laplace whose productive years extend beyond the first quarter of the nineteenth century. Characteristically, some form of the term *mechanism* frequently appears in the titles of the major works of these mathematical physicists. For example, we have the *Mécanique analytique* of Lagrange, the *Mécanique céleste* of Laplace, and *L'Homme machine* by the French physician Lamettrie. It is here, in these works, that the notion of absolute deterministic causality, in the form of mathematically conceived eternal laws, finds its most explicit formulation. The clearest exponent of this view is Laplace, who writes,

We may conceive the present state of the universe as the effect of its past and the cause of its future. An Intellect who at any given instant knew all the forces that animate nature and the mutual position of the beings who compose it, were this Intellect but vast enough to submit his data to analysis, could condense into a single formula the movement of the greatest body in the universe and that of the lightest atom; to

---

16. Russell, *History*, pp. 36–37.
17. Whitehead, *Science*, p. 59.

such an Intellect nothing would be uncertain, for the future, even as the past, would be ever present before his eyes.[18]

This position constitutes a summation of the intellectual climate of the century in which "the notion of the mechanical explanation of all the processes of nature finally hardened into a dogma of science."[19] Parenthetically it may be noted that the above idea of causality is far removed from causality in twentieth-century physical science, especially quantum mechanics. The distinction made by Northrop in his Introduction to Heisenberg's *Physics and Philosophy* is between the older "strong" causality inherent in Laplace's statement, and the "weaker" type of causality of modern quantum mechanics, which is "mechanical but not deterministic."[20] It may also be noted that Einstein's final aspiration, never completely realized, was the unified field theory which aimed at uniting all natural phenomena, whether on the quantum or relativity levels, as deductions from the four-dimensional space-time geometry. In this sense Einstein belongs to the tradition of Laplace and Newton, the latter saying at one time, "Would that the rest of the phenomena of nature could be deduced by a like kind of reasoning from mechanical principles."[21] But realizing the finiteness of man, and revealing thereby the humility of his character, not unlike that of Einstein's, he made this memorable utterance just before his death:

> I do not know what I may appear to the world, but to myself I seem to have been only like a boy playing on the seashore, and diverting myself in now and then finding a smoother pebble or a prettier shell than ordinary, whilst the great ocean of truth lay all undiscovered before me.[22]

The acute stage of mechanistic determinism is reached in two works, both by French authors: the *Système de la nature* (1770) by d'Holbach and *L'Homme machine* (1748) by Lamettrie. In these two works all of nature, both animate and inanimate, is

18. Quoted by Tobias Dantzig in *Number: the Language of Science* (New York: The Macmillan Company, 1930; reprinted by Doubleday & Company, Inc., Anchor Books, Garden City, N. Y., 1954), p. 138.

19. Whitehead, *Science,* p. 59.

20. Werner Heisenberg, *Physics and Philosophy* (New York: Harper & Brothers, 1958; reprinted by Harper Torchbooks, 1962), p. 15.

21. Quoted by Basil Willey in "How the Scientific Revolution of the Seventeenth Century Affected Other Branches of Thought," in *A Short History of Science* (Garden City, N. Y.: Doubleday Anchor Books, 1959), p. 65.

22. Sir David Brewster, *Memoirs of the Life, Writings and Discoveries of Sir Isaac Newton, The Sources of Science,* vol. 2, no 14 (New York and London: Johnson Reprint Corp., 1965), p. 407.

reduced to an unremitting, rigid determinism involving only matter in motion. Nothing was left to chance, and such concepts as the soul, spirit, and consciousness were rejected outright as superstitions or imaginary illusions, unless they had direct material concomitants. Thus, according to Willey's interpretation of d'Holbach,

> Nature is a realm of complete determinism; it knows no "order" and "disorder." We call "disorder" what disturbs or afflicts us, but all is in truth "order," in the sense that all occurs by fixed causation; order is just simply "what happens."[23]

Man fits into this deterministic scheme as merely another phenomenon of nature completely foreordained in his behavior. If he

> believes himself free, he is merely exhibiting a dangerous delusion and an intellectual weakness. It is the structure of the atoms that forms him, and their motion that propels him forward; conditions not dependent on him determine his nature and direct his fate.[24]

Lamettrie's notion of the living organism, as the title of his book suggests, is likewise on completely mechanistic and deterministic lines. His observation that the "mental state of a patient was often dependent upon his bodily conditions," and that "decapitated animals were capable of some sort of motion, like machines working imperfectly without one of their parts," led him to the idea that "the brain secreted thought, just as the liver secreted bile, and he believed that the progress of mankind depended upon the advance of medicine."[25] It should be noted that these ideas, although considered to be radical in their time in most quarters, and regarded by some as extreme even today, are the very foundation of contemporary medicine and psychology. In other words, the mechanistic hypothesis underlying all biological processes is an operational necessity of all research in the life sciences, even though this assumption has currently been enhanced by our greater appreciation of the immense and, to a large extent irreducible, complexity of living organisms, and by our consequently more holistic approach to the problem of

23. Paraphrased by Basil Willey, *The Eighteenth Century Background* (New York: Columbia University Press, 1940; reprinted by the Beacon Press, Boston, 1961), p. 158.
24. Cassirer's paraphrase of d'Holbach, in *Philosophy*, p. 69.
25. Mason, *History*, pp. 319–20.

life.[26] It should also be noted that Lamettrie's and d'Holbach's ideas are logical conclusions derived from the Cartesian notion of mechanism, diverging from Descartes only by explaining away "mind" or "soul" as a function of the body.

The present chapter has presented the major outlines of the prevailing logico-mechanistic theory of nature which commences with the Copernican Revolution in the mid-sixteenth century. It was established that this theory was fully formulated by Newton (*Principia*), and that by *ca.* 1750 its basic postulates were extended to all of nature, past and present (Laplace), inanimate and animate (d'Holbach, Lamettrie). It was further determined that the attendant epistemology of this theory dealt primarily with those cognitive factors which are capable of rational quantification in the form of absolute and universal laws of nature. As a consequence, the phenomenal world of sensed experience, along with its infinitude of qualitative gradations, of such cardinal importance to the romantic artist, was placed on the lowest scale of knowledge as mere appearance.

By no means is it here suggested that the mechanistic cosmology and its attendant deductive method account for one hundred percent of the evidence during the period under consideration. "No epoch is homogeneous," i.e., *completely* homogeneous, says Whitehead.

> Whatever you may have assigned as the dominant note of a considerable period, it will always be possible to produce men, and great men, belonging to the same time, who exhibit themselves as antagonistic to the tone of their age.

But at the same time Whitehead concedes that each age does have "a dominant note," a "dominant preoccupation; and during the three centuries in question [i.e., 1600-1900], the cosmology derived from science has been asserting itself at the expense of older points of view with their origins elsewhere."[27]

The men who are "antagonistic to the tone of their age" are Francis Bacon, Bishop Berkeley, and David Hume, all from the British Isles, where the empirical tradition with respect to such widely divergent domains as musical practice (*gymel*) and political institutions (government by precedent), goes back to the Middle Ages, to the thirteenth century, to be precise. Bacon

---

26. See especially Walter M. Elsasser, *The Physical Foundation of Biology* (New York: Pergamon Press, 1958); and *idem, Atom and Organism.*
27. Whitehead, *Science,* pp. 64, vii.

clearly displays this predilection in his *First Book of Aphorisms,* where in Aphorism XXXVI he writes,

> One method of delivery alone remains to us; which is simply this: We must lead men to the particulars themselves, and their series and order; while men . . . must force themselves for awhile to lay their notions by and begin to familiarise themselves with the facts.[28]

Berkeley's empirical attitude is mirrored in his dictum *"esse est percipi,"*[29] while Hume's radical empiricism is clearly evident in the opening sentence of his *A Treatise of Human Nature* (1739), which reads, "All the perceptions of the human mind resolve themselves into two distinct kinds, . . . impressions and ideas,"[30] meaning by ideas not something supersensible and abstract, but a less vivid version of the impressions. To underscore the fact that the form of empiricism advocated by Bacon has remained in the background of Western thought up to the so-called Romantic Era, we repeat Whitehead's observation that not until the nineteenth century was "the prophecy of Francis Bacon" fulfilled. Likewise, with respect to the radical empiricism of Hume and, implicitly, of Berkeley, which, if pursued to its logical conclusion would make science impossible, we read, "some variant of Hume's philosophy has generally prevailed among men of science. But scientific faith has risen to the occasion, and has tacitly removed the philosophic mountain,"[31] which is here construed to mean that "scientific faith" in an order of nature in the form of a uniformly rational scheme is a necessary presupposition of science, notwithstanding Hume's logical conclusion that such a scheme is not directly warranted by the empirical data. It may here be noted that the empirical turn of mind, so characteristic in British philosophy, is evident even in Bertrand Russell, and this despite his collaboration (with Whitehead) on the most important logical treatise of the twentieth century, the *Principia Mathematica.*

In the following chapter several cultural domains will be explored in the light of the preceding analysis of the dominant theory of nature during the seventeenth and eighteenth centuries.

28. Quoted in Stuart Hampshire, *The Age of Reason: the 17th Century Philosophers,* selected, with Introduction and Commentary, by Stuart Hampshire (New York: The New American Library, Mentor Books, 1956), p. 26.
29. Quoted in Northrop, *Meeting,* p. 113.
30. David Hume, *A Treatise of Human Nature,* bk. 1, *Of the Understanding,* ed. with Introduction by D. G. C. Macnabb (Cleveland and New York: The World Publishing Company, Meridian Books, 1962), p. 45.
31. *Science,* pp. 91, 12.

3

The Implications of Eighteenth-Century Cosmology in the Humanities

Presently the manner in which several cultural domains are related to the cosmology of the Enlightenment will be elucidated in explicit terms. An indication of the extent to which thought in the mathematico-physical sciences was transferred to thought in nonscientific areas is given in the following passage by Barzun:

> Seeing the beautiful demonstrations of Descartes and Newton as they explained the heavens with their coordinates, the great classical minds sought to rival this perfection and simplicity on earth. Philosophers used the geometrical method to arrive at moral and religious truth; social scientists reduced government to mechanics; the tragic muse imitated the tight deductive gait of Euclid; and I am not merely playing upon words when I say that poetry itself adopted one common meter as if scientific accuracy depended upon it.[1]

The above observation is directly confirmed by the eighteenth-century man of letters and popularizer of Cartesianism, Fontenelle, who writes in his characteristically entitled *On the Usefulness of Mathematics and Physics,*

> The geometric spirit is not so bound up with geometry that it cannot be disentangled and carried into other fields. A work of morals, of politics, of criticism, perhaps even of eloquence, will be the finer, other things being equal, if it is written by the hand of a geometer.[2]

---

1. Jacques Barzun, *Classic, Romantic and Modern* (Boston: Little, Brown and Co., 1963), p. 40.
2. Quoted by John H. Randall, *The Making of the Modern Mind* (New York: Houghton Mifflin Co., 1926), p. 254.

This spirit is in fact the ruling factor in the political philosophy of Thomas Hobbes. Antedating Fontenelle by two generations, Hobbes completely absorbed the new notion of mechanism and its attendant method as developed by Galileo in mathematical physics and as applied to physiology by William Harvey. He was likewise profoundly influenced by Descartes. Hence, just as Harvey applied Galileo's notion of mechanism to physiology, so Hobbes extrapolated the same idea to political thought. Agreement concerning this process is reached by several writers. For example, W. N. Watkins, in his essay "Philosophy and Politics in Hobbes," writes,

> Harvey and Galileo were men whose work won Hobbes' rare admiration. Each had, in his view created a new science—a science for the human body and a science of moving bodies—just as he, Hobbes, had created a new science of the body politic.

And further, commenting on the all-pervasive theory of motion, and Hobbes's appropriation of this theory into his political system, Watkins adds,

> The idea of motion permeates all Hobbes' thought: geometry studies motion; thought is motion; imagination and memory are inertial motion; "life itself is but motion"; . . . If the *Republic* may be called the political expression of the Pythagorean theory of the tuned lyre, the *Leviathan* may be called the political expression of the Galilean theory of motion.[3]

A similar observation with respect to the connection between Hobbes's political philosophy and the mechanistic theory of nature as developed by Galileo and applied to physiology by Harvey, is made by Richard S. Peters in his Introduction to an anthology of Hobbes's writings entitled *Body, Man, and Citizen*. He writes,

> Hobbes became increasingly excited by the prospect of deducing new consequences from the law of inertia. Harvey had tackled the circulation of the blood. Could not the theory of motion be extrapolated in considerable detail to psychology and politics? And so his imaginative idea gained momentum: "For seeing that life is but motion of limbs. . . . For what is the heart but a spring; and the nerves but so many strings; and the joints but so many wheels, giving motion to the whole body, such as was intended by the artificer?" Man is a natural machine and the state an artificial one.[4]

---

3. W. N. Watkins, "Philosophy and Politics in Hobbes," *Hobbes Studies,* ed. K. C. Brown (Oxford: Basil Blackwell, 1965), p. 242.
4. Thomas Hobbes, *Body, Man, and Citizen,* ed. Richard S. Peters (New York: Collier Books, 1962), p. 10.

And finally Ernst Cassirer, noting Hobbes's use of the idea of matter or "body," in addition to his use of the concept of motion, asserts that

> The fundamental principle of his [Hobbes's] political theory, that the state is a "body," means just this: that the same process of thought which guides us to an exact insight into the nature of physical body is also applicable without reservation to the state. Hobbes' assertion that thinking in general is "calculation" and that all calculation is either addition or subtraction also holds for all political thinking.[5]

Hobbes died in 1679, and thus represented the political philosophy of the seventeenth century. However, just as the theory of nature developed in the same century by Galileo, Kepler, and Newton continues into the eighteenth with few modifications, so political thought makes the same transition into the Enlightenment essentially unchanged. Fontenelle's Cartesianism and its possible application to politics, among other areas, has been mentioned earlier in the chapter. The same attitude is detectable in such eighteenth-century thinkers as Condillac, Montesquieu, and Thomas Jefferson. Hence, Jefferson in the *Declaration of Independence* appeals to "the laws of nature and of nature's God" as a basis for national autonomy; and he further writes that "we hold these truths to be self-evident, that all men are created equal." This, according to Bertrand Russell, is thought modeled on the method of Euclid. "The eighteenth-century doctrine of natural rights is a search for Euclidian axioms in politics."[6] In fact it may here be suggested that the century as whole, in its political, sociological, and artistic philosophy, bases itself on the self-evident universality of axioms deduced from the force of natural law. The theory of the social contract, for example, even though "derived from ancient and medieval thought," is transformed "in a manner characteristic of the influence exerted by the modern scientific view of the world."

> Sociology is modeled on physics and analytical psychology. Its method, states Condillac in his *Treatise on Systems* [1749], consists in teaching us to recognize in society an "artificial body" composed of parts exerting a reciprocal influence on one another. This body as a whole must be so shaped that no individual class of citizens by their special prerogatives

5. Ernst Cassirer, *The Philosophy of the Enlightenment,* trans. F. C. A. Koelln and J. P. Pettegrove (Princeton, N.J.: Princeton University Press, 1951; reprinted by The Beacon Press, Boston, 1964), p. 27.

6. Bertrand A. Russell, *History of Philosophy* (New York: Simon and Schuster, Inc., 1965), p. 36.

shall disturb the equilibrium and harmony of the whole, that on the contrary all special interests shall contribute and be subordinated to the welfare of the whole. This formulation in a certain sense transforms the problem of sociology and politics into a problem in statics.

Condillac's social equilibrium between various classes of citizens, formulated on the analogy of an equilibrium between purely physical forces, likewise appears to be the basis for the structure of the American Constitution, with its balance of powers distributed equally among the legislative, executive, and judicial branches of government. These three branches, with their built-in checks and balances, almost suggest the three terms of a Newtonian equation with its balanced contextuality of force. Montesquieu, in his political theory, discloses essentially the same methodology employed by Condillac. Even to a greater extent does he transform political problems into physical problems of statics, according to Cassirer. In his *Spirit of the Laws* (1748), for example, "the aim is not simply to describe the forms and types of state constitutions . . . , it is also to construct them from the forces of which they are composed." Furthermore, one must know these forces, if they are to be employed in the structure of constitutions, in such manner as to realize the greatest amount of freedom:

> Such freedom . . . is possible only when every individual force is limited and restrained by a counterforce. Montesquieu's famous doctrine of the "division of powers" is nothing but the consistent development and the concrete application of this basic principle. It seeks to transform that unstable equilibrium which exists in . . . imperfect forms of the state into a static equilibrium; it attempts further to show what ties must exist between individual forces in order that none shall gain the ascendancy over any other, but that all, by counterbalancing one another, shall permit the widest possible margin for freedom.[7]

Here too the principles developed and advanced by Montesquieu, especially his doctrine of the division or separation of powers, became part and parcel of American political philosophy. However, it must not be forgotten that the political theories of such French thinkers as Condillac and Montesquieu were not completely indigenous to French soil. Both thinkers, as well as numerous others, by the middle of the eighteenth century were completely saturated with the political philosophy of John Locke. And if we remember that Locke, personal friend of Newton,

---

7. Cassirer, *Philosophy*, p. 20.

wrote "with a knowledge of Newtonian dynamics"[8] then it should not be surprising that the Newtonian theory of nature, in its content and epistemology, became the exemplary paradigm of thought in the political philosophy of Condillac, Montesquieu, and our founding fathers.

The new cosmology and its attendant method equally finds its way into aesthetics. As stated previously, already Descartes, in his ideal of "universal knowledge," or *mathesis universalis,* implies an aesthetic system. "And the further the spirit of Cartesianism spread . . . , the more forcefully the new law is proclaimed in the realm of aesthetic theory." Such theory, in Cassirer's opinion, depends for its success on its ability to reduce the great multiplicity of heterogeneous data in the various arts to one principle. This conviction is expressed and realized in a work by Batteux, predictably entitled *The Fine Arts Reduced to a Single Principle,* the principle being imitation. Accordingly,

> the course of seventeenth and eighteenth century aesthetics was . . . indicated once and for all. It is based on the idea that, as nature in all its manifestations is governed by certain principles, and as it is the highest task of the knowledge of nature to formulate these principles clearly and precisely, so also art . . . is under the same obligation. As there are universal and inviolable laws of nature, so there must be laws of the same kind and of the same importance for the imitation of nature. And finally all these partial laws must fit into and be subordinate to one simple principle, an axiom of imitation in general.

Further referring to Batteux's work, Cassirer comments, "the great example of Newton exerts its influence here too. The order which he achieved in the physical universe should be sought also in the intellectual, the ethical, and the aesthetic universe." The "Newton of art," however, was not Batteux, but the French poet and literary critic Boileau, "the law-giver of Parnassus." His chief and most influential work, *L'Art poetique* (1674),

> seemed finally to elevate aesthetics to the rank of an exact science in that it introduced in the place of merely abstract postulates concrete application and special investigation. The parallelism of the arts and sciences, which is one of the fundamental theses of French classicism, now appeared to have been tested and verified in fact. Even prior to Boileau this parallelism had been explained on the grounds of the common derivation of the arts and sciences from the absolutely homogeneous and

---

8. A. N. Whitehead, *Science and the Modern World* (New York: The Macmillan Company, 1925; reprinted by The New American Library, Mentor Books, New York, 1959), p. 55.

sovereign power of "reason." This power knows no compromise and tolerates no qualification.

An attitude similar to the one present in Boileau's work is expressed by the critic d'Aubignac. In his *Theatrical Practice* (1669) he writes, "in all matters which depend on reason and common sense, such as the rules of the theater, . . . license is a crime which is never permitted." And another French critic of the period, Le Bossu, thinks in similar fashion when he says in his *Traité du poème épique* (1675), "the arts have this in common with the sciences, . . . that the former like the latter are founded on reason and that in the arts one should allow himself to be guided by the lights which nature has given us." Needless to say, *nature* and *reason* were synonymous terms in the seventeenth and eighteenth centuries, for the laws of nature in their abstract, mathematical form were arrived at by primarily rational means, with only indirect empirical verification. Thus the Enlightenment concepts of "natural religion" and "natural morality" were supplemented by the idea of a "natural aesthetics," i.e., an aesthetics which depends on certain rules derived from abstract rational thought. "Truth and beauty, reason and nature, are now but different expressions for the same thing, for one and the same inviolable order of being, different aspects of which are revealed in natural science and in art." The uniformity and continuity of aesthetic thought in the seventeenth and in the eighteenth centuries is revealed by the following passage from a poem entitled *"La Raison"* by the French poet M. J. de Chénier (1764-1811):

> It is good sense, reason, which achieves all: virtue, genius, spirit, talent, taste. What is virtue? It is reason put in practice. And talent? Reason brilliantly set forth. Spirit? Reason well expressed. Taste is simply refined good sense, and genius is reason sublime.

The affinity of the ideas expressed by Chénier, whose life-span extends into the nineteenth century, with the ideas of the seventeenth-century Batteux, Boileau, and Le Bossu, is clearly evident from the above. All of them rely on reason, which is regarded as being coterminous with the exactitude and universality of natural law. Hence, writes Cassirer,

> Like mathematics and physics, critical theory too recognizes the rigorous ideal of exactness, which constitutes the necessary correlate and presupposition for its requirement of universality. Here again we find

complete harmony between the scientific and artistic ideals of the epoch. For aesthetic theory seeks only to follow the same way that mathematics and physics had taken and pursued to the end.

And later again, speaking of the abstract, quantitative, and purely relational character of eighteenth-century cosmology and its attendant epistemology, Cassirer writes that "classical aesthetics was modeled after this theory of nature and after this mathematical theory point by point."[9] Admittedly, Batteux, Boileau, Le Bossu, *et al.*, extrapolate the implications of natural into aesthetic law in a somewhat naïve and uncritical manner. However, their relatively uncritical approach to this problem can be partially accounted for by the current adherence to ancient classical standards which, in the two centuries under consideration, were customarily equated with the principles of the cosmology as evolved by Galileo, Kepler, and Newton. It is this self-conscious association with Greece and Rome, and the feeling that the Age of Reason and the Enlightenment were but a continuation of Classical culture temporarily interrupted by the allegedly barbaric Middle Ages, which explain Alexander Pope's famous lines, "Those rules of old discovered, not devised/ Are nature still, but nature methodized."

There is a striking contrast between the seventeenth- and eighteenth-century view of law in art which, like law in nature, is assumed to admit of no exceptions, and the twentieth-century view as formulated by the composer and music theorist Arnold Schoenberg. At first sight Schoenberg would appear to take the diametrically opposed position with respect to artistic law when he writes that "laws of art are conspicuous mainly for their exceptions," while it is only laws of nature which are "true without exception." Therefore, continues Schoenberg, "(universally valid) artistic principles have so far eluded me (as well as others) and it is doubtful whether any such will soon be formulated. Attempts to base art entirely on nature will continue to be abortive."[10] The last sentence indicates that Schoenberg's position regarding the relation between laws of art and laws of nature is still largely consonant with the eighteenth-century view; for he writes that art based *entirely* on nature is bound to be misguided. Hence, with respect to culture, Schoenberg exhibits

---

9. Cassirer, *Philosophy*, pp. 279–84.

10. Quoted and translated by John F. Spratt, "The Speculative Content of Schoenberg's *Harmonielehre*," paper read at the American Musicological Society Convention, South Central Chapter, March 1968.

the weaker type of causality characteristic of contemporary science.[11] Regarding science, on the other hand, Schoenberg, with
his implicit view of natural law as absolute and unchanging,
appears to reflect the scientific determinism of the previous era.

We now turn to the effect of the mechanistic theory of nature
on literature. Most authors of literature and literary criticism
refer to the eighteenth century as the Age of Prose in contradistinction to the more poetic Romantic Era, and the pre-Enlight-
enment period of Shakespeare, Donne, and Milton. For example,
Basil Willey, in describing the transition during the seventeenth
century from a predominance of poetry to one of prose, writes
that the century

> begins with Shakespeare and Donne, leads on to Milton, and ends with
> Dryden and Swift: that is to say, it begins with a literature full of
> passion, paradox, imagination, curiosity and complexity, and ends with
> one distinguished rather by clarity, precision, good sense and definiteness
> of statement. The end of the century is the beginning of what has been
> called the Age of Prose and Reason, and we may say that by then the
> qualities necessary for good prose had got the upper hand over those
> which produce the greatest kinds of poetry.[12]

Poetry in this period, despite such figures as Dryden and Pope,
held generally little esteem among the educated strata of society.
It was actually regarded as something useless and arbitrary,
something lacking in cognitive content. This was a widely held
opinion, and among its followers we find scientists, philosophers,
and authors. Newton, for example, reputedly stated that poetry
"was a kind of ingenious nonsense," while Locke said that "at
the best it was a pleasing cheat, supplying 'pleasant pictures and
agreeable visions.' "[13] Hume was more extreme. In his estimation
"poetry is the work of professional liars who seek to entertain
by fictions." A generation later, Jeremy Bentham made the distinction between poetry and prose by saying that "all the lines
except the last extend to the margin" in prose, "whereas in poetry
some of them fall short." He continues in this sarcastic vein,
writing that "poetry . . . proves nothing; it is full of senti-
mentalism and vague generalities. The silly jingling might satisfy

11. See further Northrop's Introduction to Werner Heisenberg, *Physics and
Philosophy* (New York: Harper Torchbooks, 1962), pp. 1–26.
12. Basil Willey, "How the Scientific Revolution of the Seventeenth Century
Affected Other Branches of Thought," in *A Short History of Science* (Garden
City, N. Y.: Doubleday Anchor Books, 1959), p. 61.
13. C. J. Horne, "Literature and Science," in *From Dryden to Johnson*, ed.
Boris Ford (Baltimore: Penguin Books, 1963), p. 189.

the ears of a savage but would make no impression on a mature mind." The unanimity of opinion by these scientists and philosophers concerning the value of poetry clearly reflects the contemporaneous view of nature. And it will be recalled that this view is based chiefly on the abstract, deductively formulated primary qualities of the real world as developed by Galileo, Descartes, and Newton. Poetry, on the other hand, depends for its effectiveness and power on imagery which recalls and intensifies the vividness of the phenomenal world, of the very same transitory secondary qualities which are only a hindrance to accurate mathematical formulation of natural law. Hence the criterion of value in eighteenth-century literature, and implicitly in culture as a whole, was rational cognitive content, and this content was based on the Cartesian "clear and distinct ideas" of mathematics, not on the infinitude of immediate sense experience. Even the poets of the era swayed under the pressure of the rational climate of opinion. For example, Dryden, in his *Apology for Heroic Poetry and Poetic License,* wrote that "we should be pleased with the images of poetry but not cozened by the fiction." Addison, clearly manifesting his absorption of the current epistemology with its distinction between the primary qualities of the material world and the illusory secondary qualities of sense experience produced in our minds by the interaction between matter and mind, finds it necessary to defend poetry by writing that

> if the material world were endowed with only those qualities *which it actually possesses* it would make a joyless and uncomfortable poetic figure. Fortunately, a kindly Providence has given matter the power of producing in us a whole series of delightful *imaginary* qualities so that man may have his mind cheered and delighted with agreeable sensations.

Fontenelle's geometric spirit, cited earlier in the chapter, makes itself felt in poetry also, just as Fontenelle had envisaged. Besides aiming at mathematical objectivity, with a minimum of subjective sentiment, a poet, in order to be "complete and excellent," writes Dryden, "should be learned in several sciences, and should have a reasonable, philosophical and in some measure, a mathematical head." Another mathematical influence may be seen in the heroic couplet which, due to the uniformity and regularity of its cadence, became the standard means of versification. According to Kline,

> The heroic couplet won favor because of its balance and symmetry, and,

extreme as this view may seem to us, because the form was analogous to a series of equal proportions. The heroic couplet was regarded as the essence of cadenced regularity. Beauty, to the literary critics of the age, consisted in adherence to these strict rules of versification.[14]

Thus, the eighteenth-century poets followed nature in their creative impulses, but nature as formulated by the mathematical physicist, not as perceived with the senses by the natural-history biologist. Here too, as in aesthetic theory, to follow nature meant to follow the classics. For example, Alexander Pope in his *Essay on Criticism,* describing Virgil's aspiration to surpass Homer in epic poetry, writes "But when t'examine every part he came,/ Nature and Homer were, he found, the same." In fact the entire period embracing Dryden, Pope, and Addison is referred to as the "Augustan Age,"

and the men of that time really felt that they were living in an epoch like that of the Emperor Augustus—an age of enlightenment, learning and true civilisation—and congratulated themselves on having escaped from the errors and superstitions of the dark and monkish Middle Ages.[15]

In sum, the criteria for excellence in poetry were artistic axioms deduced from natural law, reason, and the ancients, and "to follow one was to follow all. The rules of art were 'nature methodized.' "

In consonance with the view of poetry outlined above, the faculty of the imagination, whatever meaning one may attach to this term, was regarded as antithetical to the aims of the eighteenth-century poets relevant to our discussion. It was either rejected outright as something dangerous and opposed to reason, or its value was acknowledged, but with the severest qualifications. Dryden, for example, wrote that imagination "is a faculty so wild and lawless that like a high-ranging spaniel, it must have clogs tied to it, lest it outrun the judgment."[16] Boileau similarly writes that "the law governing art as such is not derived from and produced by the imagination; it is rather a purely objective law which the artist does not have to invent but only to discover in the nature of things." And Malebranche's opinion is that "to keep the imagination in check and to regulate it deliberately, is the highest goal of all philosophical criticism." Cassirer, in his

14. Morris Kline, *Mathematics in Western Culture* (New York: Oxford University Press, 1964), pp. 277–78, 280.
15. Willey, "Scientific Revolution," p. 61.
16. Kline, *Mathematics,* pp. 279, 280.

commentary on Malebranche, continues, "the imagination appears not as a way to the truth but as a source of all the delusions to which the human mind is exposed, in the realm of natural science and in that of moral and metaphysical knowledge.[17] This low estimate of imagination in the creative process contrasts sharply with Coleridge's view of this faculty. In opposition to the entire logico-mechanistic cosmology of the seventeenth and eighteenth centuries, and in harmony with the emerging life sciences and their attendant idea of evolution, Coleridge placed imagination at the very zenith in the hierarchy of creative faculties, as the one which constitutes spontaneous, vegetative genius.[18]

It was stated earlier in this chapter that the Enlightenment was the age of prose rather than poetry. The principal literary forms were the novel, essay, memoir, biography, satire, and a great deal of historical writing. Smaller forms, usually associated with the widespread journalistic activity of the period, were the pamphlet, periodical essay, diary, and much critical writing. The preponderance of prose in various forms was stimulated by the rational temper of the times, which demanded, above all, accuracy, clarity, and economy. That this was ultimately traceable to the "Newtonian spirit" is attested to by Kline. He writes that

> mathematicians . . . were set up as literary models in the eighteenth century. Descartes' style was extolled for its clarity, neatness, readability, and perspicuity, and Cartesianism became a style as well as a philosophy. The elegance and rationality of Pascal's manner . . . were hailed as superb attributes of literary style. Writers in almost all fields began to . . . [imitate] as closely as their subject matter permitted the works of Descartes, Pascal, Huygens, Galileo, and Newton.[19]

However, aside from the influence of the natural sciences, the demand for directness and clarity of style is also attributable to the rise of journalism and an attendant large reading public composed of the growing middle classes. Hence, we find that most of the leading authors writing during the period, Defoe, Swift and Fielding, Samuel Johnson and Oliver Goldsmith, had at one time or another extensive journalistic experience. The sociological factors which generated the above trend are to a large extent responsible for the growth of public concerts and the concomitant simplification of musical style. Here too musical

---

17. Cassirer, *Philosophy*, pp. 285, 283.
18. See further M. H. Abrams, *The Mirror and the Lamp: Romantic Theory and the Critical Tradition* (New York: Oxford University Press, 1953; reprinted by W. W. Norton & Co., New York, 1958), pp. 201–25.
19. *Mathematics*, p. 275.

clarity, rationality, and intelligibility were of the utmost importance if a large and varied musical public was to be satisfied.
These features were preeminently fulfilled by the mature works
of Haydn and Mozart.

Together with the unpoetic character of the era, the profusion
of prose literature, and the demands for clarity and intelligibility
in all writing, the English language itself was subjected to a
reform whose aim was uniformity and standardization of usage.
Already in the seventeenth century the Royal Society had proposed the formation of an academy for the " 'improvement of
speaking and writing.' "[20] Thomas Sprat, the first historian of
the Society, writes that "the only remedy for past extravagances"
was

> a constant Resolution to reject all the amplifications, digressions, and
> swellings of style: to return back to the primitive purity, and shortness,
> when men deliver'd so many *things,* almost in an equal number of *words.*
> They [the Society] have extracted from all their members, a close, naked,
> natural way of speaking; positive expressions; clear senses; a native
> easiness; bringing all things as near the Mathematical plainness, as
> they can.[21]

Perhaps nowhere is the movement toward standardization and
uniformity of usage more evident than in Samuel Johnson's
Dictionary. Here too the model was the uniformity of natural
law and the exactitude of the mathematical sciences. Kline notes
that Johnson "undertook to regulate a language which had been
'produced by necessity and enlarged by accident.' " Furthermore,
by establishing clear meanings and by drawing clear distinctions
between them, Johnson intended to achieve a degree of permanence of definition comparable to the permanence in the definition
of a triangle, which "has meant precisely the same thing for
thousands of years." In short, "he set about to do for the English
language what had already been started in all spheres of activity,
namely, to determine and establish the most reasonable, most
efficient, and most permanent standards." The desire for uniformity and accuracy of expression can also be seen in the work
of Leibniz and Jeremy Bentham. Leibniz "sought to facilitate
reasoning" by converting language into a system of symbols,
while Bentham's "ideal language would resemble algebra; ideas
would be represented by symbols as numbers are represented by

---

20. *Ibid.,* p. 274.
21. History of the Royal Society, as quoted by Horne in Ford, ed., *Dryden to
Johnson,* p. 192.

letters. Thereby ambiguous or inadequate words and misleading metaphors would be eliminated."[22]

We now proceed with an analysis of the visual arts. The emphasis on those features in painting which correspond to the newly emerging world view in the seventeenth century, i.e., the emphasis on line, structure, and geometrical order, may be seen in the work of Poussin, who was an exact contemporary of Descartes. As in the cultural domains discussed previously, the influence of classical culture is also a major contributing factor to Poussin's style. In a letter to his friend and patron Chantelou, extrapolating the principle of Greek musical modes to painting, he writes that " 'Mode' means actually the rule or the measure and form, which serves us in our productions." And this results in a "certain determined manner or order, and includes the procedure by which the object is preserved in its essence."[23] It is uncertain to what extent Poussin was directly influenced by Descartes; yet Poussin's stress on such abstract features as "measure," "form," and "order" strongly suggests that such influence was present at least indirectly. Furthermore, Platonic philosophy, which Poussin knew, likewise emphasizes the very same entities. Consequently, Poussin's landscapes are frequently described as a reduction of the phenomenal "disorder of nature . . . to the order of geometry," where even "trees and shrubs are made to approach the condition of architecture."[24] It is no wonder that Cézanne, who desired "to make of Impressionism something solid and durable," and who said that the painter ought to "treat nature by the cylinder, the sphere, [and] the cone,"[25] also "wanted to do Poussin again, from Nature."[26]

The tradition of Poussin, regarding both his adherence to classical standards and his implicit reflection of the Cartesian world view, is continued in the eighteenth century by Sir Joshua Reynolds. Reynolds had a high esteem for Poussin, and was strongly influenced by him. In the work incorporating his aesthetic principles, *The Discourses on Art*, Reynolds also exhibits

22. *Mathematics*, pp. 273–74.
23. Elizabeth G. Holt, ed., *Literary Sources of Art History: an Anthology of Texts from Theophilus to Goethe* (Princeton, N. J.: Princeton University Press, 1947), p. 380.
24. Michael W. L. Kitson, "Poussin, Nicolas," *Encyclopaedia Britannica* 18 (1964) : 383.
25. Letter to Emile Bernard, 15 April 1904, quoted in Herschel B. Chipp, ed., *Theories of Modern Art* (Berkeley: University of California Press, 1968), p. 19.
26. Peter Murray and Linda Murray, *A Dictionary of Art and Artists* (Baltimore: Penguin Books, 1963), p. 54.

his allegiance to the classics and to the world view created by Descartes, Galileo, and Newton. Thus, with regard to the classics he repeatedly appeals to the work of Phidias as representing an "abstract idea" of form and an "Ideal Beauty," meaning thereby that Phidias, by abstracting from the radically empirical details of any one particular human being, arrived at an ideal beauty and universality symbolizing mankind as a whole. The analogy between this type of beauty and the universality of abstract Newtonian law need not be belabored here. It is enough to say that Reynolds was just as acutely aware of the geometrical spirit of his time as he was of the classicism of Phidias. For example, in the "Seventh Discourse" he writes,

> It is the very same taste which relishes a demonstration in geometry, that is pleased with the resemblance of a picture to an original, and touched with the harmony of musick. All these have unalterable and fixed foundations in nature, and are therefore equally investigated by reason.[27]

Moreover, his statement that "the essence of beauty is the expression of universal laws"[28] is further indication of the influence which Reynolds absorbed from Newtonian cosmology.

The *Discourses* were written in the second half of the eighteenth century, the "First Discourse" having been published in 1769 and the "Fifteenth Discourse" in 1790. Thus the views expressed therein, especially as we approach the turn of the century, are to some extent anachronistic, considering the change in the intellectual climate of these years. The change involves the gradual replacement of logocentric by biocentric thought, and is discussed at length in chapter 1 above. Reynolds's anachronism, however, may in large measure be attributed to the fact that he was an academician, and the academic viewpoint regarding established standards and regulations has always been on the conservative side.

It has been noted earlier that empiricism has continually been a strong undercurrent in the predominantly rational seventeenth and eighteenth centuries, especially in the British Isles (see chapter 2). This tendency, in contrast to Reynolds's rational orientation, may be seen in the art and aesthetic attitude of William Hogarth, who antedates Reynolds by almost a generation. For example, in the Introduction to Hogarth's *The Analysis*

27. Sir Joshua Reynolds, *Discourses on Art*, ed. Robert R. Wark (San Marino, Calif.: Huntington Library, 1959), pp. 44–45, 122.
28. Kline, *Mathematics*, p. 285.

of Beauty, Joseph Burke writes that Hogarth manifests a "frank appeal to the senses" and that this was a revolutionary feature in the "entrenched neo-classicism" of the period. Burke further notes that "Hogarth," in his time "stands out as a solitary phenomenon. He, alone of artists, attaches himself to the great tradition of English empirical philosophy."[29]

29. William Hogarth, *The Analysis of Beauty,* ed., and intro. by Joseph Burke (Oxford at the Clarendon Press, 1955), pp. liv–lv.

4

The Place of Baroque Music
in the Age of Reason

The discussion in the foregoing chapter regarding the relationship between several cultural phenomena and the mechanistic theory of nature has been centered on the seventeenth and eighteenth centuries. It was disclosed that these two centuries are basically homogeneous with respect to the manner in which literature, political philosophy, aesthetics, and other areas of endeavor were conceived. The common denominator of these widely divergent domains was a logocentric epistemology, i.e., an epistemology which dwelt heavily on reason, system, law, and, generally speaking, on those factors in knowledge which depend primarily on abstract deductive formulation. It was likewise shown that this method corresponds to, and is mirrored in, the Newtonian world view, which in similar fashion was based on certain primitive and deductively arrived-at abstract postulates. Knowledge gained through sensory experience alone, on the other hand, was relegated to an inferior cognitive status and, in philosophy, was designated as constituting the so-called secondary qualities of the appearance of reality. The purpose of the present chapter is to demonstrate that a parallel development occurred in the music of the same period, i.e., that the concept of music shares the same common denominator of rational and systematic thought exhibited in areas discussed previously.

The implementation of rationalism is immediately apparent in the so-called doctrine of affections (*Affectenlehre*) of the Baroque era (*ca.* 1600-1750). According to this doctrine human emotions are susceptible of categorization into clear and distinct stereotypes, such as joy, anger, love, hatred, and so on. These emotions, or emotional states, are in turn translatable into a certain number of musical motifs (figures) by means of which (in addition to the text) the desired emotions are expressed by the composer. The static and schematized nature of this system, and the fact that it was a typical product of the rational environment of the seventeenth century, is noted by Bukofzer. He writes that "the means of verbal representation in baroque music were not direct, psychological, and emotional, but indirect, that is, intellectual and pictorial." Furthermore, in the absence of the modern dynamic psychology of human emotions "feelings were classified and stereotyped in a set of so-called affections, each representing a mental state which was in itself static." It was the responsibility of the composer to match the desired emotion with the corresponding musical formula, for "according to the lucid rationalism of the time, the composer had at his disposal a set of musical figures which were pigeonholed like the affections themselves and were designed to represent these affections in music."[1] That this was no mere isolated theory with little influence on the actual composition of music, and that the *Affectenlehre* was in fact a viable system implemented universally from Monteverdi through J. S. Bach, is attested to by the noted musicologist Friedrich Blume.

> Thus, from its outset the Baroque developed a systematic vocabulary which could be taught and could be translated into musical terms. It was fostered by the great Italian masters and was disseminated throughout Europe by a multitude of disciples. It was embodied in Bach's *Orgelbüchlein,* in his passions and cantatas.

Moreover, lest it be thought that baroque music, with its restless and intense emotionality, appears "to have sprung from the personal excitement and 'sympathies' of the composer," Blume adds that, on the contrary, "in reality the primary concern was with the manipulation of rules and words, and with the rational translation of the extra-musical ideas into musical notation. . . . Thus musical composition was primarily an intellectual process, rather than an intuitive expression of emotional excitement."[2]

The doctrine of affections constitutes the musical rhetoric of the Baroque. It is a systematic vocabulary having its origin on

1. Manfred F. Bukofzer, *Music in the Baroque Era* (New York: W. W. Norton & Company, Inc., 1947), p. 5.
2. Roy E. Carter, "'Barock,' by Friedrich Blume: a Translation" (Master's thesis, School of Music, Florida State University, 1961), pp. 45, 60.

the one hand in the ancient art of oratory and its linguistic figures, and on the other in the mechanistic psychology of the seventeenth century. It deals chiefly with a uniform and rational scheme for the expression of a given text and its emotional content through a certain predetermined set of musical formulas said to "represent" the corresponding human emotion. Not surprisingly, the doctrine of affections and its implementation in music throughout the Baroque is implicit in the work of Descartes. For example, in his youthful treatise *Compendium musicae* (1618), Descartes writes, "regarding the different passions that music can excite in us by its various measures, I say in general that a slow measure produces slow passions in us, such as languor, sadness, fear and pride, etc.: and that a fast measure, on the other hand, gives rise to fast and more lively passions, such as joy and gladness, etc."[3] The author of the article on Descartes in *Die Musik in Geschichte und Gegenwart* goes even further. He says that Descartes was the real founder of the rationalistic doctrine of affections, whose direct influence on the philosophy of music is manifest as late as 1739, the year of Mattheson's *Der vollkomene Kapellmeister*. In this work Mattheson refers to the *Traité des passions de l'âme* (1649), Descartes's last work and a further elaboration of the theory of human emotions initiated in the *Compendium musicae*. Hence, in conformity with the Cartesian rational and mechanistic view of nature and man, music was one of two things: 1) from the standpoint of its emotional effect on man, it was a "psycho-physiological" phenomenon, while 2) from its purely acoustical properties it was a "mathematico-physical" phenomenon.[4]

Additional evidence corroborating the rational nature of the doctrine of affections, its universal adoption, and its twofold derivation from the art of oratory and from the Cartesian mechanistic psychology is disclosed in *The Art of Music*. Thus, write the authors,

a reduction of the art of oratory to "scientific," mechanistic principles inevitably affected the theory and practice of music which had adopted oratory as its preceptor. The fusion of the doctrine of Musica Poetica and the mechanistic psychology of Descartes is most clearly revealed in a periodical, *Der critische Musicus* . . . founded by Johann Scheibe

3. John M. Eddins, "A Study of Cartesian Musical Thought, with a Complete Translation of the *Compendium musicae*" (Master's thesis, School of Music, Florida State University, 1959), p. 79.
4. Rudolf Stephan, "Descartes, René," *Die Musik in Geschichte und Gegenwart* (Kassel und Basel: Bärenreiter-Verlag, 1949–68), vol. 3, cols. 209–10.

(1708–1776). Scheibe insists that the end of music is "to move the spirit, in particular to rouse or still the passions." To attain this goal we must study the principles of composition in a scientific way. The musician must first learn how the passions manifest themselves and what motions are involved in them. This he can learn from speech.

Furthermore, according to Scheibe, the "sounds of emotional speech are equivalent to the tones of melody" which serve as a vehicle for the direct and immediate expression of the passions. Harmony, contrary to Rameau's principles, "is only a secondary, though necessary, factor which ennobles the melodic idea." Therefore, the period from *ca.* 1720 to 1760 constitutes a curious admixture of the old and the new with respect to the philosophy of music, the conservative elements being represented by the supporters of the mechanistic doctrine of affections and its concomitant melodic supremacy, while the progressive elements were advanced by those musicians who advocated the spontaneous and direct expression of emotions by the simplest musical means. Harmony, in this respect, already promoted by Rameau's *Treatise* (1722), gained a hitherto unprecedented prominence. The full implications of this shift, however, were not fully realized until the advent of Impressionism, which simultaneously destroyed the major-minor harmonic system. Continuing with the rational nature of music during the period in question, we read further in *The Art of Music,*

> By the beginning of the eighteenth century the art of creating music had become almost entirely rationalized. The older humanistic conception of the intimate relationship of words and tone still remained, but this relationship now rested upon physical laws. Music represented the passion contained in the words in terms of sounds in motion.[5]

Bukofzer in essence concurs with the above observation, describing the affections, conjoined to a set of musical figures, as being elaborately systematized, "static," and "non-psychological." He further writes,

> The distinctly rational and intellectual connotation of the doctrine of figures was a direct outgrowth of the highly characteristic attitude toward concrete and abstract concepts in baroque thought, which tried to render abstract ideas concretely and concrete things abstractly. A strictly musical idea was therefore . . . an abstract affection in concrete form, and for this reason the figure had a structural significance for

5. Beekman C. Cannon, Alvin H. Johnson, and William G. Waite, *The Art of Music* (New York: Thomas Y. Crowell Company, 1960), pp. 252–54.

the entire composition. The profound respect for the figures in music is solemnly affirmed by Bernhard who bluntly puts it like this: "What cannot be justified by figures should be banished from music as a monstrosity."[6]

The foregoing has been an analysis of a major phase of baroque musical thought dealing with the manner in which words and music were combined. It has been shown that here, as in cultural realms previously discussed, the exaltation of reason in musical composition is a cardinal moving factor. Descartes's role in the formulation of the doctrine of affections, and the implementation of this doctrine in the musical practice of the Baroque, clearly illustrates that music is inseparable from the Cartesian world view and its abstract rationalistic epistemology. It is no wonder that "Descartes was called 'the conscience of his century'. . . . He clarified and formulated the thoughts of his contemporaries," and, with respect to music,

> The standardization of musical forms, the acceptance of the major-minor tyranny, . . . a general objective attitude towards the use of tonal materials—, all these fit so well the aesthetics of Descartes that one cannot avoid considering the music of the seventeenth century as a very definite expression of those principles that motivated man's thoughts and actions in the Age of Reason.[7]

The rational and systematic approach is no less apparent in purely instrumental music of the Baroque. This is especially evident in the music of J. S. Bach, who simultaneously represents the synthesis and culmination of the Baroque era. Thus, when we examine such works as the forty-eight preludes and fugues of the *Well-Tempered Clavier* (Book I, 1722; Book II, 1744), the *Musical Offering* (1747), the *Goldberg Variations* (1742), and the *Art of Fugue* (1749), the conspicuous feature is the systematic and logical exploitation of a musical idea. The *Well-Tempered Clavier*, for example, illustrates in systematic fashion the employment of all twenty-four major and minor keys made possible by the contemporaneously developed equal-temperament tuning. In themselves the very development and application of equal temperament reflect the method of Newtonian physics, in the sense that both constitute a necessary oversimplification of natural phenomena, if these are to be controlled and implemented

6. Bukofzer, *Baroque*, pp. 388–90.
7. Arthur W. Locke, "Descartes and Seventeenth-Century Music," *The Musical Quarterly* 21 (1935): 430–31.

in practical applications. Parenthetically it may here be pointed out that the profound modification in Newtonian cosmology during the early part of the twentieth century, and the recent development of electronic music combined with the influence of Oriental philosophy, suggests that equal temperament has become inadequate for contemporary musical expression.

The concern for order in the music of Bach is even more clearly manifest in the *Goldberg Variations*. Here every third of the thirty variations is in the form of a canon (in itself a highly abstract technique) at successive intervals from the unison through the ninth, the last variation being a *quodlibet*. The transcendent order and logic imposed on this work, an order which goes beyond audible sound, are noted by Bukofzer. He writes,

> Only intellectual playfulness can account for the order of the nine canons in the *Goldberg Variations*. . . . While it is of course true that the sequence of canons at different intervals can be grasped by ear, the idea of correlating the numerical order of the canons with their intervallic order is a clever intellectual pun, possible only because musical intervals happen to be called by numerals.

And further,

> The . . . intellectual principles were all . . . devices to secure inner unity and consistency that in themselves were not audible. . . . They materialized at times only on the printed page, like certain puzzle canons. . . . The devices were logical . . . and they could be intellectually understood but not intuitively experienced.

Thus instrumental music in the Baroque period was something more than sound, more than a mere " 'aggregation of auditory stimuli.' " It was above all a rational system governed by "abstract principles of order," to a large extent a "supramusical order" as revealed in the *Goldberg Variations*.

> We must recognize the speculative approach to music as one of the fundamentals of baroque music and baroque art in general without either exaggerating or belittling its importance. . . . Audible form and inaudible order were not mutually exclusive or opposed concepts . . . but complementary aspects of one and the same experience: the unity of sensual and intellectual understanding.

The pinnacle of baroque contrapuntal art and, in the opinion of some writers, of counterpoint since its inception, is found in Bach's two final masterpieces, the *Musical Offering* and the *Art of Fugue*. Both works are based on one theme. Here, to a greater extent than in any of his previous works, a highly abstract and supra-sensory scheme is the conspicuous feature. The series of ten canons in the *Musical Offering,* for example, seems to exhaust all the possibilities of this contrapuntal technique, and constitutes the severest test in abstract inferential thought, almost suggesting thought processes in mathematical physics. For example, we have canon in contrary motion, canon by augmentation and contrary motion, canon in contrary motion invertible in double counterpoint, and retrograde canon. The succession of canons and fugues in the *Art of Fugue* presents similar techniques with further intensification and complexity. Here the sixteenth fugue in three parts (Kalmus Edition) is accompanied by its mirror version, although the two versions are to be performed separately; the eighteenth fugue discloses the same technique, except this time in four parts. It is said that Bach planned to conclude the entire cycle with a quadruple fugue, all parts of which were to be invertible. The absence of any specified instrumentation, the notation in open score with the old *c* clefs, and the general designation *contrapunctus* for each of the nineteen items in the cycle is further evidence that Bach intended something transcendent and supra-sensory in this undertaking. With this in mind, it does not appear to be remote to suggest that implicit in the *Art of Fugue* is a cosmos regulated by impersonal and universal law, not unlike the orderly universe postulated in Newton's *Principia.* The same attitude of lawful regulation is given expression in Bach's final aspiration to achieve "a regulated church music," i.e., "regulated in accordance with the precepts of . . . both sacred and secular music. For a composer who conceived music as 'the reflection and foretaste of heavenly harmony' . . . it was no sacrilege to use in the church the *concertato* style or even opera style."[8]

Therefore, just as the doctrine of affections furnished a complete rational basis for vocal music in such diverse forms as opera, cantata, and oratorio, so Bach in his instrumental music reveals an essentially rational method of composition consistent with the predominantly logocentric world view of the seventeenth and eighteenth centuries. His frequent indifference to medium of performance indicates a habit of mind which is more concerned with principle than with sonority. That in his last years he was criticized by his sons and others (Scheibe, for example) for undue "intricacy" and "artificiality," and for obscuring the

---

8. Bukofzer, *Baroque,* pp. 368–69, 272.

" 'natural beauty' of the music,"[9] is symptomatic of a trend which was not fully materialized until the advent of Romanticism in the nineteenth century.

With respect to baroque harmony and rhythm, certain features are discernible which are also the product of the same rational mentality. Turning to harmony first, we notice that by the year 1680 the harmonic anarchy of the early part of the century had been stabilized and reduced to a predictable system of chordal relations known as major-minor tonality, and frequently described since the late nineteenth century (H. Riemann) as functional harmony. The essence of this system is a tonal center (key) with neighboring "satellite" tonalities which "gravitate" toward the center. The degree of attraction between the tonal center and the neighboring tonalities may be said to be directly proportional to the distance between the two, figured by the circle of fifths. Thus, the degree of attraction between the tonal center c and its nearest neighbor g (one fifth apart) is fivefold greater than the attraction between c and its more distant neighbor b (five fifths apart). There is a clear analogy between this description of tonality and the Newtonian operation of the solar system with its inverse square law of gravitational attraction between the sun and the planets. It is noted by no less a scholar of baroque music than Bukofzer that, "It is no mere metaphor if tonality is explained in terms of gravitation. Both tonality and gravitation were discoveries of the baroque period made at exactly the same time." Described further by Bukofzer,

> The functional or tonal chord progressions are governed by the drive to the cadence which releases the tension that the movement away from the tonic produces. The technical means of achieving key-feeling were, aside from the cadence itself, diatonic sequences of chords that gravitated toward the tonal center. The degree of attraction depended on the distance of the chords from the tonic, and this distance was measured and determined by the circle of fifths.[10]

There is a striking parallel between the life cycle of the major-minor tonal system and the mechanistic theory of nature. The year 1550 may here be taken as a convenient starting point for both domains. In the music of this period (especially secular) the existing modal harmony was progressively being eroded by the chromatic alterations of *musica ficta*, with the result that an in-

9. Jacob Opper, " 'Klassik' by Friedrich Blume: a Translation" (Master's thesis, School of Music, Florida State University, 1965), p. 27.
10. *Baroque,* pp. 12, 220.

creasing number of harmonic progressions approached the sound of modern tonality. Simultaneously the music theorist Zarlino, in his *Instituzioni armoniche* (1558), came close to reducing the enlarged system of twelve modes to two by giving special prominence to those modes (Ionian and Aeolian) which are most like the major and minor scales (the Ionian mode being a major scale without alterations). Zarlino's further assertion that "the basic variety of all part-music derives from the major and minor harmonies"[11] points in the same direction. Accordingly, these events in the practice and theory of music may be termed the embryonic stage in the development of major-minor tonality. Contemporaneously with these developments in music, the *De revolutionibus orbium coelestium* of Copernicus was published in 1543, thus heralding the speculative stage of the mechanistic cosmology. With the appearance of Newton's *Principia* in 1687, and with the music of Corelli composed in the 1680s, the stage of formulation comes to a close in the theory of nature and in harmonic practice, although the final codification of the major-minor tonal system had to wait until 1722, when Rameau had his *Traité de l'harmonie* published. The following two hundred years witness a period of application in science to the extent that Newtonian mechanics was made explicit in almost every area of technology, while music underwent an exhaustive exploitation of those tonal relationships implicit in Rameau's *Traité*, thus stretching the harmonic system to its inherent limitations. By 1887, the year of the Michelson-Morley experiment, Newtonian cosmology was faced with an increasing number of unaccountable discrepancies which paved the way for Einstein's modifications. At the same time Wagnerian harmony in music extended the boundaries of major-minor tonality to such an extent that it was frequently absurd to speak of a clearly defined tonal center to which subsidiary tonalities gravitated. And with the contemporaneous music of Debussy, tonality, in terms of predictable functional chordal relations, disappears completely. Hence, the last two decades of the nineteenth century witness a dissolution of major-minor tonality and of Newtonian cosmology, both having undergone parallel stages of development, and both displaying strikingly analogous principles of operation.

Rameau's *Traité* deserves special attention, since here, more clearly and explicitly than heretofore, the relation between musi-

---

11. Gustave Reese, *Music in the Renaissance* (New York: W. W. Norton & Company, Inc., 1959), p. 377.

cal thought and the physical sciences, with their attendant mechanistic cosmology, is established. The first thing to notice is the
full title of the work (rarely reproduced), which runs as follows:
Traité de l'harmonie reduite à ses principes naturelles (*Treatise
on harmony reduced to its natural principles*). The likeness of
this title to Newton's *Philosophiae Naturalis Principia Mathematica* (*Mathematical Principles of Natural Philosophy*), published thirty-five years earlier, is unmistakable, and it is quite
probable that Rameau upheld Newton's work as a model of
rational procedure. Both titles share the words "natural" and
"principles," while the words "mathematical" and "reduced" are
synonymous in the sense that they are indicative of primarily
deductive methodology. Therefore, it may safely be inferred that
Rameau, in the tradition of Descartes, Huygens, and, implicitly,
Newton, is here regarding music and musical composition not as
something arbitrary and dependent on mere personal choice, but
as a physical phenomenon which can be known properly only if
it is treated as a mathematical and deductive science reduced to
its basic axioms. This methodologically rational and anti-empiri-
cal attitude is made unequivocally clear at the outset of the
Traité when Rameau in the first sentence of the Preface writes,
"Whatever progress the art of music may have made amongst
us, it would appear that the more the ear becomes sensible to its
marvellous effects the less is the desire manifested to understand
its true principles, so that one may say that reason has lost its
rights, while experience alone has acquired any authority."[12]
Implicit in this sentence is a Cartesian epistemology which is
always suspect of building on empirical data that have not been
subjected to a thoroughgoing process of ratiocination.

That Rameau was actually saturated with Cartesian thought
is borne out throughout his theoretical writings. The *Traité*,
for example, is filled with references to Descartes's *Compendium*,[13] while in the *Démonstration du principe de l'harmonie*
(1750) we find a clear expression of Cartesian doubt with
respect to traditional knowledge of music, a distrust for "hit-
or-miss" empiricism, and a single-minded faith in knowledge
deduced from natural principles. Accordingly, he writes, regarding the empirical chaos in music theory existing before him,

---

12. Quoted in Matthew Shirlaw, *The Theory and Nature of Harmony* (Box 91-C,
RR #1, Sarasota, Fla. 33577: Dr. Birchard Coar, 1970), p. 64.
13. See Jean-Philippe Rameau, *Complete Theoretical Writings*, ed. Erwin R.
Jacobi (n.p.: American Institute of Musicology, 1967), 1 : 33, 37, 38, 41, etc.

Has anyone so far sought in Nature . . . some invariable and steadfast principle from which one may proceed with certainty, and which would serve as the basis of melody and harmony? Not at all! It has been a case rather of fumbling about, of compiling facts, of multiplying signs. After much time and trouble all that there was to show was a collection of phenomena without connection, and without succession.

We read further of Rameau's subjecting himself to doubt and rejecting all traditional formulations, preconceptions, and prejudices after reading Descartes's *Méthode*.

Enlightened by the *Méthode* of Descartes, which I had fortunately read, and with which I was much impressed, I began by subjecting myself to a process of self-examination. I attempted to put myself in the place of a child who tries to sing for the first time; essayed various fragments of melody, and examined what were the effects produced on my mind and by my voice.

The above passages are ample evidence that Rameau regarded himself as a naturalist in the tradition of Descartes, Huygens, and Newton, rather than a music theorist formulating arbitrary laws not grounded in the theory of nature. As Shirlaw observes, "He has approached his task in the spirit of the scientist, of the *savant*. His theoretical principles are to be *natural* principles; they must have their source in Nature and have, therefore, all the certainty of natural laws." It must be remembered that nature here is not the phenomenal world of sense experience, but the noumenal world of quantitatively expressed relations. Addressing himself to the *Académie des Sciences*, Rameau considers "harmony to be a physico-mathematical science of sufficient scientific importance to merit the attention of the most eminent *savants* of his day." He writes in the *Génération Harmonique* (1737),

Music . . . is for most people an art intended only for amusement; as respects artistic creation and the appreciation of artistic works, this is supposed to be only a question of *taste;* for you however Music is a Science, established on fixed principles, and which, while it pleases the ear, appeals also to the reason.

The basis of Rameau's theory of harmony is found in what he terms the "sonorous body" (stretched string or organ pipe), which provides the fundamental tone and the series of overtones requisite for the formation of chords. It is the simultaneous sound of the fundamental and of the partials, what he describes

as "the most perfect harmony" of nature, that ultimately caused
him to postulate that all musical elements are secondary to, and
derivative from, harmony. Shirlaw comments in this respect,

> From this sounding body, which breaks itself up into sections, there
> proceeds "the most perfect harmony" of which the mind can conceive.
> This now becomes the fact of primary importance for Rameau. From
> this time onwards the nature of the sonorous body is the theme which
> is hardly ever absent from his lips. . . . He champions it as the key
> to the theory of harmony. That a musical sound is not simple, but
> composite, and that in a well developed musical sound we hear not
> only the primary fundamental tone, but other secondary tones, which
> unite with it, and together form the "perfect harmony" . . . the har-
> mony of Nature, that it is in this natural phenomenon that the whole
> of art of music and of harmony have their origin, and from which they
> take their development—on these things Rameau lays the greatest
> possible stress, and dwells on them with almost tiresome iteration.

The parallel between Galileo's moving body, Hobbes's "body
politic," and Rameau's vibrating "sonorous body" comes here to
mind. All operate according to mechanistic principles and all
exhibit properties which, in the final analysis, are reducible to
numerical proportions. Rameau thus stands in relation to music
as Galileo and Newton stand to physics and as Harvey and
Descartes stand to biological organisms. All conceive their respective realms in terms consistent with the mechanistic theory
of nature of the seventeenth and eighteenth centuries.

Further indication that Rameau, as a music theoretician, placed
himself in the category of the natural scientists is borne out by
his references to the Dutch mathematician and astronomer Chris-
tiaan Huygens, whose theoretical works on music include the
Novus Cyclus Harmonicus and the *Cosmotheros,* and to Isaac
Newton. With respect to the latter Rameau speculates that, had
Newton postulated a harmony of colors, he, like Rameau, would
have "inquired whether each of these colours ought . . . to be
considered as forming a bass, a generator, whereby the colours
form themselves into pleasing groups."

In his later years Rameau was increasingly concerned with
the extrapolation of the mathematical proportions inherent in
the vibrations of the sonorous body into other arts. For example,
with respect to architecture he writes in the *Nouvelles Réflexions
sur la Démonstration du principe de l'harmonie,* "M. Briseux, the
architect, . . . intends shortly to publish a treatise, in which he
is to demonstrate, . . . that the beautiful edifices of the ancient

Greeks and Romans . . . were constructed according to the proportions derived from Music." This led him to believe that the natural principles of music constitute the foundation of all the arts. He writes further,

> I have long held, that in Music there is unquestionably to be found the principle of all the arts of taste, . . . it is from the regular division of the string in its several parts that arise the proportions, each in its order of pre-eminence, or of subordination . . . a fact which ought to guide one with greater certainty than has hitherto been possible towards establishing the basis of a most noble and sublime philosophy.

Ultimately Rameau came to regard the natural principle of harmony produced by the vibrating body as an all-embracing cosmic law. "There is one principle underlying all things; this is a truth which has presented itself to the minds of all thinkers, but the more intimate knowledge of which has been attained by none [because] the phenomenon of the sonorous body was absolutely unknown to them."[14]

In view of what has been said, it is no wonder that Rameau was considered by his contemporaries to be the "Newton of music." This, for example, is the express opinion of the French violinist and composer Jean-Benjamin de la Borde.[15] Rameau, more clearly than any other single musician of the Enlightenment, reflects a clear connection between the Newtonian cosmology and the theory of music founded on purely physical and numerical properties of sound.

> Rameau made it his principal task to demonstrate, not only that all music, whether melodic or harmonic, is governed by certain laws, but that these laws are derived from "natural principles," which, he endeavoured to prove, reside in musical sound itself, are neither more nor less than the natural relations which may be observed to exist in a sonorous body capable of producing an appreciable musical sound.

It is interesting to note the reaction of the nineteenth-century composer Berlioz to Rameau's theory of harmony. On the whole Berlioz praises Rameau, taking exception only to what is and what is not natural, or in nature, respecting music. For example, he criticizes Rameau for deducing his natural principles from sonorous bodies such as the string or the organ pipe, which in themselves are not products of nature. In this connection he

---

14. Shirlaw, *Harmony*, pp. 65, 64, 155, 135, 215, 262, 264.
15. See Rameau, *Complete Writings*, 1 : xi; see also Erwin R. Jacobi, "Rameau, Jean-Philippe," *Die Musik in Geschichte und Gegenwart* (1962), vol. 10, col. 1899.

observes, "Instrumental music . . . is not natural, because Nature does not make instruments!" Moreover, Rameau's use of man-made and highly selective vibrating bodies is the reason, according to Berlioz, why Rameau had so much difficulty in accounting for the minor third on the basis of the overtone series. He writes: "the majority of large bells make us hear quite distinctly the minor third above its fundamental tone! How this fact would have consolidated his theory!" Of course Berlioz fails to mention that bells are also man-made instruments; however, his assumption appears to be that a bell more closely approximates a natural sonorous body, such as a stone or a hollow log, whose more complex partials would account for the minor third.

More in accord with his own time, which placed a greater emphasis on the individual and personal experience as an aesthetic criterion rather than the formulation of general and universal artistic laws characterized by the Enlightenment, Berlioz writes that

> musical harmony is the result of a *choice* of sounds, according to the different impressions that they make on our ear in such and such combinations, with particular conditions as to their successive connection, and to recognize finally that the science of chords has no other *raison d'être* than that of our organization, and no other basis than that which he denies to it, namely, *Experience.*[16]

This represents a striking contrast to Rameau's Cartesian view, described above, that experience alone leads to confusion.

We now turn our attention to rhythm and meter. The principal difference between the rhythmic organization of Baroque and Renaissance music was the accented uniformity of the former and the free-flowing nature of the latter. In more technical terms, the distinction resides in the difference between Baroque metrical rhythm, where the measure is the constant and a given note value the variable, and Renaissance measured rhythm, where the implicit measure (if any) is the variable while the note value (usually the so-called *tactus*) is the constant. The result of this change is a reduction of all metrical schemes to a factor of two or three. Descartes, with his customary insight, grasped immediately the elemental nature of this reduction. He notes that it is easiest for us to perceive duple or triple time (and multiples thereof), while temporal divisions which go beyond these proportions, as for example when "five notes of equal value" are

---

16. Shirlaw, *Harmony,* pp. viii, 165–66.

placed "against one single note," are most difficult to comprehend. He notes further, "from these two kinds of proportion in time have come the two measures that are used in music: division into triple and duple time."[17] Hence, the Baroque, besides evolving the major-minor tonal system which provided Western music with a rational harmonic scheme not superseded until the end of the modern era, likewise furnished a rational basis for the rhythmic organization of music, a basis which extended for the same duration of time. Only in the twentieth century did composers revive the measured rhythm of the Renaissance and of the Middle Ages, eliminating thereby the rhythmic regularity of the Baroque, Classical, and Romantic periods.

In late Baroque music, especially in solo concerti and in concerti grossi, the rhythmic uniformity throughout a concerto movement is frequently described as being "mechanical." Bukofzer repeatedly reverts to this term in his analysis of Baroque rhythm. For example, he writes that the Renaissance "*tactus* was transformed" in the Baroque "to mechanically recurrent pulsations," while the reputed " 'fire and fury of the Italian style' " was primarily due to the "mechanical and ceaselessly progressing beats." Torelli's concerto style is characterized by a "relentless mechanical beat," and Bach invested his Passacaglia in C minor with "quasi-mathematical permutations" and "mechanical patterns which appealed so strongly to baroque speculation."[18] Blume likewise refers to the relentless rhythmic energy of late-Baroque music as late-Baroque "Motorik."[19]

Bukofzer's earlier analogy between a gravitational tonal center and physical gravity, concurrent products of the Baroque, suggests that a similar analogy may be made here, i.e., an analogy between the mechanical uniformity of Baroque temporal organization and the uniform flow of Newtonian time. For time, in Newton's mechanics, was not the immediately sensed experience which "varies from person to person, and even for a single person passes very quickly under certain circumstances and drags under others." On the contrary, time in Newtonian mechanics is " 'absolute, . . . true and . . . mathematical' " flowing " 'equably without relation to anything external.' "[20] There appears to be something equally objective and impersonal about the uniform

17. Eddins, "Cartesian Thought," p. 77.
18. Bukofzer, *Baroque,* pp. 13, 222, 229–30, 279.
19. Carter, "Barock," p. 86.
20. F. S. C. Northrop, *The Meeting of East and West* (New York: The Macmillan Co., 1946), p. 76.

rhythmic flow in a Bach concerto movement suggesting the mathematical uniformity of an eternally moving object in space and time. By no means is this to be understood as a literal identity. We are only making the observation that the underlying ideas of uniformity and rationality in the Newtonian physical world have their concomitants in the rhythmic uniformity and rationality of late-Baroque music, especially the music of J. S. Bach. Leibniz's statement that music is " 'the unconscious counting of the soul' " is a further indication of the role mathematics played in Baroque musical thought. Leibniz, in Bukofzer's words, was "convinced that the unconscious realization of mathematical proportions was the ultimate cause of the sensuous effect of music." The concept of *ratio* was in itself a leading idea of Baroque music. "Sauveur's discovery of the overtone series or what has been termed the 'chord of nature' " gave a further impetus to this idea. "Like tonality and gravitation," the overtone series "was a discovery of the late baroque period; it revolutionized the science of music and led to the substitution of the physical properties of sound for . . . purely speculative rationalizations."[21]

Despite the predominance of reason and the importance of abstract thought in Baroque culture, late-Baroque music, particularly that of Bach and Handel, approaches what is here termed epistemological optimality, that is, a balance of rational and empirical elements in musical composition. For example, the highly relational and inferential techniques employed by Bach in most of his fugal and canonic writing, are contrived in such fashion as to render the relationships audible without undue effort. Admittedly, certain fugues and canons in the *Musical Offering* and the *Art of Fugue* disturb this balance in the direction of recondite relationships accessible more to the intellect than to the ear. These isolated cases notwithstanding, the continuing viability of Bach's music is at bottom due to his ability to combine the most abstract counterpoint, the *logos* of Western music, with an acute sensitivity to instrumental sonority. The six *Brandenburg Concerti*, each exploiting the coloristic properties of different instrumentation yet each invested with the highest contrapuntal skill, are a good example of this. The preludes and fugues for organ are another example. Here the frequently rhapsodic prelude serves as a vehicle for realizing the phenomenal world of sound inherent in the various registers of the instrument, and in the technical ability of the performer, while the

21. Bukofzer, *Baroque*, p. 392.

more relational, abstract features are manifested in the fugue. Hence, if Bach, as is frequently asserted, represents the synthesis of the Baroque, then synthesis, in the highest sense of the word, means the union of the abstract and the sensory in a viable equilibrium. The same balance of cognitive factors, termed by Northrop "epistemic correlation,"[22] is at the basis of Galilean and Newtonian science, where empirical evidence is always connected to deductive thought. Whitehead regards this balance as a "paradox" in the sense that "the utmost abstractions are the true weapons with which to control our thought of concrete fact."[23]

22. See further F. S. C. Northrop, *The Logic of the Sciences and the Humanities* (New York: The Macmillan Company, 1947; reprinted by Meridian Books, Inc., New York, 1959), pp. 119-32.

23. A. N. Whitehead, *Science and the Modern World* (New York: The Macmillan Company, 1925; reprinted by The New American Library, Mentor Books, New York, 1959), p. 37.

5

Musical Classicism Reflected in
Enlightenment Mentality

The intent of the present chapter is to introduce evidence supporting the thesis that music in the second half of the eighteenth century was still dominated by rationalism and the logocentric world view formulated by Galileo, Descartes, and Newton. It will be demonstrated that musical classicism, as exemplified by such composers as Haydn, Mozart, and Beethoven, is in principle basically logical in nature, respecting formal processes and means of achieving unity. Admittedly, the stylistic changes which occurred around the midpoint of the century were profound and embraced all phases of musical expression. Numerous forms disappeared, to be replaced by new ones. The *Affectenlehre,* with its indirect "representation" of emotional states, was superseded by a more direct expression of human feelings. The *basso continuo* became extinct, and the modern symphony orchestra with its disciplined precision of playing and its great dynamic and coloristic contrasts replaced the small court and church ensembles. Yet, when reduced to the most basic epistemological and perceptual considerations, late-baroque and classical music share an essential identity with respect to their primarily rational and logical nature. In Darwinian terms, moreover, it may be argued that these forms of musical expression did not actually become extinct, but were severely modified to meet the new environmental necessities of simplicity, immediacy, and spontaneity of expression, and of intensification in the technical production of sound, all requisite to reach a wider middle-class public. Classical music may thus be said to reflect the Enlightenment just as

Baroque music reflects the Age of Reason, if that philosophical distinction be recognized.[1]

The simplification of style in early classical music, alluded to above, is frequently emphasized by musicologists, and a comparison is sometimes made between this stylistic change and the change of *ca.* 1600, from renaissance to baroque music. Blume, for example, describes early classicism as "a conscious primitivization unprecedented in the history of music."[2] Parenthetically, the designation "classical" regarding eighteenth-century music does not here mean the imitation of Greek and Roman models (none existed), as was the case in architecture and the visual arts, except perhaps in the sense of excellence and in the criterion of value implicit in these models. The term classical, when applied to music, is rather used in contrast to the excesses of Romanticism, and always connotes something optimal and balanced. Hence classical music, by definition, has always implied a superior product. Its attributes, as opposed to those of Romanticism, are balance, proportion, control, stability, unity, and above all, a certain perceptual and epistemological optimality or "rightness." Any of these factors, alone or in combination, depends primarily on logical processes, thus further supporting my contention that Classicism is largely an analogue of the type of knowledge fostered by the mathematical physicists of the seventeenth and eighteenth centuries.

The unity and integrity of classical music, and the means by which they are achieved, has been a controversial issue of widespread speculation and discussion. The source of this controversy is an apparent paradox: classical music, such as a sonata or symphony, consists of numerous disparate and heterogeneous elements (on a small and large scale), yet its formal integrity and unity are generally recognized to be on the highest artistic level. The question then arises, how can things disparate and unlike fit together to form an "organic" and inseparable whole? There are various schools of thought which have been concerned with this question, yet none of them offers a completely satisfactory solution.

The first school attributes the unity in classical music to what

1. This distinction is made in the Mentor Philosophers series, where *The Age of Reason* by Stuart Hampshire is devoted to seventeenth-century philosophers, while *The Age of Enlightenment* is devoted to the philosophers of the eighteenth century.

2. Jacob Opper, " 'Klassik' by Friedrich Blume: a Translation" (Master's thesis, School of Music, Florida State University, 1965), p. 27.

may be summarized by the Latin maxim *discordia concors,* or a general principle of unity by contrast. This is not fallacious, but the principle of unity by contrast—i.e., asserting that two or three things belong together because of their contrasting nature— does not constitute a real explanation. There is an infinite number of things, musical or nonmusical, which could be selected at random to form contrast; however, their mere contrasting or disparate nature is no assurance of unity. To this first school belong such writers as Donald J. Grout, William S. Newman, Reinhard G. Pauly, Hans David, and Hugo Leichtentritt, although authors generally opposed to the idea that two or more disparate entities can produce unity also occasionally support this view. In his description of the first movement of the *Eroica* Symphony, Grout writes that Beethoven's "capacity to organize a large amount of contrasting material into a unified musical whole is one of the chief marks of Beethoven's greatness."[3] Pauly, noting the essential features of sonata form (the chief formal pattern of the Classical period), writes that "the concept of one or more clearly defined themes, coupled with certain principles of harmonic progression and contrast, is essential to the sonata form." And further, "Most movements in sonata form contain at least two clearly defined themes . . . frequently of contrasting character." This "thematic dualism," according to Pauly, is an "essential structural element in Classic music."[4] The suggestion that the principle of contrast and the unity resulting therefrom is a cardinal feature of classical music is implicit in Hans David's statement that the "concept of form . . . in the classic structures of Haydn and Mozart" depends on "each section [fulfilling] a different function within the whole."[5] Newman, like David, Pauly, and Grout, also places great importance on contrast as a structural principle in the classical sonata. Using as an example the "Alla Turca" finale from Mozart's Sonata in A major, K. 300i, he writes, "diametric contrast . . . in its purest form, "phrase grouping"—that is, the apposition, opposition, or other juxtaposition of relatively complete "sentences"—tends to generate a polythematic hierarchic design of sections within sections." Newman also observes that the "dualistic contrast" be-

3. Donald J. Grout, *A History of Western Music* (New York: W. W. Norton & Co., 1960), p. 480.

4. Reinhard G. Pauly, *Music in the Classic Period* (Englewood Cliffs, N. J.: Prentice-Hall, Inc., 1965), pp. 39–40.

5. Hans David, "Principles of Form in Use from the Middle Ages to the Present Day," *Bulletin of the American Musicological Society* (1947), nos. 9–10, p. 10.

tween the initial and second theme represents "one of the most conspicuous features" of the classical sonata. Dualism, however, "is but another term for the polarity of variety and unity, [and] some kind of dualism must exist in all music. It is not the fact of it but how it is achieved that distinguishes the dualism of Classic 'sonata form.' "[6] A more complete and general statement concerning the polarity between variety and unity is encountered in another work of Newman:

> The one principle that underlies all art forms is that of *variety within unity*. Something must persist sufficiently to hold the form together (unity), yet something must differ sufficiently to give it interest (variety). Like hot and cold, positive and negative, east and west, variety and unity are interdependent concepts. Theoretically neither is any more possible by itself than is an absolute vacuum. A painting so unified that it is nothing but one solid mass must still impart a certain variety by contrast with its frame, or the wall, or the room where it is hung. A painting so varied that no color or line repeats must still reveal a certain unity in the very persistence with which its elements disagree. But we can acknowledge at once that either extreme leads to monotony. What is wanting is that all important sense of proportion between variety and unity by which any art work must stand or fall.[7]

Noteworthy in this passage is Newman's implication that variety results from a basically logical relationship of components, such as hot and cold, east and west, and so on. This relationship, it will be remembered, constitutes Aristotle's "forms by privation," primarily an inferential type of knowledge.[8] Newman, however, does not adequately explain the logical nature and the logical relationship of the elements which create variety and unity. Furthermore, the terminology "variety and unity" is too vague and inaccurate, in the sense that the precise nature of the musical components which fit together to form an "organic" whole is not identified.

Hugo Leichtentritt likewise recognizes the logical relatedness of contrasting components and their resultant unity. In more explicit terms he writes, "Two phrases may belong together not only by virtue of their rhythmic and melodic similarity, but in their differences they may even complement each other like light and shadow, day and night." Still more emphatically, "Aesthetic

6. William S. Newman, *The Sonata in the Classical Era* (Chapel Hill, N. C.: The University of North Carolina Press, 1963), pp. 113–14, 152.
7. William S. Newman, *Understanding Music* (New York: Harper & Row, 1961), p. 134.
8. See further F. S. C. Northrop, *The Meeting of East and West* (New York: The Macmillan Co., 1946), p. 269.

effects and logical connections are derived not from the similari-
ties, but from the differences."[9]

Not committed to this school of thought, but still conceding
that classical music, at least in part, depends for its effect on the
union of disparate entities are Josef Rufer and Arnold Schoenberg. With respect to Beethoven, Rufer writes,

> One can clearly see from any Beethoven sonata that the elements of
> tension in tonal music are not produced merely by the harmonic scheme,
> but arise at least equally strongly from the opposition of contrasting
> ideas and themes, and from the varying "density" of the different sections.
> After all, in a work of art which is shaped as a unity, how could an
> effect be due to only one of its components?[10]

Schoenberg, in an article defending the German origin of his
music, writes that his teachers were, "in the first order, Bach
and Mozart," and "in the second order Beethoven, Brahms and
Wagner"; and that from Mozart he learned what he terms
"the union of heterogeneous entities in a thematic whole" ("*die
Zusammenfassung heterogener Charaktere in eine thematische
Einheit*").[11] These are striking assertions from thinkers whose
musical aesthetic is generally incompatible with an idea of unity
generated by disparate elements.

Curiously, the notion of contrast as an aesthetic principle of
unity in music was recognized as far back as the eighteenth century, when Burney wrote the following about J. C. Bach:

> Bach seems to have been the first composer who observed the law of
> *contrast*, as a *principle*. Before his time, contrast there frequently was,
> in the works of others; but it seems to have been accidental. Bach in his
> symphonies and other instrumental pieces, . . . seldom failed, after a
> rapid and noisy passage to introduce one that was slow and soothing.[12]

The second school of thought dealing with the problem of
unity in classical music (and music in general) rejects outright
the idea that heterogeneous entities, having no affinity of any
sort with one another, can be fused to form a unified whole.
Here we have such writers as Rudolph Reti, Hans Keller, the
musicologist Karl Marx and, with the exceptions cited, Josef

9. Hugo Leichtentritt, *Musical Form* (Cambridge, Mass.: Harvard University
Press, 1951), p. 233–34.
10. Josef Rufer, *Composition with Twelve Tones* (London: Rockliff, 1954), p. 27.
11. *Ibid., Das Werk Arnold Schönbergs* (Kassel: Bärenreiter-Verlag, 1959),
p. 138.
12. Charles Burney, *A General History of Music* (New York: Harcourt, Brace
and Company, n.d.) [first published, 1776–89], vol. 2, p. 866.

Rufer and Arnold Schoenberg. All of them are related, in one way or another, to the thought of Heinrich Schenker, and all of them are biocentrically oriented in their aesthetic formulations. The main thesis of these authors is that all great masterpieces of music, regardless of period or style, exhibit a thematic homogeneity on all levels of magnitude, and that this homogeneity is, in the final analysis, traceable to a basic melodic germ, kernel, or shape. Thus, not only are the four movements of a typical symphony by Haydn, Mozart, or Beethoven thematically related, but all the themes within each movement must disclose a similar type of connection. The alleged intra- and inter-movement contrast of themes, and the resultant unity therefrom are only illusory phenomena, dispelled by a deeper analysis of the musical masterpiece. This analysis will always reveal that, no matter how disparate the themes are, their origin can always be traced to some fundamental thematic motif. To quote from Reti's chief work expounding these ideas, ". . . in the great works of musical literature the different movements of a composition are connected in thematic unity—a unity that is brought about not merely by a vague affinity of mood but by forming the themes from one identical musical substance." Furthermore, "the different themes of *one* movement—in fact all its groups and parts—are in the last analysis also but variations of one identical thought." Reti continues,

> The general view would hold almost the opposite. For instance, the first and second subjects of a sonata are usually considered as contrasting, certainly not as identical or even related, manifestations. In reality, however, they are contrasting on the surface but identical in substance. In fact, it is this being "different on the surface but alike in kernel" in which is centered the inner process of musical structure of the last centuries.

The last centuries are those which begin with the classical style, where the principle of "thematic transformation," as differentiated from the principle of "contrapuntal imitation" in former periods, manifests itself. Indeed, the apparent contrast between themes is produced by the transformation of the basic musical germ, transformation and its artful manipulation being one of Reti's leading principles.

Despite the common source of all thematic ideas from the basic germ theme, Reti considers their apparent contrast desirable, for in the advanced symphonic style, the era of genuine thematic transformation, a composer's ability to form a theme from a preceding one must be considered the more effective, the less the outer similarity of the two themes is recognizable, in spite of identity in kernel.

In this style, therefore, it must be the composer's endeavor not to emphasize the identity but to conceal it. To state this in a way perhaps still more appropriate: a thematic transformation must be regarded as most impressive from a structural angle if the identity is rooted strongly and firmly in the depths of the shapes in question and at the same time is as inconspicuous and little traceable as possible on the surface.

Hence, notwithstanding the allegedly superficial thematic contrast in an extended multi-movement work, Reti depends primarily on a literal principle of identity in his attempt to "explain" the unity of a musical composition. For, as he says, "unless the thematic shapes themselves are . . . connected through deep inward affinities," it is impossible "to forge different groups into a musical whole." Reti is thus diametrically opposed to the first school of writers who in varying degrees suggest, without actually giving a satisfactory explanation, that the unity in a classical composition depends on a principle of contrast, inherent in this principle being a more abstract and inferential principle of identity.

The evidence Reti adduces to validate his theory is questionable at best. In order to give the reader some notion of Reti's methodology for showing thematic identity, it will be advisable at this point to reproduce some of his musical examples accompanied by his commentary.

In Mozart's Symphony in C major ("Jupiter") . . . the thematic figure of its opening (a) is in the last movement transformed into the serenely floating Finale theme (b):

. . . But to understand the full meaning of this shaping, we must compare the fugue [theme] (a) with the second theme of the first movement (b):

(a)

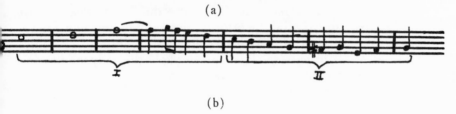

(b)

As has already been indicated, the fugue theme is itself a transformation of the first theme of the symphony's opening movement. Now it becomes apparent that it is also a transformed reiteration of the second theme. And by this process of thematic merging, the original themes become entirely weightless musical lines, dancing through space. Again the dramatic resolution of the work is focused on thematic transformation.

The description of themes as "weightless musical lines, dancing through space" does not strike one as the product of a self-avowedly analytical mind. The same type of analysis is applied to Beethoven's Sonata in G major, op. 14, no. 2. Here, by adding, omitting and changing notes (what he terms "slight melodic license"), by inverting themes, and by ignoring tempo changes and the presence or absence of rests, Reti proceeds to "prove" that the opening themes of the first and second movements are of identical thematic substance.[13]

(a)   (b)

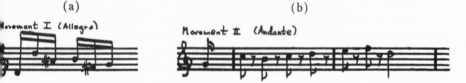

Admittedly, there is some similarity in the contour of these two motifs. However, experientially this similarity appears to be remote.

Concerning the above and, by inference, the Mozart examples, Nordmark makes the apt observation that "we do not experience

13. Rudolph Reti, *The Thematic Process in Music* (London: Faber & Faber, 1961), pp. 4–5, 58, 161–62, 75–77.

the two themes as related at all," hence the "fatal weakness of his [Reti's] and similar theories." Illustrating the same fallacy of creating thematic identity where none exists, Nordmark quotes C. C. Pratt, who writes, "It is hardly likely that anyone hearing the last three notes of God Save the Queen will be brought up with a start at the end by noting the resemblance to the first measure of Three Blind Mice, or vice versa." It is clear from what has been said so far that Reti, in manipulating the evidence to suit his theory, totally ignores perceptual factors when attempting to establish thematic relationships. That his theory of thematic kinship's permeating an entire work holds little validity is particularly borne out by the following passage from Nordmark regarding the works of Beethoven:

> There is abundant evidence in the sketchbooks to show that the thematic process is but a figment of Reti's imagination. Nottebohm, who published many of the sketches, has disclosed that Beethoven transferred the original finale of the *Violin Sonata in A major,* Op. 30, to the *Kreutzer Sonata,* partly because it was, in the composer's own words, too brilliant, and partly because he had no time to write a new finale for the *Kreutzer Sonata,* a public performance already having been arranged. The *Alla danza tedesca* movement of the *B-flat Quartet,* Op. 130, was originally intended for the *A-minor Quartet,* Op. 132, and even worked out in A major. For its last movement the latter quartet appropriated, almost without a change, the theme originally planned to be the main theme of the instrumental finale of the *Ninth Symphony.* Since Reti has analyzed the *B-flat Quartet* at great length, has found therein "a proof of almost mathematical conclusiveness" of his thesis, and has devoted two pages to show that the *Danza tedesca* is derived from the basic theme of the Quartet, grave doubts are cast on the methods of the analytical school.

Nordmark appears to align himself with the first school of thought concerning the manner in which a musical work is formed into a composite whole. Noting Beethoven's haphazard fashion of jotting down various thematic scraps, and using them *ad hoc* as opportunity arose, he writes, "The reasons for his choice of melodies can be described best in terms of balance, proportion, affinity, or contrast of mood or character, etc."[14]

Reti's hypothesis is further refuted by similar examples in the music of Mozart. Blume, for example, informs us that "several of Mozart's symphonies written for the Italian public originally consisted of three movements; later, however, for performances

14. Jan Nordmark, "New Theories of Form and the Problem of Thematic Identities," *Journal of Music Theory* 4 (November 1960): 214, 216–17.

in Salzburg he added the minuets (as for example in K. 73n, 111b)."[15] In view of this fact it seems unlikely that Mozart composed the minuets in such manner as to fit the overall thematic plan of the work, if a plan of this sort existed at all. Better known than the above examples is the Symphony no. 33 (K. 319 in B flat major). The Minuet of this symphony was written three years later (1782), and we are told by Jens Peter Larsen that "it is . . . in complete accord with the other movements, and properly speaking only with its composition was the symphony complete."[16] Listening experience and an examination of the score confirm Larsen's assertion and disclose no thematic connections.

Related to these events, and further weakening Reti's argument respecting thematic homogeneity in classical music, is the suggestion of some writers that movements of two different symphonies or sonatas by the same composer could be interchanged, or even that movements by two different composers could undergo this alteration, with little or no damage to unity. This is clearly the opinion of Günther von Noé, who writes that "it is conceivable in the early works of Haydn or Mozart to exchange individual movements of different symphonies or other multi-movement works without violating structural principles." (*"Noch bei den Frühwerken Haydns oder Mozarts wäre es denkbar, Einzelsätze verschiedener Symphonien oder anderer zyklischer Werke neu zu gruppieren, ohne Strukturgesätze zu verletzen."*)[17] Blume likewise remarks that "the replacement of an existing or almost completed movement still frequently occurs in Mozart's music."[18] Newman goes even further. According to him (and also to Noé) corresponding movements of two different composers, such as Haydn and Mozart, could be interchanged. He writes: "one must acknowledge that a sonata movement by Haydn can usually be interchanged with an equivalent one by Mozart without serious detriment to either sonata cycle, and perhaps without detection," i.e., provided they have not previously been bound "together through habit of memory."[19] It is not our intent to pass judgment as to the aesthetic soundness of the above

15. Opper, " 'Klassik,' " p. 88.
16. Jens Peter Larsen, "The Symphonies," in *The Mozart Companion,* ed. H. C. Robbins Landon and Donald Mitchell (New York: Oxford University Press, 1956), p. 181.
17. Günther von Noé, *"Der Strukturwandel der Zyklischen Sonatenform,"* Neue *Zeitschrift für Musik* 125, no. 2 (1964): p. 55.
18. Opper, " 'Klassik,' " p. 94.
19. Newman, *Understanding,* p. 221.

observations. These assertions, combined with the practice of adding or exchanging movements by such masters as Mozart and Beethoven, do, however, point to serious misgivings with respect to the validity of Reti's ideas concerning thematic uniformity. Clearly, unity in the music of the Classical era must reside in a different principle.

Reti's unyielding dogmatism that formal unity in a musical work can be generated only by thematic homogeneity, and his insistence that thematic differentiation, based on the metamorphosis of the germ theme, constitutes a criterion of excellence, leads him to the untenable conclusion that many works of Haydn are inferior because frequently his second subject in sonata-form movements is only a slight modification of the first. As he himself observes, "Haydn in his symphonies sometimes introduces a theme that according to all signs of the outer proportions represents a second theme but proves to be a mere repetition of the first theme. In the light of the ensuing evolution, however, this must be considered a problematic shaping."[20] Reti here ignores, or is not aware of, the so-called closing theme which Haydn habitually uses to provide the necessary contrast. This is true even in his late works, such as the *Military* and *London* Symphonies. Concerning this problem Alvin Bauman, in his vitriolic review of *The Thematic Process in Music,* notes that, according to Reti's standards, "we shall have to reevaluate those (Haydn) symphonies which use the same first and second subjects, for, according to Dr. Reti, one of the most important standards of a great work in the classic period is that the second theme be a 'new utterance, a transformation' of the first."[21]

Hans Keller is in essential accord with Reti in his approach to form and in his account of unity in classical music. He in fact lists Reti as one of the four men "who would seem to have provided my method with stimulating incentives,"[22] the other three being Schenker, Schoenberg, and Oskar Adler. If there is any difference between Reti and Keller, it resides in the latter's being more tendentious, presumptuous, and sometimes even arrogant toward the musical community and to those who might possibly question his "analytical" method.

Keller's ideas on music are expounded in two extended articles

---

20. Reti, *Process,* p. 57.
21. Alvin Bauman, review of *The Thematic Process in Music* by Rudolph Reti, *Journal of the American Musicological Society* 5 (Summer 1952) : 140–41.
22. Hans Keller, "The Chamber Music," *The Mozart Companion,* p. 93.

on Mozart.[23] It is on these that the following discussion is based. Keller opens his musical disquisition by making the methodological distinction between "tautological description" and "verbal or symbolic analysis." The former is unnecessary because it "gives a verbal account of what you hear," while the latter "shows . . . the elements of what you hear." We are further told that

In a great piece, these are always the elements of unity, not of diversity, because a great piece grows from an all-embracing idea. Great music diversifies a unity; mere good music unites diverse elements. As soon as you have analysed the unity of a great work, its variety explains itself, whereas when you describe its, or indeed any work's diversity, nothing is explained at all.

This constitutes Keller's first statement respecting the unity of a musical work and that it "grows from an all-embracing idea." The similarity of this position to the one espoused by Reti is unmistakable, and its more explicit formulation will become increasingly clear. Keller indulges in a debatable analogy between the notion of unity in the psychology of dreams and unity in music. According to him, Freud's *Interpretation of Dreams* "demonstrated the unity of the most chaotically diverse dream by analysing the *latent* content of the *manifest* dream, and demonstrating that behind all the dream contrasts there was the single-minded, basic motive of wish fulfillment." In like fashion, Keller tells us, it is "the *latent* basic motifs, and generally the unitive forces behind the *manifest* music" upon which his observations are based. After asserting that "Mozart was no prodigy at all," and that "the eruption of his original creative force was retarded by his . . . technical facility and his passive and eclectic character," Keller proceeds to analyze the early quartets, writing that "extreme latent unity beneath extreme manifest variety is the mark of genius," and that "all great music is latently monothematic and, if in more than one movement, cyclic."

At this point it is appropriate to acquaint the reader with Keller's analytical method, whereby it is allegedly "proven" that all themes within a movement or within an entire multi-movement work are latently related. What follows is an excerpt from Keller's analysis of Mozart's string Quartet in G major, K. 387:

---

23. In "The Chamber Music," and in "K. 503: The Unity of Contrasting Themes and Movements," *The Music Review* 17 (1956): 48–58, 120–29.

The melodic evolution of K. 387 . . . immediately shows both the master and the genius; every note is overdetermined, and everything springs from the basic motif (x).

The basic fourth is at once reversed and filled up scale-wise (x^1), in which basic shape it serves as main thematic material. The first half of the second bar represents, in diminution, a retrograde version of the first bar, while the cadential motif of its second half is a straight (con)sequence of the first bar's second half, and just as a semitone is here replaced by a whole tone, a whole tone has been replaced by a semitone in the four-quaver motif. x^1 appears in straight form in the second half of the third bar, but in the first half it develops towards what is ultimately to become the second subject [which is here presented for comparison].

The shake itself increases the oscillating motion that is to become the characteristic rhythmic feature of the subsidiary theme [see above]; whereas the semi-quaver diminution of x^1 establishes the actual rhythm of this feature, whose notes (mediant and sharpened supertonic) come from bar 4's cadential motif, itself a crab of x^1's cadential notes (g ' ' — f ♯ ' '), though from the standpoint of rhythmic structure, its immediate model is bar 2's cadential motif, to which it forms the formal and harmonic complement.

This type of writing continues for another twelve pages, where Keller allegedly proves that the themes of all four movements of K. 387 are latently related to motif (x). For the reader's inspection and comparison the opening themes are herewith reproduced.

There is no need here to quote Keller's involved commentary proving that these themes are related by originating from one common motif. It is enough to say that his *"gesucht"* way with musical structure and analysis is tantamount to the abstruse method of medieval scholasticism, whereby it could conceivably be proven that all of Mozart's works and, beyond that, all of West-

ern music, has its genesis in one basic motif. After all, within the inherent limitations of the major-minor tonal system and of equal temperament tuning, and with the application of the type of reductionism present in Reti's and Keller's work, the quantity of intervallic relations can be reduced to three (the second, third, and fourth with their respective inversions). This is especially the case in Reti's work, where notes are arbitrarily added, changed, or ignored to suit his purpose. But more important than the above criticism is Reti's and Keller's total neglect of perceptual considerations. For on the experiential level Mozart's four themes neither exhibit thematic homogeneity nor spring from the (x) motif by any stretch of the imagination. Only the rigid adherence to a literal principle of thematic identity as the sole unifying agent, the deliberate disregard of experience, and the violation of the uniqueness of the phenomenon can lead to conclusions arrived at by Reti and Keller. Indeed, Keller's and Reti's observations do describe the preponderance of nineteenth-century music as exhibiting the cyclical technique and the metamorphosis of themes; and these two principles were still the leading ideas of Schoenberg and his school. However, the indiscriminate projection of these chiefly biocentrically oriented principles of unity to the more logocentrically oriented Classical period can at best be regarded as being misguided.

Keller does not endear himself to the general reader by his statement that he is addressing himself primarily "to the string quartet player, who hears the heart-beat of chamber music," and by his incessant and gratuitous advice to the performer. For example, with respect to the opening movement of Mozart's K. 387, we read that "both the unity and the diversity of the second subject must be brought out in performance." And this is to be done by "an infinitesimal retardation, . . . introduced by a slightly more noticeable widening-out of tempo in the cadence of the bridge passage." And further, "we must not lose aural sight of . . . the upper octave." Still later we read, "The chief point is to have a clear idea of the phrase, rather than take a narcissistic joy in one's wrist."[24] Such advice suggests that string quartet playing is for Keller just as esoteric an activity as the "discovery" of latent formal unity.

The article on Mozart's Piano Concerto K. 503 need not be discussed in great detail since here, as in Keller's analysis of Mozart's chamber music, the same ideas are introduced. Aside from the reiterated assertion that a great work grows "from an all-embracing basic idea" and that by virtue of this idea "contrasting motifs and themes belong together," Keller, apparently as a final recourse in "proving" thematic homogeneity, resorts to serial analysis. Thus he writes that the "second subject phrase" of

the slow movement is "but a variation of the first subject's first

24. Keller, "Chamber Music," pp. 90–107.

consequent . . . as soon as we listen to the phrase serially."
And further, "Serial listening means being prepared for de- and
re-rhythmicizing and octave transpositions."[25] It is fitting at this
point to close with Eric Blom's comment that Keller's "serious-
ness and missionary zeal to impose a new religion with faults far
greater than those of the native one" creates "an unbridgeable
gap between his approach to music and sensitive experience
of it."[26]

It has been mentioned previously that Schoenberg and Rufer
also espouse views on musical unity similar to those of Reti and
Keller. In view of Schoenberg's statement concerning Mozart,
quoted earlier, however, and in view of his observations on contemporary music, it is doubtful that Schoenberg would unre-
servedly extend the principle of thematic homogeneity to all
music, especially to that of the Classical era. Admittedly, Schoenberg's central principle in serial music is the transformation of
the basic tone-row, thus constituting cyclical form and the metamorphosis of themes. Yet his assertion that the value of contemporary music may consist of a different type of formal unity such
as "the *variety* and *multitude* of the ideas, the manner in which
they develop and grow out of germinating units, how they are
contrasted and how they *complement* one another" (italics added), shows that he adhered by no means to one formal law.
Furthermore, in the chapter entitled "Criteria for the Evaluation
of Music" he writes that the expert

> values a composition more highly only if its themes and melodies are
> significantly formulated and well organized; if they are interesting
> enough to hold the attention of a listener; *if there is a sufficiently great
> number of ideas;* if they are well connected so as not to offend musical
> logic; if they are restricted by subdivision to a conceivable size; *if monot-
> ony is avoided by good contrasts;* if all ideas, however contrasting, can
> be proved to be only variations of the basic idea, thus security unity.[27]
> [Italics added.]

25. Keller, "K. 503," pp. 50, 127; see same for complete analysis of above.
26. Eric Blom, review of *The Mozart Companion,* in *Music and Letters* 37
(July 1956):287.
27. Arnold Schoenberg, *Style and Idea* (New York: Philosophical Library,
1950), pp. 86–87, 189.

In view of these observations it would appear that Schoenberg represents a synthesis of the principles concerning musical unity advanced by Newman *et al.* on the one hand, and Reti and his school on the other.

Josef Rufer, a pupil of Schoenberg's, despite his earlier statement, concerning the "opposition of contrasting ideas" (see above), follows Reti's line of thought with respect to unity. If anything, he is more adamant in his insistence that a *Grundgestalt* forms the basis of a multi-movement work. Referring to Beethoven's Sonata op. 10, no. 1, he writes,

> The whole collection of themes in a work, though apparently independent of one another, can be traced back to a single basic idea, . . . whether or not one can recognise and demonstrate these relations in every case. This corresponds to the thesis that a work of art is a unity, the unity existing even where it cannot be exactly demonstrated.

Rufer's statement vitiates his own argument. To assert that all themes in a musical work are related, regardless of whether this relation is empirically demonstrable or not, and then to add further that this follows from the thesis that the art work is a unity, likewise undemonstrable, is to indulge in a kind of blind mysticism not characteristic of twentieth-century thought, especially of the ostensibly analytical method of Rufer, Reti, and Keller. More significantly, Rufer's specious argument obtains from the naïve premise that unity must rest on a literal principle of identity. ("Only things which belong together and possess affinity can cohere, that is, become a form.") That this is the case in numerous manifestly cyclical works of the nineteenth century is not contested here. Empirical evidence will disclose, however, that the preponderance of classical music exhibits unity based on a more abstract and logical principle of identity.

It is clear that writers like Rufer, Keller, and Reti rely excessively on Schoenberg's principle of row transformation in their analysis and evaluation of classical music. Rufer, for example, repeatedly draws on parallels between structural processes in the music of such composers as Beethoven and Brahms and the principle of the basic row and its transformations in Schoenberg's music. He writes,

> even in the music of the youthful Beethoven [Piano Sonata Op. 10, No. 1, in C minor] . . . the creation of the themes of a whole work follows an idea of construction which is also of fundamental importance for Schoenberg's music in general, and for twelve-tone music in particular;

it is the idea that, in order to ensure the thematic unification of a work and thus the unity of its musical content, all the musical events in it are developed, directly or indirectly, out of one basic shape.

A similar analogy is made between the music of Brahms and serial music:

> the original shape [theme] which a basic idea assumes already contains the characteristics of the whole piece, both directly and indirectly. For . . . the whole thematic material of the piece [Paganini Variations] is developed from this shape. We therefore call this the "basic shape" (*Grundgestalt*); it corresponds in its significance and functions to the "basic series" of twelve-note music.

And finally, "Just as the thematic material of a tonal work is derived from the basic shape, similarly in twelve-note music it arises out of the basic set (series)."[28] Keller's reference to serial technique in his analysis of Mozart's music has been noted. His article entitled "Strict Serial Technique in Classical Music"[29] is a further indication of this.

Musicologist Karl Marx will be considered next in his reply to an article by Günther von Noé entitled *"Der Strukturwandel der zyklischen Sonatenform."*[30] Noé's thesis is that beginning with the middle works of Beethoven there appears an increasing number of works manifesting the cyclical recurrence of themes, whereas the Classical period is conspicuous by the relative absence of this technique. Marx attempts to refute Noé's argument, presenting evidence which, he states, is limited to only several characteristic examples from the works of Haydn and Mozart (*"Ich . . . beschränke meine Ausführungen auf Haydn und Mozart, wobei nur einzige besonders charakteristische Beispiele aus der Fülle der möglichen herausgegriffen werden."*)[31] The validity of Marx's evidence is (with a few exceptions) dubious. To begin with, he presents the opening themes of the two-movement sonata by Mozart, K. 46d, which run as follows:

(a)

28. Rufer, *Composition*, pp. 29, 25, 45.
29. *Tempo*, Autumn 1955.
30. *Neue Zeitschrift für Musik* 125, no. 2 (1964) : 56–62.
31. Karl Marx, *"Über die zyklische Sonatenform,"* *Neue Zeitschrift für Musik* 125, no. 4 (1964) : 142.

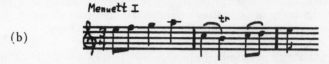

(b)

The thematic relationship is here relatively convincing, although Marx concedes that in this case the cyclical treatment is a vestige of the baroque variation suite of such composers as Froberger and Peuerl. Marx's next example is the Divertimento in D major, K. 136. According to him, the opening theme of the first movement corresponds to the initial theme of movement three.

(a)

(b)

The resemblance between these two themes is also apparent, although Marx does not account for the second movement. This omission is likely because the thematic material of the second movement does not fit his cyclical hypothesis, thus proving that Mozart was not consistent in his application of the cyclical technique, using it only in isolated cases. Furthermore, in view of the early date of this work (1772), it too may be a remnant of the Baroque variation suite, although Marx does not acknowledge this. The next example, Mozart's Violin Concerto in D major, K. 218, is striking. Here the theme of the last movement is clearly related to the main theme of the second movement which, in

(a)

(b)

turn, has its origin in the following theme of the first movement:

Simultaneously, this theme gives rise to the initial theme of the last movement.

Whether this constitutes a conscious use of cyclical thematic recurrence is not known and is perhaps irrelevant. The fact remains that, without recourse to a Reti type of analysis, a perceptually felt thematic connection here exists. Considering, however, the infrequent presence of such examples in classical music and, conversely, in view of the statistically overwhelming incidence of cyclical form in the nineteenth century, this example, and others of its kind, must be regarded as isolated cases, Reti, Keller, and Rufer notwithstanding. In most of the remaining illustrations Marx indulges in a type of analysis characteristic of the authors just mentioned. Thus, he tries to show that these three themes from Mozart's "Prague" Symphony are related:

Admittedly, the general contours of these themes are alike; experientially, however, in the course of listening to the work, these alleged thematic relationships are meaningless. Moreover, had Mozart really planned to create unity by a deliberate thematic homogeneity, the remaining themes of the work would also manifest at least some semblance of thematic kinship. That this is not the remotest case may be inferred from Marx's omission of the work's remaining thematic material, both from discussion and analysis.

The remainder of Marx's article is devoted to Mozart's String Quintet K. 614, and several works of Haydn. Aside from disclosing the relation between the slow introduction and the allegro of Haydn's "Clock" Symphony (this is a habitual practice of Haydn; see also his Symphonies nos. 98, 100, 102, and 103), Marx's illustrations of alleged thematic interrelations are unconvincing. He, like Reti and Keller, omits notes, disregards tempo change, and generally violates the uniqueness of the phenomenon in attempting to show literal relations where none exist and where none need to exist.

The third and final group of writers concerned with unity in classical music consists of authors who recognize the problem but offer no solution. Monroe C. Beardsley, for example, writes,

> One of the most puzzling problems about musical unity arises in connection with compound, or several-movement, compositions. It is reasonably clear in what the unity of each movement consists. But what makes a group of movements, as in a sonata or suite, constitute a coherent whole? The movements offer contrasts in tempo and key, and may make an interesting pattern in sequence, but so do the various members on a concert program, and a concert is not a single composition. But Beethoven's *C minor Symphony* is one composition, and so is Handel's *Water Music,* and Brahms' *Clarinet Quintet.*[32]

After stating the problem, Beardsley introduces Reti's hypothesis as a possible solution, submitting as an illustration the opening themes of the first, second, and fourth movements of Mozart's *Eine Kleine Nachtmusik*. These are here presented for the reader's consideration:

(a)

32. Monroe C. Beardsley, *Aesthetics: Problems in the Philosophy of Criticism* (New York: Harcourt, Brace & Co., 1958), p. 199.

(b)

(c)

Needless to say, these three themes, on the level of experience, are not heard as related entities. Their disjunct contour may simply be an indication of Mozart's predilection for triadic themes in this composition. Furthermore, these disjunct themes in isolation, i.e., without their consequent conjunct and hence complementary character, do not make much sense. It is also significant that here, as in Reti's previous examples, the third movement is not accounted for, thus undermining the consistency of his hypothesis.

Walter Nallin, on the other hand, simply regards the method of grouping movements in the works of Haydn, Mozart, and early Beethoven as a structural weakness which was not rectified until the nineteenth century.

> For several decades after the symphonic pattern was formulated, no one was apparently much concerned that its movements existed as individual entities. In effect symphonies of this era were constituted from an association of disjunct parts connected by only two tenuous threads: a utilization of common or related keys and adherence to a conventional pattern of movement successives. Such a casual assemblage suggests that the symphony had serious internal weaknesses, of course, but it was not until the time of Beethoven (c. 1800–1825) that tangible steps were taken to rectify this condition.

Nallin then lists three measures which were taken to provide greater unity in the symphony: 1) elimination of the pause between movements, 2) cyclical treatment of thematic material, and 3), the use of a *motto* theme throughout a symphony.[33] The implication that these features *ipso facto* render a representative nineteenth-century symphony superior to the mature products of Haydn, Mozart, and, to a large extent, Beethoven, cannot be taken seriously. The consensus of opinion in musical scholarship and criticism, and of the listening public at large, would seem to

---

33. Walter Nallin, *The Musical Idea* (New York: The Macmillan Co., 1968), pp. 498–99.

hold the opposite view. Nallin's error, like the error of writers previously discussed, resides in an excessively literal principle of identity which, in turn, has its source in a naïve view of reality.

Abraham Veinus, on the other hand, although here describing Baroque music, does recognize that the unity of a contrapuntal texture is based on the union of disparate elements. This unity he considers a contradiction, since each of the contrapuntal lines is a distinct and independent musical entity. In principle this is analogous to the classical sonata, except that here the contrast is simultaneous whereas in the sonata it is successive. Veinus writes,

> Indeed, the organic cohesiveness, the sense of oneness instantly evident in Bach's polyphony depends upon the clearest projection of each of the simultaneously sounded and apparently self-contained lines of musical thought. The unity of a polyphonic work rests upon a contradiction, i.e., the ability of several equal parts to fuse together into a single impression despite emphasis on their equality and on the lack of subservience of one part to another.[34]

Veinus's observation is not without merit, since contradiction, contrast (note identical prefixes), union of opposite or heterogeneous entities, all point in the right direction. His observation does not, however, constitute a satisfactory explanation of why and how several equal parts fit together, and why it is desirable in the first place to have a principle of identity and unity more abstract in nature than the one advocated by Reti et al.

Polish phenomenologist Roman Ingarden, here discussing the positive structural role played by the silent pauses between the movements in a musical work, also observes, without submitting an explanation, that a sonata or a symphony is in fact a composite of four different works. He writes, "is it not truly the case that a sonata, for example, consists of four different works, and that it is merely a matter of custom and convention to play them successively and to separate them by short intervals of time?" ("Ist es wirklich nicht so, das wir es z.B. bei einer Sonate mit vier verschiedenen Werken zu tun haben, wobei es konventionell üblich ist, diese Stücke in kurzen Abständen nacheinander zu spielen?")[35]

Although Leonard Meyer does not, strictly speaking, belong to any of the three categories of writers discussed, his observa-

---

34. Abraham Veinus, *The Concerto* (New York: Doubleday, Doran & Co., Inc., 1945), p. 61.
35. Roman Ingarden, *Untersuchungen zur Ontologie der Kunst* (Tübingen: Max Niemeyer Verlag, 1962), p. 112.

tions and criticism with respect to theories of musical unity,
especially those generated by Schenkerian thought, are noteworthy. Meyer first of all distinguishes between "static" and
"dynamic conceptions of musical process."[36] Curiously, Schenker's
conception of the creative process in music, despite its biocentric
orientation,[37] is regarded by Meyer as being static because of its
drastic reductionism. He writes that there are

> dangers of concentrating too much attention upon the structure of a
> musical work as a single sound term interpreted as a stable whole. The
> disciples of Schenker have not been sufficiently aware of this danger.
> Too much emphasis upon the highest architectonic level not only tends
> to minimize the importance of meanings as they arise and evolve on
> other architectonic levels but it also leads to a static interpretation of
> the musical process.

More specifically, Meyer is critical of Felix Salzer's idea that
modulations in a tonal work are merely intensifications of one
(the principal) key. This, it will be noticed, is basically the same
method used by Reti to show that all tunes of a work are transformations of one germ theme. Meyer writes,

> Felix Salzer's condemnation of the concept of modulation is symptomatic
> of this essentially static view of musical meaning. It is true that, when
> we consider the evident and determinate meaning of the whole work,
> modulations can be regarded as passing intensifications of the main key.
> But this view ignores that the entire meaning of the work includes the
> meanings of the several parts and the various architectonic levels.

"Several parts and various architectonic levels" appears to be
essentially synonymous with Schoenberg's union of heterogeneous
elements and Rufer's opposition of contrasting ideas. Meyer continues by equating this "static" approach with a mechanistic
notion of unity. Implicitly attacking Reti's and Keller's ideas,
he writes that "theories of music which imply that melodic similarity results in musical unity of necessity adopt a more or less
mechanistic conception of what constitutes aesthetic unity."[38] In
order to show that this is not true, i.e., that musical unity does
not result from basing an entire composition on a single tonality
or a single thematic kernel, Meyer quotes a passage by Henry
D. Aiken, here reproduced:

36. Leonard B. Meyer, *Emotion and Meaning in Music,* Phoenix Books (Chicago: University of Chicago Press, 1965), p. 52.
37. Processes in biology governing change, such as growth and metamorphosis,
are generally thought to be more dynamic, those in classical physics more static.
38. Meyer, *Emotion,* pp. 52–54.

What is required if the elements of a work of art are to be compounded into an aesthetic whole is the presence of an ordering system of beliefs and attitudes which make them mutually relevant to one another; and conversely, the materials handled in a work of art and the emotions which they express, may vary indefinitely without endangering the integrity of the whole so long as they are held together by a controlling system of expectations.[39]

Aiken, although not writing specifically about music, expresses basically the same ideas offered by Grout, Pauly, and Newman concerning musical unity. The key phrases here are "ordering system," the infinite varying of the material, and a "controlling system of expectations." The corresponding phrases in Grout and Newman are "unified musical whole" through the organization of a "large amount of contrasting material," a "principle of contrast," and a "polythematic hierarchic design." "Controlling system of expectations" suggests that a certain degree of predictability based on logical relations is desirable in a work of art. In contrast to this, Meyer, obviously alluding to such writers as Reti *et al.*, writes that

these scholars, in their intricate and ingenious attempts to derive all the melodic materials of a musical work from a single motivic "germ" . . . , have with Talmudic tenacity confused . . . uniformity with unity.[40]

The foregoing discussion has been an exposition of the manner in which the problem of structure and unity in classical music has been approached by various writers. Methodologically these writers fall into two basic categories: on the one hand we have authors such as Newman, Leichtentritt, Pauly, *et al.,* who suggest in various degrees that unity in classical music rests on the juxtaposition of heterogeneous and contrasting elements, both on a micro- and macro-level (measures, movements). The logical nature of this juxtaposition and the resultant unity therefrom has been noted by Newman and Leichtentritt. None of these writers, however, offers a complete and satisfactory explanation of unity in the above terms, and none of them recognizes the abstract and inferential principle of identity operating in this formal process. On the other hand we are confronted with such authors as Reti and Keller, who reject the notion that musical entities not related by some sort of affinity or likeness can be united to form a whole.

39. Henry D. Aiken, "The Aesthetic Relevance of Belief," *Journal of Aesthetics* 9 (1950), pp. 305–6, quoted in Meyer, *Emotion,* p. 54.
40. Meyer, *Emotion,* p. 161.

These writers (especially Reti and Keller) do give a complete
explanation of their theories, going to great lengths and frequently
employing abstruse methods in their attempts to "prove" the
presence of thematic homogeneity in the works of Mozart, Beethoven, and Haydn. Their well-meaning intentions notwithstanding, the efforts of Reti, Keller, *et al.*, must here be regarded as
misguided, due chiefly to their uncritical projection of the nineteenth-century, biocentrically oriented, literal principle of identity
on the more logocentrically oriented classical music of the eighteenth century. The application of such biological metaphors as
"germ" theme, thematic "kernel," and the "metamorphosis" of
themes is a clear indication of this biocentric view. A still more
explicit indication of the profound influence of the biological
sciences and their attendant world view on musical aesthetics may
be seen in Heinrich Schenker's chapter heading entitled "The
Biological Nature of Form," where we read,

> within . . . larger formal units, the biological momentum of music
> recurs in an amazing way. For what is the fundamental purpose of the
> turns and tricks of the cyclical form? To represent the destiny, the real
> personal fate, of a motif or of several motifs, simultaneously. The sonata
> represents the motifs in ever changing situations in which their characters
> are revealed, just as human beings are represented in a drama.

An even more striking example of a biologically derived literal
principle of identity in music occurs earlier in Schenker's *Harmony*. Here he writes:

> Man repeats himself in man; tree in tree. In other words, any creature
> repeats itself in its own kind, and only in its own kind; and by this
> repetition the concept "man" or the concept "tree" is formed. Thus a
> series of tones becomes an individual in the world of music only by
> repeating itself in its own kind; and, as in nature in general, so music
> manifests a procreative urge, which initiates this process of repetition.
>   We should get accustomed to seeing tones as creatures. We should
> learn to assume in them biological urges as they characterize living beings.
> We are faced, then, with the following equation:
>   In Nature: procreative urge → repetition → individual kind;
>   In music, analogously: procreative urge → repetition → individual
> motif.[41]

It will be remembered that Schenker was the ideational progenitor
of Reti and of the school of musical analysis he represents.
   By no means is it here suggested that Schenkerian analysis has

---

41. Heinrich Schenker, *Harmony,* trans. Elizabeth Mann Borgese, ed. Oswald
Jonas (Chicago: The University of Chicago Press, 1954), pp. 12, 6–7.

no value in the study of music. We merely assert that Schenker's
ideas, being chiefly derivative from the nineteenth-century view
of nature, are applicable to that century respecting formal processes and principles of unity. It is this century which clearly and
unequivocally manifests the cyclical treatment of themes, thematic
metamorphosis, and, generally, the idea that a musical work
evolves from a germ motif in the way that a tree grows from
a seed. Additional evidence concerning this will be submitted in
a later chapter. That the nineteenth century was dominated by
the biological sciences and their attendant cosmology has already
been disclosed in the first chapter of this study. Further and
more specific evidence with respect to the change from the mathematico-physical sciences of the eighteenth century to the biologico-
evolutionary sciences of the nineteenth will be adduced in the
ensuing chapter. What is maintained, rather, is that the application of Schenkerian, biocentrically oriented ideas of form to
the still logocentrically dominated eighteenth century is fallacious.
It is for this reason that Schenker's disciples, such as Reti and
Keller, have to resort to such questionable methods in order to
prove thematic homogeneity in the works of Haydn, Mozart,
and Beethoven. Clearly, a different principle of unity must here
be sought, one which does not violate the musical phenomenon,
and one which will be consistent with the dominant philosophical
mentality of the eighteenth century.

The idea submitted here, which would account in a satisfactory
manner for the apparently insoluble paradox involving the unity
of heterogeneous entities in classical music, is designated as the
principle of *logical complementarity*. As an illustration of this
principle, I present the opening four measures from Mozart's
Jupiter Symphony.

It is immediately apparent that the initial theme comprising these
measures consists of two strikingly disparate musical ideas. On
the one hand we have a highly animated motif rendered with
the full force of the entire orchestra, on the other a calm and
restrained musical idea played only by the strings. The parameters constituting the contrasts between these two motifs are
manifold, and are here termed *complementary variables*. They
entail, 1) duration of notes (quarter notes and sixteenth-note

triplets in the first motif, dotted quarter notes, a half and a quarter note in the second); 2) volume (*forte* in the first, *piano* in the second); 3) frequency change (low register in the first, high in the second); 4) sound and the absence thereof (the first motif is punctuated by eighth-note rests, the second lacks rests); 5) timbre (the first is scored for full orchestra, the second for strings alone); 6) intervallic differentiation (the first motif, repeated twice, consists of a descending fourth followed by two ascending major seconds and a minor second, while the ensuing motif is comprised of a repeated note, a descending minor second, an ascending fifth, and a descending major second); 7) tonal direction (the first motif is more stable by its emphasis of the tonic, while the second creates tension by moving to the dominant). By no means is this claimed to be an exhaustive analysis of these four measures. Furthermore, it is not intended to burden the reader with "tautological description," since an examination of the score and an auditory experience of the music will disclose these parameters in a much more palpable fashion. What I do aim to illustrate is that these two motifs form a whole by virtue of their disparate nature and by virtue of the fact that one "logically" complements, i.e., completes, the other. The term *logical* here designates the most fundamental conditions of cognitive and perceptual experience, and is in principle analogous to Aristotle's *forms by privation*. For example the quality "cold" can be known in one of two ways: 1) we can sense this quality directly by touching a cold object, such as a window pane (this is the positive form); or 2) we can also know this quality indirectly by inferring that the window pane is not hot (this is the negative form). The logical nature of this relationship has been noted by Northrop.

> It is the character of any positive form or quality which we immediately sense that it is logically related to its opposite. It is because the immediately sensed qualities or positive forms are not mere bare data, but are logically connected to their opposites by the relation of opposition, that in sensing the window pane to be cold we are also able to assert that the window pane is not hot.[42]

Thus, potentially the sensed quality "cold" implies its opposite, "hot." It is here contended that the relationship between the contrasting motifs of the above theme by Mozart possesses essentially the same logical structure. In this sense motif one, by

42. Northrop, *Meeting*, p. 269.

exhibiting the set of parameters described above (the positive form, so to speak), logically generates motif two with its unique set of parameters (negative form), thus setting up a predictable sequence of events and an attendant expectation in the listener. Mozart fulfills this expectation by juxtaposing the two motifs and thereby providing a self-contained and logically complete musical unit.

The term *complementarity* or *complementary* means that the two motifs, by reason of their logical relationship, and by reason of the fact that one derives its meaning and identity from the presence of the other, complete one another and form an epistemologically and perceptually intelligible whole. The motifs are the variables, since a change in one implies a change in the other, if this logical relation is to be maintained. This reciprocity renders either motif in isolation meaningless, i.e., incomplete in the sense discussed. Complementary variables, then, and their logical juxtaposition, form the basis of unity and completeness in the opening theme of Mozart's *Jupiter* Symphony.

The principle of logical complementarity also operates on a larger scale within the first movement of the symphony. This accounts for the contrasting and logically related character of the first and second themes with their attendant sections. The second theme runs as follows:

Note here a similar logical relationship of two contrasting motifs forming a complete whole. The order of the motifs, however, is in this case reversed. Whereas the first motif of theme one is animated, and the second characterized by repose, here the converse is true: the first motif displays repose, whereas the second is more animated. The two themes and their attendant sections are thus related not by one identical musical substance and its diversification, as Reti and Keller would have us believe, but by a number of thematic and other musical parameters which form a complete whole by virtue of their logical contrast. In view of what has been said it is appropriate to examine the third thematic component of this movement in order to explore the manner in which it is related to the two themes so far discussed.

The conspicuous feature of this theme is its rhythmic uniformity, whereas the chief trait of the first and second theme is a highly differentiated rhythm. Here the uniform rhythmic flow consists of primarily one note value (the eighth note, with only three quarter notes). In theme one, on the other hand, we have five different note values, and in theme two, six. Moreover, the uniformity and continuity of the closing theme is further intensified by the absence of rests, whereas the opening and second theme are punctuated by eighth, quarter, and half rests, thus further delineating their discontinuous character. One final contrast: whereas the first and second themes are differentiated by an alternately ascending and descending melodic movement, theme three tends to revolve around the note *b*, thus lending it a relatively static quality.

All of these contrasts are of a logical nature, in the sense herein attributed to the word *logic*. They invariably entail the consequent generation of a complementary variable demanded by the presence of its reciprocal opposite, or negatively and hence inferentially, by the presence of this opposite potentially, i.e., by privation. It must be further observed that the unity and completeness resulting from these contrasts go far beyond thematic unification, which is Reti's and Keller's bone of contention. They involve the manifold variables of rhythmic uniformity and differentiation, sound and silence, volume, tone color, ascending and descending melodic movement, disjunct or conjunct thematic structure, and so on. All of these variables, in a classical work, are endowed with a Cartesian clarity and distinctness requisite for a logically coherent and complete whole.

Unity, based on the principle of logical complementarity and involving complementary variables, has so far been discussed on the magnitude of one theme and of one movement. When thus understood, the separate movements of a classical symphony are not like "the various members on a concert program," like a "casual assemblage" "of disjunct parts," or like "four different works"[43] which are played in a certain order according to mere custom. If this were the case, unrelated juxtaposition would be

43. See above: Beardsley, Nallin, and Ingarden.

the result. And the juxtaposition of logically unrelated variables cannot, in our framework of reference, produce completeness. On the contrary, the four movements of a classical symphony form a completely unified whole because each movement, within this whole, operates to fulfill a specific function, i.e., the movements logically complement each other in such manner as to form a complete and perceptually optimal musical structure. Here again, the parameters are manifold: tempo, thematic contrast, rhythm, dynamic contrasts, timbre, and so forth. Considering once again the *Jupiter* Symphony, we notice that the tempo of the first movement is fast (*Allegro vivace*), that of the second relatively slow (*Andante cantabile*), that of the third moderate (*Allegretto*), and that of the last very fast (*Allegro molto*). Now in itself this is an obvious fact, hardly constituting "news." Yet when these four tempi are seen as complementary variables, logically completing each other to form a perceptually satisfying whole, then indeed this appears to be newsworthy. The same observation holds for the themes of the four movements. In no way is there evidence that they are related to one germinal motif, unless one wishes to employ Reti's questionable methods; their relationship, on the contrary, is a logical one constituting the principle of logical complementarity.

It is relevant to consider, in the light of what has been said, the possibility of movement interchange in classical music, noted earlier by Noé, Blume, and Newman. Assuming the validity and desirability of this practice, it appears that movement interchange would produce unrelated juxtaposition and thus weaken our argument respecting unity based on the above premises. However, the factor which would prevent this unrelatedness, and make movement interchange possible, is the relative stylistic uniformity in the works of Haydn, of Mozart, and of Beethoven in his early years. An illustration of this uniformity is encountered in the frequent inability of music students to distinguish readily works composed by these three masters. As a reflection of eighteenth-century mentality, uniformity of musical style corresponds in large measure to the Enlightenment ideal of a "universal language" of music accessible to all mankind.[44] It is also consistent with the view that nature and man operate according to certain uniform and universal laws discoverable by human reason and applicable to the improvement of humanity.[45] In contrast to this,

44. See further Opper, " 'Klassik,' " p. 40.
45. That this view was the dominant intellectual force during the eighteenth century has been demonstrated in chapter 2 above.

the nineteenth-century glorification of originality and uniqueness, together with the romantic conception of art in general as the expression of the individual inner self, implies stylistic features which would render interchange of movements more problematic. Further, and more important, however, is the frequent application in this century of the cyclical recurrence of themes, and the elimination of the pause between movements, rendering movement interchange impossible. It is not unlikely that the drastic decline in the production of large-scale works, and, conversely, the striking proliferation of the miniature "character piece" during the Romantic era, is in large measure traceable to the creative demands made by the musical aesthetic of originality and self-expression.

The related juxtaposition of complementary variables, as heretofore described, constitutes *successive logical complementarity*, since the contrasting musical entities are presented sequentially, one after another. Almost as important in classical music (and of cardinal importance in the music of the Baroque) is *simultaneous logical complementarity*. As the term implies, in the presence of simultaneous logical complementarity the logically contrasting complementary variables appear at the same time in contrapuntal combination. Again Mozart's *Jupiter* Symphony, here the last movement, serves as a preeminent example.

This combination appears after the five themes have been presented successively, in the following order of appearance: 1, 5, 3, 2, 4. Once again the unity and completeness of this passage do not depend on thematic homogeneity, but on the union of heterogeneous and logically related thematic entities. Note here that the logic and rationality of this passage, and of counterpoint in general, rests on the proportional relationship of note values. For example, theme one consists of whole notes, theme two primarily of half notes, themes three and four chiefly of quarter notes, and theme five mainly of eighth notes, constituting the rational progression 1:2:4:8. It will further be observed that this proportional relationship exists in every measure (except the first and last), i.e., every measure contains simultaneously at least one whole, one half, one quarter, and one eighth note. Clearly, the unity of this passage does not depend on an identical musical substance, as Reti and his followers would assert; neither does it depend on a contradiction, which was Veinus's way of "explaining" the problem.[46] On the contrary, the unity and completeness of the Mozart example, and similar contrapuntal textures, depends on the logical relation of simultaneously presented individual themes which complement each other in the sense that one theme "is logically . . . what the other is not."[47]

That the principle of simultaneous logical complementarity forms the basis of late baroque polyphony (or of any true polyphony) should be clear from the above analysis. The following passage from J. S. Bach's Fugue in C sharp minor (*Das Wohl-temperirte Clavier*, bk. 1, no. 4), illustrates the point. (For purposes of clarity only the relevant parts are here given.)

The three constituent parts are heterogeneous in nature, and are related in the manner described in the Mozart example. Thus

---

46. See *The Concerto*.

47. See further Gene F. Taylor, "Culturally Transcendent Factors in Musical Perception" (Ph.D. diss., The Florida State University, Tallahassee, 1969), p. 19.

theme one consists of whole and half notes, theme two of quarter notes, and theme three of eighth notes (with minor exceptions). Their individuality and uniqueness depend on this fact. Yet each theme, by virtue of its singular properties, contributes to a larger and more complete whole. Here also the relation of the themes to one another is logical (not literal) in the sense that one theme "is logically . . . what the other is not." And the relation of their note values, as in the example by Mozart, is also in the ratio of $1:2:4:8$. The triple fugue under consideration actually exhibits both, successive and simultaneous complementarity, since the three themes in question were initially presented successively before being combined in triple invertible counterpoint. Still, if a distinction between baroque and classical music be made in the above terms, then baroque music is characterized by a greater preponderance of simultaneous logical complementarity, while classical music, with its greater dependence on homophony, manifests to a greater extent successive logical complementarity.

The purpose of the above analysis has been to demonstrate that classical music, in its structure and principle of unity, discloses an essentially logical and rational character consistent with the predominantly logocentric mentality of the eighteenth century. It was shown that attempts to impose principles of unity chiefly derivative from nineteenth-century, biocentrically oriented thought, were misplaced because the authors advocating these principles had failed to examine the fundamental presuppositions of eighteenth-century thought, presuppositions which have their sources in the philosophy of nature of that period. The consequence of this misapplication was the Procrustean attempt to explain the unity in a classical work by means of a biologically derived literal principle of identity,[48] in the sense that all themes of a given work by Haydn, Mozart, or early Beethoven, were purportedly traceable to one thematic motif. That this is fallacious on phenomenological grounds has been elucidated. It has likewise been demonstrated that the unity and structure of classical music rest on a more abstract, and hence a more inferential, principle of identity, in the sense that unity and completeness, on both a large and small scale, are the result of juxtaposing logically related musical entities. This has been designated as the principle of logical complementarity.

---

48. Note such biological metaphors as "germ" theme, thematic "kernel," and "metamorphosis" of themes; see also Schenker's comment in *Harmony,* quoted above.

Although no operatic music has been discussed in this analysis, it may be shown that in this domain also a literal principle of identity is more characteristic of the nineteenth century, whereas eighteenth-century opera rests on a more abstract principle of identity. Thus Wagner, for example, identifies his characters at various points in the opera with the same, although frequently modified, tunes (as in *The Ring* cycle, for example). Mozart, on the other hand, identifies his characters with the same *type* of music, rather than with the same tune. For example, the child-like Papageno, in the *Magic Flute,* is consistently characterized by simple-minded music, whereas the noble Sarastro is depicted with music appropriate to his personality. Here we see an exemplification of the eighteenth-century predilection for the general, the abstract, and the universal, as distinguished from the nineteenth-century proclivity for the particular, the individual, and the local. That the first group of features existed in a period dominated by abstract Newtonian law formulated in mathematical equations and applicable to the cosmos, and that the second group of features emerged in an environment characterized by the study of the unique flora and fauna of the Galápagos Islands, and by the exhaustive examination of microorganisms under the microscope, cannot be regarded as mere coincidence.

It has been suggested in a recent study by Taylor that the principle of logical complementarity is not merely a cultural phenomenon of Western music, but a natural one which transcends cultural boundaries, since its basis resides in the neurophysiological constants of the human organism. Logical complementarity, in this context, is the human organism's demand for completeness and optimality in its perceptual and cognitive experience, musical or otherwise, completeness and optimality in turn being a reflection of the organism's desire for homeostasis. The other principle introduced by Taylor is designated *compensatory change,* i.e., "that change which compensates for completeness, sameness or homogeneity but does so through a more or less literal principle of identity." In more abstract terms, logical complementarity may be designated as completeness achieved by the union of the complementary variables x, y, and z (these letters representing logically contrasting themes, sections, or movements), while compensatory change mitigates the relative absence of completeness, by the variables x, x', x'', and so on. These variables stand for the modification or transformation of a given thematic entity. It should be clear that the union of the variables x, y, z is more logical and abstract, whereas change through the variables x, x', x'' is more literal. These principles reflect the two basic needs in human perception: completeness and change. Further, a balance of these is requisite if the extremes of "sensory deprivation" or "sensory overload" are to be avoided. Therefore, the human organism seeks "sensirostasis" in its musical experience, and in experience in general. It is here suggested that "sensirostasis" is a conspicuous feature of musical classicism, while romantic music distorts this balance in the direction of sensory overload. It is this predicament which prompts Taylor's observation that in the Romantic period "little attempt is made to achieve a perceptually optimal condition as concerns the whole. Rather, this condition is sacrificed to the achievement of intensity of experience at local points in the music.[49]

That an epistemological equilibrium is a cardinal feature of classical music may also be inferred from Cassirer's assertion that beginning with Newton the goal of aesthetics is "to free the mind from the absolute predominance of deduction" and "to make way . . . for the phenomena, for direct observation—not to the exclusion of deduction but side by side with it."[50] True, the mature classicism of Haydn and Mozart did not manifest itself until the 1780s, almost fifty years after Newton's death. At the same time, one should not expect to encounter an exact contemporaneity between the ideas and methods generated by science and their implementation in the arts. The process whereby these ideas are propagated into the intellectual climate of an era is subtle and extended in time. The epistemological balance between deduction and direct observation, or in F. S. C. Northrop's terms, between the "theoretic and aesthetic components"[51] in knowledge, is what in essence constitutes classicism, musical or otherwise. Classicism, in this sense, exhibits a logical formal structure without neglecting the phenomenal attributes of sound. It manifests the very optimality and perceptual completeness which characterizes the biological organism, and which the organism actively seeks in order to preserve its well-being. Romanticism, in contradistinction to this, destroys this optimality in the direction of the

---

49. Taylor, "Transcendent Factors," pp. 17, 65–123, 131.
50. Ernst Cassirer, *The Philosophy of the Enlightenment,* trans. F. C. A. Koelln and J. P. Pettegrove (Princeton, N.J.: Princeton University Press, 1951; reprinted by the Beacon Press, Boston, 1964), p. 131.
51. *The Logic of the Sciences and the Humanities* (New York: The Macmillan Company, 1925; reprinted by The New American Library, Mentor Books, New York, 1959), pp. 103–18.

phenomenal at the expense of the logical and rational. It remains to demonstrate in a future chapter of this study that romantic music, having largely abandoned the logical and rational methods of the eighteenth century, rests primarily on the more literal principle of compensatory change.

To conclude this chapter, a recent study involving temporal proportion in the music of Mozart will be considered.[52] The author of this study, after conducting a statistical investigation of the ratios between the lengths of the exposition and of the combined development-recapitulation sections in the sonata-form movements of the Mozart piano sonatas, concludes that Mozart innately leans toward the so-called "golden section ratio," a geometrical (rather than arithmetic) proportion commensurable only in the square. Ghyka has asserted that this ratio, whose numerical value to the nearest thousandth is the irrational number .618, is not only fundamental to the Pythagorean and Platonic idea of the beautiful, but also plays a leading role in gothic and renaissance art and architecture.[53] Hambidge, who terms this ratio "dynamic symmetry" (from the Greek *dynamei symmetroi*, or commensurable only in the square), likewise concluded that a preponderance of Hellenic art manifests this proportion.[54] Furthermore, the desirability of this ratio in the formal properties of various arts has also been recognized by no lesser figures than Vitruvius, Leonardo, Dürer, and Kepler, to mention the most important names. It has also been found that a striking number of natural forms (such as the human body, various shells, and the seed pattern of the sunflower plant) exhibit this ratio.[55] Setting aside any mysticism which might be associated with these findings, it appears that a certain formal optimality and balance are attributable to the golden section ratio, at least in the art of the past twenty-five hundred years.

The recently disclosed presence of this ratio in a large body of Mozart's music corresponds to numerous assertions made

52. Jane P. Camp, "Temporal Proportion: A Study of Sonata Forms in the Piano Sonatas of Mozart" (Ph.D. diss., The Florida State University, Tallahassee, 1968).

53. For a history of this ratio and its application to Western art, see Matila Ghyka, "The Pythagorean and Platonic Scientific Criterion of the Beautiful in Classical Western Art," in F. S. C. Northrop, ed., *Ideological Differences and World Order* (New Haven: Yale University Press, 1949), pp. 90–116, *passim*.

54. Jay Hambidge, *The Elements of Dynamic Symmetry* (New Haven: Yale University Press, 1959).

55. See D'Arcy W. Thompson, *On Growth and Form* (New York: The Macmillan Company, 1943), pp. 748–61, *passim;* also see Theodore A. Cook, *The Curves of Life* (New York: Henry Holt and Company, 1914), pp. 414–32.

during the last two centuries by various writers about this composer's sense of form and timing. For example, we read such statements as "classical proportion," "perfect symmetry," an "infallible taste for saying exactly the right thing at the right time," and so on. It is also reported that Mozart, since his earliest childhood, had an unusual affinity for numbers, and that this affinity, in turn, may have had an effect on his sense of proportion. Regardless of the conclusions that one may draw from the above evidence, the suggestion emerges that the source of Mozart's organicity of form,[56] his sense of balance, timing, and formal intelligibility, resides in the abstract, rational properties of mathematics, not in the more literal principles of "organic" unity encountered in nineteenth-century music. This would tend further to confirm my original proposition that, epistemologically, musical classicism is an analogue of eighteenth-century science centered chiefly on mathematical physics.

---

56. Camp, "Proportions," pp. 1–2, 111–25, 78.

6

The Primacy of the Life Sciences
in the Nineteenth Century

The aim of the present chapter is to trace synoptically the development of the life sciences during the eighteenth and nineteenth centuries. It is argued that not until the nineteenth century did the various branches of biology attain some sort of autonomy in approach and method, the previous centuries being on the whole dominated by paradigms established elsewhere. It is also argued that in terms of influence on the intellectual climate of the nineteenth century the biological sciences, in conjunction with the idea of evolution, occupy a preeminent position, just as mathematical physics prevailed over all provinces of thought in the preceding era. The distinction in subject matter is of obvious importance in determining the character of these periods; equally important, but less obvious, is the corollary epistemological distinction governing these two domains. Thus it has been shown that the primacy of abstract deduction in the physical sciences was the key factor in shaping seventeenth- and eighteenth-century culture. It remains to be demonstrated in the remainder of this study that a similar process occurred in the nineteenth century, where the inductive method of natural history biology played the decisive role.

The biological sciences in their scope and influence during the period contemporaneous with the activities of Galileo, Descartes, and Newton were relatively insignificant when compared with the advances made in mathematics and physics by the above men. True, considerable progress in biology was made at this time (chiefly due to the activities in Northern Italy at the universities of Padua, Bologna, and Pisa) by such men as Harvey (circulation of the blood), Borelli (muscular mechanics), and Malpighi (animal and plant microscopy). Despite these achievements, biology failed to attain the autonomy and status of the physical sciences, serving primarily to corroborate and further extend the mechanical principles elaborated by the physicists.

During the eighteenth century we witness a progressive acceleration in the study of the life sciences. At this time, however, as in the subsequent century, it is unintelligible to speak of biology apart from geological investigations and the emerging doctrine of evolution. Despite great controversy concerning some leading and widely divergent ideas in these domains, biology and geology, the latter in its paleontological implications, are found in a continuous state of cross-fertilization culminating in the evolutionary hypothesis, which accounted in a unified and comprehensive manner for the origin and development of the animate world.

The outstanding natural-history biologist of Newton's generation is John Ray (both were members of the Royal Society). Ray's work deals primarily with the description and classification of plants and animals (*Historie plantarum generalis*, 1686-1704; *Synopsis methodica animalium*, 1693; *Historia insectorum*, 1710),[1] thus paving the way for the classification systems of such naturalists as Linnaeus and Cuvier. Characteristically, reflecting the static world view created by Galileo, Descartes, and Newton, Ray's classificatory scheme is predicated on a corresponding statically conceived fixity of species, i.e., on a permanent *scala naturae*. Writing in an intellectual climate increasingly inimical to revealed religion, Ray asserts in his *The Wisdom of God Manifested in the Works of the Creation* (1691) that the works of nature are "the Works created by God at first, and by him conserved to this Day in the same State and Condition in which they were first made." J. C. Greene, commenting on the above passage, notes that

These words expressed the prevailing conviction of the stability of the fundamental structures of nature—stars, mountains, oceans, species, and the like. In Ray's mind there was no *scientific* problem concerning the origin of these structures. They were created by God in the beginning. If one wished to know why they had the particular shapes, patterns, and properties which they exhibited, the answer was to be sought, not in

1. See further René Taton, ed., *History of Science*, vol. 2: *The Beginnings of Modern Science from 1450 to 1800* (New York: Basic Books, Inc., 1964), pp. 338 and 363.

the daily operations of nature, but in the purposes which God had intended them to serve when he created them.[2]

Hence, the uniqueness in structure and environmental adaptation of the organic world was explained in terms of a naïvely conceived teleology, by the so-called argument from design, not by an evolutionary process of natural selection.

That Ray's conception of the animate world is a special case obtaining from Newton's mechanistic cosmology is implicit in Dampier's assertion that Ray "as a biologist . . . supports the view of Newton and his disciples as astronomers."[3] And Newton himself explicitly enunciates an order of nature invested from its inception with an immutable preestablished harmony:

> God in the Beginning form'd Matter in solid, . . . moveable Particles of such Sizes and Figures, and with such other Properties, and such Proportion to Space, as most conduced to the End for which he form'd them. . . . For it became who created them to set them in order. And if he did so, it's unphilosophical to seek for any other Origin of the World, or to pretend that it might arise out of a Chaos by the mere laws of Nature; though being once form'd, it may continue by those laws for many Ages.[4]

The same view is manifest in Descartes's thought, even though his physical theory of cosmic vortices fashioning the world from primordial matter might at first sight give the impression of an evolutionary process. That this is not the case is attested to by Mason who writes that Descartes emphasized that "any possible world of primordial matter would necessarily assume the present configuration of our world . . . , as the laws of mechanics would always operate in the same way. Thus our present world was the predetermined end of any cosmic system; it was in fact the only possible world." Comparing Descartes with Newton concerning this conception of the universe, Mason further asserts that Newton's notion of the origin of the cosmos was even less evolutionary than Descartes's.

> For Newton, God had created the world in the form in which it is found today, and only then had the laws of mechanics come into oper-

---

2. Reproduced by permission from *The Death of Adam: Evolution and Its Impact on Western Thought,* by John C. Greene, © 1959 by The Iowa State University Press, Ames, Iowa; reprinted by The New American Library, Mentor Books, 1961), p. 15.

3. Sir William C. Dampier, *A Shorter History of Science* (New York: The Macmillan Company, 1944), p. 87.

4. Quoted in Greene, *Adam,* pp. 22–23.

ation to sustain the cosmic machine. These were phenomena, Newton thought, which were not entirely explicable in terms of the laws of mechanics, but Laplace towards the end of the 18th century tied up these loose ends, and showed the solar system to be mechanically stable.[5]

Therefore, it may be asserted that just as Harvey's discovery of the circulatory system constitutes a special case derived from Galilean mechanical principles and applied to a gross physiological process, so Ray's conception of the living world constitutes a special case derived from the Newtonian world-machine. It might be noted in passing that despite Ray's general acceptance of corpuscular mechanism as the ultimate constituent of matter, in the province of life he was compelled to add a vitalistic principle conjoined to Aristotelian final causes. For example, we read, "For my part, I should make no scruple to attribute the Formation of *Plants,* their growth and nutrition to the vegetative Soul in them; and likewise the formation of *Animals* to the vegetative power of their Souls."[6]

John Ray, who died in 1705, was followed by Linnaeus, perhaps the greatest natural history biologist of the eighteenth century. In Linnaeus's taxonomical system, the fixity and immutability of species appear to have been established for all time to come. Founding his systematic classification of the animate world on the work of Ray, and further extending it, Linnaeus, according to Greene, aspired "to reduce the earth to order as Newton had the heavens." Greene further notes:

"God created, Linnaeus arranged" went an eighteenth-century saying, and Linnaeus himself noted in his diary that his *System of Nature* was unique, "a work to which natural history has never had a fellow." In it, for the first time, every terrestrial production was assigned its place in one great system of classification. Nothing could have been more contrary to the idea of organic evolution than Linnaeus' aspiration to place every creature in its proper niche.[7]

This aspiration rested in large measure on the "conviction that the world constituted a perfect *Scala Naturae,* with each type of plant filling a necessary niche in an overarching pattern . . ." , and "on a faith in the strict orderliness of the divinely created world of living things. Since this created world was orderly, a

5. S. F. Mason, "The Ideal of Progress and Theories of Evolution in Science," in S. Lilley, ed., *Essays on the Social History of Science* (Copenhagen: Ejnar Munksgaard, 1953), pp. 93–94.
6. Quoted in Greene, *Adam,* p. 20.
7. *Ibid.,* p. 136.

perfect natural system of classification was possible."[8] These assertions clearly indicate that Linnaeus, more systematically and to a greater extent than his predecessor Ray, regarded the animate world as a fixed, nonevolving entity corresponding to the static, mechanistically conceived universe of Galileo, Descartes, and Newton.

It is to Linnaeus that we owe the so-called binomial nomenclature, i.e., the classification of plants and animals into genus and species still used today. We are told by Butterfield that Linnaeus's chief work, the *Systema naturae* (1735) gave him a reputation and influence "that lasted down to the time of Darwin." The relative synchronicity of the *Systema naturae*, Newton's *Principia* (1687), and Rameau's *Traité* (1722) may here be noted, for all of these works rest on the premise of a rationally ordered world capable of systematic treatment and ascertainability. Butterfield further affirms that Linnaeus "assumed that all individuals in a given species could be traced back to an original pair produced at the Creation, and it was to be significant that he gave the weight of his great authority to the idea of the immutability of species."[9] Accordingly Mason writes:

> Thus the formation of the world and all its inhabitants, like the place of the scientific revolution in history, was seen during the 17th and 18th centuries as a single creative event, which once accomplished, was eternally enduring and finished for all time. During the same period a similar view obtained concerning the formation of human society. For all their differences, Bodin, Hobbes, Locke, and Rousseau, thought that once upon a time isolated individual men had come together and had contracted to live with one another in human society for ever after. . . . They [also] agreed that mankind had been much the same throughout the ages after the signing of the original social contract. Hume averred in 1748 that, "mankind are so much the same in all times and places that history informs us of nothing new in this particular. Its chief use is only to discover the constant and universal principles of human nature."[10]

These assertions to the contrary, the eighteenth century, already with Linnaeus, begins to witness a progressive erosion of the idea of an immutably fixed world. For example, increasingly

8. Maurice Mandelbaum, "Scientific Background of Evolutionary Theory in Biology," in P. P. Wiener and Aaron Noland, eds., *Roots of Scientific Thought; a Cultural Perspective* (New York: Basic Books, Inc., 1957), p. 520.

9. H. Butterfield, *The Origins of Modern Science, 1300–1800* (New York: The Macmillan Co., 1951), p. 172.

10. Mason, "Progress," pp. 94–95.

in his later years Linnaeus began to encounter difficulties in making precise distinctions between closely related species, "partly because he had discovered much overlapping, and partly because he had done much in the way of hybridising in his own garden."[11] He became aware of nature's "sportiveness," in its ability to generate spontaneously new varieties and "abnormal" plants from existing forms.

> As one pursues this subject through his multitudinous writings and the ever mounting editions of the *Systema Naturae* one can trace a growing uncertainty and doubt. He sees the possibility of new species arising through crossbreeding. He confesses that he dare not decide "whether all these species are the children of time, or whether the Creator from the very beginning of the world had restricted this course of development to a definite number of species." He cautiously removes from later editions of the *Systema* the statement that no new species can arise. The fixity of species, the precise definition of the term, is no longer secure. *"Nullae species novae"* had been accepted by the world, but to the master taxonomist who had drawn the lines of relationship with geometric precision all was now wavering toward mutability and formlessness.[12]

In fact the very exhaustive and systematic arrangement of the animate world into a *scala naturae,* i.e., a chain of being ranging from the simplest organisms at the bottom of the spectrum to highly differentiated life forms at the top may have spontaneously suggested to Linnaeus some sort of developmental process.

The transition from a static to a developmental conception of organic nature, already intimated by Linnaeus, emerges more explicitly in the work of Comte de Buffon, his exact contemporary. Although both conceived of nature as a system, for Buffon this system was not "a statically ordered array of classes, but a dynamic whole." Thus he writes, *"La nature . . . est dans un movement de flux continuel."* Furthermore, it was a whole "in which individuals vary from each other in sometimes imperceptible degrees: *'la marche de la nature se fasse par nuances et par degrés.'"*[13] As a consequence of this affirmation Buffon regarded the Linnaean classificatory scheme as being artificial, erroneous, and not conducive to an understanding of nature's processes. He viewed it, in his own words, as an "error in metaphysics"[14] which

---

11. Butterfield, *Origin,* p. 173.
12. Loren Eiseley, *Darwin's Century: Evolution and the Men Who Discovered It* (New York: Doubleday Anchor Books, 1958), p. 25.
13. Mandelbaum, "Evolutionary Theory," pp. 520–21.
14. Stephen F. Mason, *A History of the Sciences* (New York: Collier Books, 1962), p. 335.

"degraded and disfigured nature instead of describing it."[15] Writing further in his chief work, the *Histoire naturelle,* begun in 1749, Buffon asserts:

> The error consists in a failure to understand nature's processes, which always take place by gradations. . . . It is possible to descend by almost insensible degrees from the most perfect creature to the most formless matter . . . there will be found a great number of intermediate species, and of objects belonging half to one class and half to another. Objects of this sort, to which it is impossible to assign a place necessarily render vain the attempt to a universal system.

We may see in this passage the transition from the study of nature in terms of its products to one centered on the idea of process, from a generic to a genetic conception of natural phenomena, from the elemental notion of being to the equally elemental notion of becoming. It was only a short step from this change to an evolutionary view of the animate world. Buffon writes in this respect,

> If the point were once gained that among animals and vegetables there had been, I do not say several species, but even a single one, which had been produced in the course of direct descent from other species . . . then no further limit could be set to the power of nature, and we should not be wrong in supposing, with sufficient time, that she could have developed all other organic forms from one primordial type.[16]

In the *Epoques de la nature* (1779), Buffon extends the idea of mutability, development, and constant change to all of nature, animate and inanimate. He writes,

> Nature being contemporary with matter, space, and time, her history is that of every substance, every place, every age; and although it appears at first glance that her great works never alter or change, . . . one sees, on observing more closely, that her course is not absolutely uniform; one realizes that she permits considerable variations, that she undergoes successive alterations, that she lends herself to new combinations, to mutations of matter and form; finally, that the more fixed she appears in her entirety, the more variable she is in each of her parts; and if we comprehend her in her full extent, we cannot doubt that she is very different today from what she was in the beginning and from what she became in the course of time: these are the different changes which we call her epochs.[17]

---

15. Mandelbaum, "Evolutionary Theory," p. 521.
16. Mason, *History,* pp. 335–36.
17. Quoted in Greene, *Adam,* pp. 81–82.

With respect to plants and animals, however, Mason observes that Buffon was not an evolutionary thinker "in the modern sense." As opposed to the Darwinian assumption that the more complex forms of life evolved from simpler organisms, he maintained that the "various organic species were so many degenerate forms of a more perfect original type," that the donkey, for example, "was a degenerate horse, whilst apes and monkeys were degenerate men."[18]

Before proceeding with the further development of the biological sciences it is well to point out that during the second half of the eighteenth century several independent streams of thought contributed to the idea of evolution before converging during the nineteenth century in the work of Darwin. These were the idea of progress, speculations concerning the origin of the solar system, studies in geology, and embryological investigations.

With respect to the idea of progress, J. C. Greene, describing his book as being centered on "the rise of evolutionary views of nature and on the decline of static creationism in the two centuries separating Isaac Newton and Charles Darwin," asserts that "as faith in the stability and wise design of the structures of nature declined, there was a compensating effort to find in the idea of progress a new world view which would give meaning to science and direction to human history."[19] The idea of progress as applied to secular man and his knowledge of the world around him is a product of the Enlightenment. Thus Hume's proposition that "mankind are . . . much the same in all times and places" notwithstanding, Fontenelle, according to Mason, suggested at the beginning of the eighteenth century that "if humanity has been much the same . . . , then mankind must progress by the sheer accumulation of knowledge throughout the ages."[20] Comparing his own culture with the culture of classical Greece, and concluding that his period constitutes an improvement over the ancient civilization, Fontenelle further writes (as paraphrased by Bury) that

truth could only be reached by the elimination of false routes and in this way the numbers of the Pythagoreans, the ideas of Plato, the qualities of Aristotle, all served indirectly to advance knowledge. [And in his own words] "We are under an obligation to the ancients for having exhausted almost all the false theories that could be formed." Enlightened

18. Mason, *History,* pp. 336–37.
19. Greene, *Adam,* pp. i–ii.
20. Mason, "Progress," p. 95.

both by their true views and by their errors, it is not surprising that we should surpass them.

And finally, suggesting a general doctrine of progress for all future time, he affirms that "we must expect posterity to excel us as we excel the Ancients, through the improvement of method . . . and through increase of experience" (Bury's paraphrase). In view of what has been said with respect to the role of mathematical physics during the seventeenth and eighteenth centuries, it is not surprising to read that "the achievements of physical science did more than anything else to convert the imaginations of men to the general doctrine of Progress."[21]

Succeeding Fontenelle, Voltaire "called for an active effort to advance mankind through the criticism of traditional beliefs and the dissemination of the newly acquired knowledge of the natural world."[22] In the *Essai sur les moeurs et l'esprit des nations* (1756), he writes further,

> We may believe that reason and industry will always progress more and more; that the useful arts will be improved; that . . . the evils which afflicted man . . . will gradually disappear among all those who govern nations.[23]

The view expressed by Voltaire was in fact the self-avowed aspiration of the *philosophes* and of the *Encyclopédie* which aimed, in Diderot's words, "To bring together all the knowledge scattered over the surface of the earth, and thus to build up a general system of thought, so that . . . our descendants, becoming *more* instructed, shall become *more* virtuous and happier"[24] (italics added). In fact, the entire encyclopedic movement of the Enlightenment had its source, according to Bury, in the belief that "man is *perfectible*," i.e., "capable of indefinite improvement." And further, "belief in Progress was their [the encyclopedists'] sustaining faith."[25]

The idea of progress, which "introduced an essentially evolutionary interpretation into features of life," was likewise extended to historical thought. It is implicit in Vico's *Scienza Nuova* (1725) which similarly rests on the notion "that the modern

---

21. J. B. Bury, *The Idea of Progress* (London: Macmillan and Co., Ltd., 1920), pp. 104, 105, 113.
22. Mason, "Progress," p. 95.
23. Bury, *Idea,* pp. 149–50.
24. Mason, "Progress," p. 95.
25. Bury, *Idea,* pp. 162, 163.

period of human culture, while dependent on previous eras, was in its essential features superior to them; thus Vico accepted both continuity and progress in cultural change."[26] It is more explicit in Turgot, who writes that "the total mass of the human race is moving always slowly forward." The same ideational tendency is discernible in the French school of economists known as the "physiocrats." They (Quesnay, Mirabeau and Turgot) "assumed . . . that the end of society is the attainment of terrestrial happiness by its members, and that this is the sole purpose of government."[27] Hence, these thinkers "of the eighteenth century," notes Scoon, "adopting a naturalistic attitude toward human culture, were led to an interpretation which emphasized . . . progress." Scoon further observes that the idea of progress spontaneously passed "into the vaguer notion of development," especially in literature and philosophy. As an example of this he quotes the following passage from Diderot's *Pensées sur l'interprétation de la nature* (1754):

> Even if Revelation teaches us that species left the hands of the Creator as they are now, the philosopher who gives himself up to conjecture comes to the conclusion that life has always had its elements scattered in the mass of inorganic matter; that it finally came about that these elements united; that the embryo formed of this union has passed through an infinitude of organization and development; that it has acquired, in succession, movement, sensation, . . . thought, . . . language, laws, and finally the sciences and arts; that millions of years have elapsed during each of these phases of development, and that there are still new developments to be taken which are as yet unknown to us.[28]

The ideas of progress and of development naturally stimulated biologists "to formulate theories of organic evolution." The formative stage of this process may be seen in the transformation of the timeless *scala naturae* "so that the chain of beings was seen not as a static hierarchy of creatures but as an evolutionary series of organisms in time."[29]

Another province of knowledge which undermined the notion of a fixed, immutable world and paved the way for evolutionary thought dealt with cosmogony. Here the most prominent and influential speculations concerning the origin of the solar system

---

26. Robert Scoon, "The Rise and Impact of Evolutionary Ideas," in *Evolutionary Thought in America,* ed. Stow Persons (New Haven: Yale University Press, 1950), p. 10.

27. Quoted in Bury, *Idea,* pp. 168, 173.

28. Scoon, "Rise," pp. 10, 11.

29. Mason, "Progress," p. 96.

belong to Immanuel Kant and Laplace. It was Kant who in 1755 first proposed the so-called "Nebular hypothesis." According to this hypothesis the earth and the solar system were to be derived "from a previous state of the system of matter in motion by the operation of mechanical laws,"[30] i.e., the very Newtonian laws upon which the permanent design of the cosmos rested. The previous state was one of a rotating, primordial, gaseous nebula, out of which the planets condensed. Kant's nebular hypothesis was further elaborated by Laplace in his *Exposition du système du monde* (1796), wherein "he tried to show how known laws would operate" to form the solar system. Laplace, however, was much more famous for his *Mécanique céleste,*

> in which a century of mathematical analysis of the solar system was summed up and extended. His demonstration of the stability of the solar system was hailed as proof positive of its divine origin, but Laplace himself drew no such conclusion. For him as for Buffon, the uniformities observable in the arrangement and motions of the planets were a challenge to scientific explanation, not a proof of divine handiwork.

In the fifth edition of the *Exposition* he writes:

> But could not this arrangement of the planets be itself an effect of the laws of motion; and could not the supreme intelligence which Newton makes to interfere, make it depend on a more general phenomenon? such as . . . a nebulous matter distributed in various masses throughout the immensity of the heavens. Can one even affirm that the preservation of the planetary system entered into the views of the Author of Nature? The mutual attraction of the bodies of this system cannot alter its stability, as Newton supposes, but may there not be in the heavenly regions another fluid besides light? Its resistance, and the diminution of its emission produced in the mass of the Sun, ought at length to destroy the arrangement of the planets, so that to maintain this, a renovation would become evidently necessary. And do not all those species of animals which are extinct, but whose existence Cuvier has ascertained with such singular sagacity, and also the organization in the numerous fossil bones which he has described, indicate a tendency to change in things, which are apparently the most permanent in their nature? The magnitude and importance of the solar system ought not to except it from this general law; for they are relative to our smallness, and this system, extensive as it appears to be, is but an insensible point in the universe.

Laplace is here clearly suggesting a general principle of cosmic evolution within the framework of Newtonian mechanics. The

---

30. John C. Greene, *Darwin and the Modern World View* (Baton Rouge: Louisiana State University Press, 1961), p. 41.

same principle was more explicitly developed during the nine-teenth century by such men as Spencer and Bergson. Commenting on the philosophical implications of the above passage, Greene writes that "the wheel had come full circle. The sense of the permanency of the structures of nature was gone and with it the belief in final causes and the argument from design."[31]

Another contributing factor leading to evolutionary ideas of the organic world was provided by the geological sciences, par-ticularly paleontology. We read that before the eighteenth cen-tury geology was a "scattered and divided subject" conceived in terms of speculative theories which were largely independent of the few facts "known to miners and others concerned with the extraction of metals, clays, coal and salts from the earth." It was only during the eighteenth century that geology gradually became an autonomous science, reaching "maturity in the early decades of the nineteenth." Therefore, temporally, the geological and biological sciences exhibit a close parallel.

Geology, during the period under consideration, discloses a variegated picture of several conflicting theories, most of which attempted to reconcile the available evidence concerning forma-tive geological processes with the Biblical account of the earth's creation. Despite their diversity, these theories naturally fall into two distinct categories designated as 1) Vulcanism (Plu-tonism) and 2) Neptunism. The first of these was based on the role of heat, the second on the role of water in the formation of geological strata. Furthermore, Vulcanism is customarily associated with the view that the earth had evolved gradually over a period of time incommensurable with the Biblical time-scale, while Neptunism assumed a catastrophic and hence sudden formative process compatible with the Mosaic flood and the Biblical time-scale.

Characteristically, such geologists as John Ray adhered to the neptunist view, according to which "fossils were widely regarded as abortive attempts of nature to produce animals and plants, or as 'sports of nature,' fortuitously resembling organic forms." To admit that they are remains of living forms now extinct would be to imply that "the great chain of living crea-tures could not be continuous and complete; there would be gaps where species had died out and thereby the world as a whole would be rendered imperfect." The neptunist (catastrophist) view was continued during the eighteenth and early part of the

31. *Ibid., Adam,* pp. 45–46.

nineteenth centuries by such men as Scheuchzer, de Luc, Werner, and Cuvier. Most of these scientists worked within the narrow confines of Biblical assumptions respecting the earth and its processes.

In contrast to the above views, which on the whole attempted to reconcile theories of geological development with the Biblical account of creation, we have the so-called vulcanist or plutonist idea that heat and volcanic processes play a greater role than water in the formation of the earth. The most important vulcanist of the period, and the founder of modern geology, was James Hutton. In opposition to the neptunist view with its Biblical time-scale extending backwards only *ca.* 6000 years, Hutton proposed the novel theory that it was mainly the "geological activity of the internal heat of the earth" which was responsible for its processes and changes, although he also "accepted the formative powers of water." A more radical and, on religious grounds, unacceptable proposition of his was that "the age of the earth was indefinitely long, with the same geological forces as are now in operation always at work, forming, breaking down, and re-forming the rocks composing the surface of the earth." This view was designated as "uniformitarianism" in contrast to the catastrophism of the Neptunists. Hutton's theory is in essence a reflection of Newtonian mechanistic cosmology, which rests on the premise that "the forces of nature are constant" and that "the solar system was mechanically stable and permanently self-sustaining." Writing in his major work, *The Theory of the Earth* (1795), Hutton asserted,

> From seeing the revolutions of the planets, it is concluded that there is a system by which they are intended to continue those revolutions. But if the succession of worlds is established in the system of nature, it is vain to look for anything higher in the origin of the earth. The result therefore of this physical enquiry is that we find no vestige of a beginning, no prospect of an end.

Hutton's geological investigations were further extended by Charles Lyell, whose principal contribution was "to connect up the scattered facts of the subject." The title of Lyell's chief work is worth quoting in full, since it reveals essentially the same uniformitarian position found in Hutton's work. It reads, *The Principles of Geology being an Attempt to Explain the Former Changes of the Earth's Surface by reference to Causes now in Operation* (1830-33). Thus, unlike the neptunist Werner, who "had started from a definite if hypothetical origin of the rocks, the primeval ocean, and had argued forwards," Lyell and Hutton "started with the present geological forces of nature and argued backwards." It has been affirmed previously that Hutton's uniformitarianism is chiefly derivative from the assumption that the laws of nature and the systems they govern are constant. In order to accommodate this view to evolutionary process and change, a shift of emphasis occurred whereby the forces of nature rather than the material systems were regarded as being constant: "Thus through the operation of the same unchanging forces the matter of the earth was transformed, and in this way the idea of geological evolution was deduced from an extension of the former unhistorical mechanical view of nature." Because of the prevailing religious sentiments with respect to the earth's age, Hutton's work at the close of the eighteenth century was almost totally ignored. By the third decade of the nineteenth century, however, when Lyell's work was published, the mounting geological and paleontological evidence that the earth was much older than hitherto believed, combined with the historical idea of progress, radically changed the climate of opinion. With respect to the influence of historical change and development we read that Lyell himself

> pointed out several analogies between geological investigations and the study of history: indeed his Uniformitarianism in geology is said to have been suggested by the gradual growth of the British Constitution. . . . Lyell averred that the geological study of the earth was strictly analogous to the archaeological study of human history, and later he went over into this field producing in 1863 his work on *The Antiquity of Man*.

A further impetus to an evolutionary view of the earth and its living forms, extinct or extant, may have come from the domain of embryology, which, like geology and the other biological sciences, was in its formative stage during the eighteenth century. The theory of embryological development, which would likely suggest evolutionary process, is known as epigenesis, i.e., the idea that the embryo develops from a relatively simple and undifferentiated protoplasm into a highly differentiated and complex organism. The first step in this process was Wolff's observation that "the embryos of a different species resembled one another much more closely than did the adult forms and that they developed in very similar ways." Wolff's follower, Kielmeyer, went further by noting that

there was a physiological parallel between the embryological development of higher organisms and the scale of perfection into which the
adult forms of organic beings were arranged. Each organism developed
up the scale to the grade of its species so that the human embryo . . .
first had only vegetative functions, then those of the lower animals
which move but do not feel, and finally those of the higher animals
which both move and possess sensation.

This trend of thought was continued when in 1797 Autenrieth
"suggested that there was also an anatomical parallelism, the
structure of an embryo passing through anatomical forms similar
to those of lower creatures on the way to its adult form." Finally,
it was proposed by Meckel in 1811 that "species might have
evolved one from the other, and that the embryos of the higher
animals during the course of their growth recapitulated anatom-
ically and physiologically the evolutionary development of their
species."[32] Thus Haeckel's biogenetic law stating that "ontogeny
recapitulates phylogeny," enunciated in the second half of the
nineteenth century, is implicit much earlier in the work of these
men, and especially in the investigations of Ernst von Baer (1792-
1876). Furthermore,

> to accept *development,* an emergence *by degrees,* in the case of the single
> individual makes it possible to accept with greater equanimity the con-
> ception that species itself may have come into existence by some more
> extended process of phylogenetic change. Thus, *indirectly, epigenesis,*
> or the developmental theory of embryonic growth, fitted, analogically,
> the theory of evolution.

The eighteenth-century theory of epigenesis, as developed by
Wolff, had to compete with a rival theory of embryological development known as preformationism. According to this theory
the germ cell, male or female, already contained in miniature the
fully formed and differentiated organism, so that embryological
growth simply meant the gradual enlargement of the preformed
embryo, or *homunculus,* as it was designated in the human species.
This theory, based largely on speculation with little empirical
evidence, was supported by such men, in the seventeenth and
eighteenth centuries, as Leeuwenhoek, Malpighi, Bonnet, Spal-
lanzani, Leibniz, and Wolff's contemporary, Albrecht von Haller.
Haller adopted an extreme form of preformationism whereby
the germ cell

---

32. Mason, *History,* pp. 385, 397, 402–3, 408–11, 368–69.

will contain not only her daughter, but also her granddaughter, her great-grand-daughter, and her great-great-grand-daughter, and if it is once proved that an ovary can contain many generations, there is no absurdity in saying that it contains them all.[33]

Curiously, William Harvey, whose *On the Generation of Animals* (1651) is said to have initiated modern embryology, was an epigeneticist, despite the fact that the intellectual environment in which he lived was more conducive to static preformationism. This turn of mind, however, is chiefly due (according to Mason) to the continuing influence of Aristotle's ideas concerning the development of living things, which Harvey adopted in the case of embryology.[34]

The foregoing has been a brief survey of the major developments in the life sciences and geology during the eighteenth century. It is to be concluded that on the whole this century, especially its first half, witnessed an attempt to incorporate the animate world into the Newtonian scheme of static mechanism. Admittedly, evolutionary ideas concerning organic nature, and nature as a whole, increasingly obtruded themselves on the mentality of the period. However, in view of Darwin's great synthesis in the ensuing century, these ideas must be regarded as being in their formative stage and hence subordinate to advances made in the mathematico-physical sciences by such men as Euler, Lagrange, and Laplace. That this predicament was reversed in the nineteenth century, i.e., that the biological sciences provided the chief impetus for thought in all provinces of human endeavor has already been discussed. Additional testimony to the biocentrism of the nineteenth century presents itself readily. For example, A. N. Whitehead writes that

> In the nineteenth century, the general influence of mathematics waned. The romantic movement in literature, and the idealistic movement in philosophy were not the products of mathematical minds. Also, even in science, the growth of geology, of zoology, and of the biological sciences generally, was in each case entirely disconnected from any reference to mathematics. The chief scientific excitement of the century was the Darwinian theory of evolution. Accordingly, mathematicians were in the background so far as the general thought of that age was concerned.[35]

We read elsewhere that "the nineteenth century witnessed the

33. Eiseley, *Darwin's Century*, pp. 367–69.
34. Mason, *History*, p. 363.
35. *Science and the Modern World* (New York: The Macmillan Company, 1925; reprinted by The New American Library, Mentor Books, New York, 1959), p. 37.

triumphant rise of biology. Everything that preceded this period could be nothing more than preparatory."[36] And still further, "The impact of evolutionary ideas on the intellectual world was monumental. . . . Evolutionary ideas swept into explorations of human life and values, social institutions, religion, and morality."[37] And finally, Arnold Toynbee observes that "the racial factor in history" was especially pronounced "in the nineteenth century, when Western minds had been rendered biology-conscious by the work of Charles Darwin and other scientific investigators."[38]

There is no need to enter here into a protracted exposition of evolutionary theory, whether it be in its Lamarckian or Darwinian version. The major postulates of both are readily available in scores of books. What the remainder of this chapter will be devoted to are certain random observations respecting the theory of evolution and certain ideas which led to its formulation. First of all, it may be noted that Lamarck's version of organic evolution (*Philosophie Zoologique,* 1809), especially his propositions that necessity produces new organs, and that these (acquired characteristics), in turn, are genetically transmitted, thus producing new species, has been rejected in the Western world due to lack of empirical evidence. Second, the role of Lyell and Malthus should be noted in Darwin's arrival at the mechanism of natural selection. With respect to Lyell, we read that his *Principles of Geology,* advocating the Huttonian theory of geological evolution, was taken by Darwin on the voyage of the *Beagle,* where he perused it with great interest. Writing home he asserted, "I am become a zealous disciple of Mr. Lyell's views, as known in his book. Geologising in South America, I am tempted to carry parts to a greater extent than he does." What Darwin likely carried to a greater extent was Lyell's discovery that "each rock stratum contains its own characteristic fossils," and that "if there had been a succession of rock strata in time, so too there must have been a succession of the organic species. In this way Lyell prepared the way for Darwinism." Concerning the economist Malthus (*Essay on Population,* 1798), Darwin wrote that

36. Maurice Caullery, *A History of Biology* (New York: Walker and Co., 1966), p. 132.

37. William Beck, *Modern Science and the Nature of Life* (New York: Harcourt, Brace and Company, 1957; reprinted by Doubleday & Company, Inc., Anchor Books, Garden City, N. Y., in cooperation with The American Museum of Natural History, 1961), p. 117.

38. Arnold J. Toynbee, *A Study of History,* abr. by D. C. Somervell (New York: Oxford University Press, 1946), 1 : 55.

In October 1838 I happened to read for my amusement "Malthus on Population," and being well prepared to appreciate the struggle for existence which everywhere goes on from long continued observation of the habits of animals and plants, it at once struck me that under these circumstances favourable variations would tend to be preserved, and unfavourable ones to be destroyed. Here then I had at last got a theory by which to work.[39]

Third, the shock experienced by the public upon the publication of the *Origin of Species* (1859) was not so much due to the evolutionary ideas and their implications for man's place in nature, as to the nonteleological mechanism of natural selection, i.e., that merely random variations in a given species are responsible for the preservation of those individuals which are adapted to the environment, and the destruction of those which are not. Hence,

the *Origin of Species* recognized no goal set either by God or nature. Instead, natural selection, operating in the given environment with the actual organisms presently at hand, was responsible for the gradual but steady emergence of more elaborate, further articulated, and vastly more specialized organisms. Even such marvelously adapted organs as the eye and the hand of man—organs whose design had previously provided powerful arguments for the existence of a supreme artificer and an advance plan—were products of a process that moved steadily *from* primitive beginnings but *toward* no goal.[40]

Darwin himself, aware of this implication in his theory, wrote in his autobiography, "There seems to be no more design in the variability of organic beings and in the action of natural selection, than in the course which the wind blows." Explaining further this predicament in a letter to Asa Gray, he wrote,

There seems to me too much misery in the world. I cannot persuade myself that a beneficent and omnipotent God would have designedly created the Ichneumonidae with the express intention of their feeding within the living bodies of caterpillars, or that a cat should play with mice. Not believing this, I see no necessity in the belief that the eye was expressly designed. On the other hand, I cannot anyhow be contented to view this wonderful universe, and especially the nature of man, and to conclude that everything is the result of brute force. I am inclined to look at everything as resulting from designed laws, with the details whether good or bad, left to the working out of what we may call chance. Not that this notion *at all* satisfies me. I feel most deeply that

39. Quoted in Mason, "Progress," p. 102.
40. Thomas S. Kuhn, *The Structure of Scientific Revolutions*, vol. 2, no. 2, of the International Encyclopedia of Unified Science (Chicago: The University of Chicago Press, 1962), p. 171.

the whole subject is too profound for the human intellect. A dog might as well speculate on the mind of Newton. Let each man hope and believe what he can.[41]

It would be unfair to conclude this chapter without making some reference to the nonevolutionary phases of nineteenth-century biological science. To begin with, we have the cell theory of living matter as elaborated by Schleiden with respect to plants (1838), and by Schwann with respect to animals (1839). The fundamental importance of this theory in our understanding of the structure and operation of living organisms cannot be easily overrated. The basic process in plant development, according to Schleiden, "was the formation of independent living cells, which once formed were arranged in a structural pattern expressive of the unity of the plant as a whole." Schwann wrote similarly "that there is one universal principle of development for the elementary parts of organisms however different, and that this principle is the formation of cells."[42] According to Whitehead, the cell theory of living matter is an extension of the atomic theory of matter in general.

> The living cell is to biology what the electron and the proton are to physics. Apart from cells and from aggregates of cells there are no biological phenomena. The cell theory was introduced. into biology contemporaneously with, and independently of, Dalton's atomic theory. The two theories are independent exemplifications of the same idea of "atomism." The biological cell theory was a gradual growth, and a mere test of dates and names illustrates the fact that the biological sciences, as effective schemes of thought, are barely one hundred years old.[43]

Of equally fundamental importance, especially in the pathology of organisms, are nineteenth-century developments in microbiology. The relevant names here are Pasteur, Lister, and Koch. Pasteur, we are told, is "the founder of microbiology."[44] His bacteriological investigations proved that microorganisms were responsible for such widely divergent phenomena as the fermentation of beer and the infection of human tissue causing disease. His further work in immunology laid the foundation for preventive medicine.[45] The implications of Pasteur's discoveries were

41. Greene, *Darwin,* pp. 44, 45.
42. Mason, *History,* p. 389.
43. Whitehead, *Science,* p. 94.
44. Mason, *History,* p. 517.
45. See further Hugh Clegg, "Pasteur and the Problems Presented by Bacteria," in *A Short History of Science* (New York: Doubleday Anchor Books, 1959), pp. 86–93.

worked out by Lister in the area of antiseptic surgery, with dramatic results: post-surgical mortality rate was reduced from forty-five to fifteen percent.[46] Koch's work (he discovered and isolated the bacteria causing tuberculosis and cholera) paralleled the activities of Pasteur and Lister in further medical applications of bacteriological and immunological findings.

Finally, mention should be made of Gregor Mendel, who initiated the study of modern genetics. His experiments with the cross-fertilization of pea plants resulted in the conclusion that there was no "variability in the plant characteristics which he had studied," thus emphasizing "the stability of the species, and 'the continuity of the germ-plasm.'" These investigations seemed to contradict evolutionary thought, with the consequence that Mendel was largely ignored in his lifetime. It is interesting to note that the Swiss botanist Nägeli rejected Mendel's findings "because he thought them 'empirical rather than rational.'"[47] The empirical or inductive nature of all of the above sciences may here be pointed out. It is unthinkable, for example, to envisage studies in microbiology without the aid of the microscope. It is equally unthinkable for Darwin to have developed his theory of natural selection without the "fact-finding" voyage of the *Beagle* (1831-36). Similarly, in Mendel's case it was experimental data obtained from the crossing of different varieties of a given plant which established the statistical predictability and mechanism of inherited characteristics. Admittedly, Newtonian science is equally dependent on the experimental or observational component of knowledge. Yet biology, as was noted by Whitehead, was in the nineteenth century almost totally divorced from the deductive method of mathematics. The cultural consequences of this predominantly Baconian epistemology will be worked out in the final two chapters of this study.

---

46. Mason, *History*, pp. 518–19.
47. *Ibid.*, p. 532.

7

The Humanities in the Light of
Romantic Biocentrism

We have ascertained, in the preceding chapter, the dominance of the biological sciences during the nineteenth century, especially as they are connected with ideas of progress, development, and evolution. That implicit in this biocentrism is a theory of nature describable only by the root metaphor of the growing and evolving organism, as opposed to the root metaphor of the nonevolving clock relevant to eighteenth-century cosmology, has already been discussed in the opening chapter. It was further affirmed at that time that Goethe, Herder, and Coleridge were the three central figures manifesting the philosophical shift from the former to the latter world view. The task of the present chapter is to render explicit the cultural implications of an organismically dominated era and its attendant mentality. Let us begin with philosophical thought.

With regard to the role of science in the formulation of "philosophical opinion," Bertrand Russell, in a chapter entitled "Currents of Thought in the Nineteenth Century," states an already familiar proposition, namely, that "What Galileo and Newton were to the seventeenth century, Darwin was to the nineteenth." We read further,

> The prestige of biology caused men whose thinking was influenced by science to apply biological rather than mechanistic categories to the world. Everything was supposed to be evolving, and it was easy to imagine an immanent goal. . . . The conception of organism came to be thought the key to both scientific and philosophical explanation of natural laws, and the atomic thinking of the eighteenth century came to be

regarded as out of date. This point of view has at last influenced even theoretical physics.

Aside from the biological influence, the romantic reaction against the rationalism of the previous era also had the consequence, particularly in the philosophy of Schopenhauer and Nietzsche, of emphasizing "the will at the expense of the intellect," and of displaying a definite hostility "to what is commonly called reason."[1] However, the most conspicuous names reflecting the biological root metaphor of the evolving organism in time are those of Hegel, Comte, and Spencer. Considerable space will be devoted to the thought of these philosophers, while briefer observations will be made with respect to Schelling, Marx, Bergson, and Whitehead.

Hegel, according to Collingwood, forms the "culmination of the historical movement which began in 1784 with Herder,"[2] and it will be recalled that the underlying ideas of Herder's thought regarding history and the world as a whole are those of progress and development in time, as "the growing tree, the struggling man, . . . pass through various stages"[3] of evolution. Hegel first delivered his lectures on the philosophy of history in 1822-23, thus antedating Darwin's theory of evolution by thirty-seven years. It should be remembered and emphasized that Darwin did not singlehandedly invent evolution and thereby cause a revolution in the history of thought. On the contrary, evolutionary ideas, usually allied to those of human progress, reach back to the very period when the concept of the universe as a fixed and immutable machine exerted an influence of the first magnitude. Hence, we frequently read that evolutionary ideas were "in the air" throughout the second half of the eighteenth century, preparing the way for Darwin's synthesis. Hegel's lectures, then, are preceded by evolutionary hypotheses of Buffon (*Histoire naturelle*, 1749), Erasmus Darwin (*Zoonomia*, 1794-96), and Lamarck (*Système des Animaux sans Vertèbres*, 1801), not to mention the Enlightenment ideas of progress. Moreover, although Hegel approaches his philosophy in general, and his philosophy of history in particular, in terms of process, development, and progress, he rejects outright the notion of organic

---

1. Bertrand Russell, *A History of Philosophy* (New York: Simon and Schuster, Inc., 1965), pp. 725, 727, 724–25.
2. R. G. Collingwood, *The Idea of History* (New York: Oxford University Press, Galaxy Books, 1956), p. 113.
3. See chapter 1 above.

evolution and, implicitly, the philosophical consequences of natural science. This is made clear in Whitehead's comment (which obviously alludes to Hegel) that "nineteenth century . . . philosophical idealism which finds the ultimate meaning of reality in mentality . . . has been too much divorced from the scientific outlook."[4] Hegel himself writes in his *Encyclopedia of the Philosophical Sciences* (1817),

> Nature is to be regarded as a *System of Grades,* of which the one necessarily arises out of the other, and is the proximate truth of the one from which it results,—but not so that the one were *naturally* generated out of the other. . . . It has been an inept conception of earlier and later *"Naturphilosophie"* to regard the progression and transition of one natural form and sphere into a higher as an outwardly actual production. . . . Thinking consideration must deny itself such nebulous, at bottom sensuous, conceptions, as in especial the so-called *origin,* for example, of plants and animals from water, and then the *origin* of the more highly developed animal organisations from the lower.[5]

Commenting on Hegel's rejection of evolution in nature and on his objection to analogies drawn between natural and historical processes, Collingwood observes that

> Hegel refuses to approach history by way of nature. He insists that nature and history are different things. Each is a process or congeries of processes; but the processes of nature are not historical: nature has no history. The processes of nature are cyclical; nature goes round and round, and nothing is constructed or built up by the repetition of such revolutions.

Collingwood continues in the ensuing paragraph that "Hegel must be given credit for having stated an important distinction," but is

> wrong to reinforce [it] by denying the doctrine of evolution. Since Darwin we have found ourselves obligated to accept that doctrine and to conceive the process of nature as resembling the process of history in a way in which Hegel thought it did not resemble it, namely by producing increments of itself as it goes on.[6]

The process by which history develops in Hegel's viewpoint is

---

4. *Science and the Modern World* (New York: The Macmillan Company, 1925; reprinted by The New American Library, Mentor Books, New York, 1959), p. 62.
5. Quoted in Robert Scoon, "The Rise and Impact of Evolutionary Ideas," in *Evolutionary Thought in America,* ed. Stow Persons (New Haven: Yale University Press, 1950), p. 34.
6. Collingwood, *History,* pp. 114, 115.

logical rather than evolutionary (in the naturalistic sense), and the stages by which it progresses are well known (thesis, antithesis, synthesis). For example, the three main stages of historical development through Hegel's own time are designated by him as 1) oriental despotism, 2) classical slavery, and 3) modern freedom, "the last of which was realized most completely in the Prussian state."[7] It will be noticed that this plan constitutes "a universal history of mankind (here Hegel follows Herder)," and exhibits "a progress from primitive times to the civilization of to-day."[8] Moreover, "Human history," for Hegel, "was in its entirety a kind of epitome of a vast cosmic process of development which was at bottom rational."[9] Thus, in contradistinction to the essentially nonhistorical eighteenth-century view of nature and culture, the so-called "Romantic idealists, and Hegel in particular, were saying . . . that the world evolves, that reality itself is in a process of evolution."[10] And evolution, process, and development are the preeminent features of life. Accordingly, Russell notes that Hegel conceived the world as a complex whole, "of the sort that we should call an organism."[11] It may here be noted in passing that Hegel's contemporary Schelling likewise postulated a historical process of development consisting of three principal stages, the stages here being 1) the "primitive, characterized by the predominance of fatalism," 2) the "active and voluntary stage, which was inaugurated by the Romans and still continues," and 3) "a future stage which will synthesize the principles of the two preceding stages." Furthermore, unlike Hegel, Schelling held that history "was parallel to the processes of development in nature and in mind, so that he finally envisaged a general scheme of cosmic development, although vaguely defined and full of fanciful rationalistic extravagances."[12]

The idea of process as manifesting itself in stages of development as in a living organism is also a feature of Comte's thought. This feature, in addition to Comte's dependence on historical progress as a cardinal factor in his philosophy, discloses a close kinship to Hegel. Hence, writes Aiken,

Comte's philosophy, like Hegel's, is profoundly impregnated with the

7. Scoon, "Rise," p. 12.
8. Collingwood, *History*, p. 114.
9. Scoon, "Rise," p. 12.
10. George H. Mead, *Movements of Thought in the Nineteenth Century* (Chicago: The University of Chicago Press, 1936), p. 154.
11. Russell, *History*, p. 731.
12. Scoon, "Rise," p. 11.

concept of historical development. His famous "law" of "three stages" of human intellectual development has an authentically Hegelian ring and he uses it, in Hegel's own fashion, as a device for subtly undermining all points of view previous to his own.

Comte terms the three stages of historical development as the 1) theological, 2) metaphysical, and 3) scientific. The theological stage is distinguished by a mentality which tends to explain the natural world and its phenomena in terms of animism and anthropomorphism, viewing everything "under the categories of purpose, will and spirit." The world, from this standpoint, "is conceived mythically as a spiritual order in which the animating purposes of things are also thought of as effective agencies which 'cause' them to behave as they do." In the second or metaphysical stage the role of divine creation by a "providential god" is abandoned in favor of a first cause or principle "which it is necessary to assume in order to account for the order of the universe." Therefore, instead of ascribing the processes and events of nature to divine will and spirit, the metaphysician posits such concepts as " 'essences,' 'tendencies,' 'potentialities,' and 'natures' " in order to explain the world. "Most characteristically . . . ," writes Comte, he "identifies 'reason' with 'cause,' and supposes thereby that by reasoning alone he may explain the causes of things." The third and scientific stage rejects the above two in favor of "positive" knowledge, i.e., knowledge which rests exclusively on explanation "in terms of empirical hypotheses or laws which describe the constant relations . . . among classes of observable phenomena."[13]

There is undeniable logic and historical plausibility in Comte's three stages of development; however, assuming the presence of the scientific or positive stage, one could argue for a reversal of the sequence, gaining thereby even greater cogency and more convincing logic. The succession of stages 1) scientific, and 2) the combined metaphysical-religious is in fact implicit in the work of such twentieth-century writers as Albert Einstein, A. N. Whitehead, and F. S. C. Northrop, writers whose mature philosophical thought can ultimately be described only in religious terms.

The account of the development of knowledge and thought as described above appeared in the *Positive Philosophy* (1830-42). The word "positive" is significant here, since it furnishes

13. Henry Aiken, *The Age of Ideology: The 19th Century Philosophers* selected, with Introduction and Interpretive Commentary by Henry Aiken (New York: The New American Library, Mentor Books, 1956), pp. 117–120.

us with another clue to the empiricist (as opposed to rationalist) tendency in nineteenth-century epistemology, this tendency having been already noted in connection with the biological sciences.

The province of knowledge which plays a central role in Comte's system of thought is sociology, a science which he founded and named. Not only was sociology the "highest science," in Comte's estimation, but it "must seek its foundation in its immediate predecessor, biology. The laws of sociology are the counterparts of those of biology."[14] Hence the connection between the biological sciences and the philosophy of Comte is clear. We read elsewhere that "although Comte did not believe in organic evolution, biology and biological analogy played a large role in his social theory." For example, according to Greene, Comte "drew from biology his distinction between the statical and the dynamical approach to the study of organisms." He thus defined social statics as "the fundamental study of the conditions of existence of society." He further extrapolated from biology "his theory of basic human nature, that nature which made possible and inevitable man's social evolution, determined its general direction of movement, and prescribed the limits of its variability." We read further,

> Thus, whereas in biology progressive gradation was conceived as being given once and for all in the organic hierarchy or great chain of being, in sociology it was regarded as evolved in the course of time, as moving gradually toward full realization. And just as in biology the progressive gradation of the organic hierarchy was thought to be recapitulated in the embryological development of the individual human organism, so the *échelle sociale,* or progressive societal development, was conceived as mirrored in the mental life history of each individual in civilized society.[15]

Perhaps the clearest example of the connection between biology and philosophical thought is manifest in Herbert Spencer. Unlike Hegel and Comte, who repudiated organic evolution, and whose interest lay "primarily in the development of human ideas and institutions," Spencer based his entire philosophy on the implications of evolution in the animate world. "In his hands," we are told, the philosophical consequences of evolutionary theory

---

14. John Herman Randall, Jr., *The Making of the Modern Mind* (New York: Houghton Mifflin Co., 1926), p. 492.

15. John C. Greene, "Biology and Social Theory in the Nineteenth Century: Auguste Comte and Herbert Spencer," in Marshall Clagett, ed., *Critical Problems in the History of Science* (Madison: The University of Wisconsin Press, 1959), pp. 425–27.

are "transformed into a grand synthesis of human knowledge, complete with a cosmology, an ethics, and a politics,"[16] even though his works were published both before and after the appearance of Darwin's *Origin of Species* in 1859. For example, such works as *Social Statics* (1851), *Principles of Psychology* (1855), and *Progress: Its Law and Cause* (1851) depend primarily on evolutionary ideas drawn from geology, paleontology, astronomy, embryology, and the notion of human progress. During these years he observed that "the time was ripe for a philosophical reconstruction which would tie together with a few leading concepts and broad generalizations the growing accumulation of empirical knowledge in the various fields of scientific enquiry," further noting that "developmental concepts had [already] invaded many fields of science, especially anatomy and physiology, but also geology, paleontology, astronomy, linguistics, and social theory." However, it was social progress as manifest in history which provided the chief impetus for his thought. Progress, he wrote, was "not an accident, not a thing within human control, but a beneficent necessity."[17] With respect to organic evolution we are informed that Spencer was a Lamarckian at this time. "He had been converted to Lamarck's theory of evolution about 1840 by reading Charles Lyell's discussion of it in his *Principles of Geology*."[18] According to Sarton, Spencer "remained a Lamarckian to the end of his life [1902]."[19] Still, it was only after Darwin's publication of *Origin of Species* that Spencer was "able to proclaim a grand synthesis of biological and social theory in terms of universal competition and survival of the fittest,"[20] a phrase, incidentally, which Spencer coined.

Spencer's system of thought is known as *The Synthetic Philosophy* which is comprised of the above-mentioned *Principles of Psychology,* in addition to *First Principles* (1862) and *Principles of Sociology* (1896). The dominating idea pervading these works is that progress in the form of evolution proceeds "from the homogeneous to the heterogeneous, from the simple to the complex, from the incoherent to the coherent, from the indefinite to the definite."[21] Moreover, this evolutionary idea was applicable not only to living organisms but to the universe as a whole.

16. Aiken, *Ideology,* p. 162.
17. Greene, "Biology," p. 436.
18. *Ibid., Darwin and the Modern World* (Baton Rouge: Louisiana State University Press, 1961), p. 93.
19. George Sarton, *The Life of Science: Essays in the History of Civilization* (New York: Henry Schuman, Inc., 1948), pp. 118–19.
20. Greene, *Darwin,* p. 93.
21. Quoted in Sarton, *Life of Science,* p. 119.

Whether it be in the development of the Earth, in the development of Life upon its surface, in the development of Society, of Government, of Manufactures, of Commerce, of Language, Literature, Science, Art, this same evolution of the simple into the complex, through successive differentiations, holds throughout. From the earliest traceable cosmical changes, down to the latest results of civilization, we shall find that the transformation of the homogeneous into the heterogeneous, is that in which Progress essentially consists.

Scoon comments on the above passage that not only was evolution "the fundamental principle throughout all nature, but also that it was inevitably toward perfection, 'towards a complete development and a more unmixed good.' "[22]

The consequences of extrapolating such concepts as the Malthusian "struggle for existence," Darwinian "natural selection," and Spencer's "survival of the fittest" to the study of man is known as Social Darwinism, a doctrine first introduced by Spencer. Accordingly, it was argued that just as in the "state of nature" organisms with favorable variations automatically survive, while those with undesirable variations perish, so in society the law of *laissez-faire* spontaneously ensures "the survival of the ablest and most efficient entrepreneur,"[23] which is translated as meaning progress. With respect to this, Spencer writes in the *Social Statics,*

> Partly by weeding out those of lowest development, and partly by subjecting those who remain to the never-ceasing discipline of experience, nature secures the growth of a race who shall both understand the conditions of existence, and be able to act up to them. It is impossible in any degree to suspend this discipline by stepping in between ignorance and its consequences, without, to a corresponding degree, suspending progress.

Furthermore, as Greene observes on the above, "such an intervention . . . would interfere with the automatic process of internal adjustment whereby the energies of the social organism are directed where they are most needed."[24]

It is suggested here that this constitutes a rather naïve and uncritical transference of nonnormative natural law to the normative needs of civilized society. Besides justifying the malpractices of absolute *laissez-faire* economics and the unremitting exploitation of labor, it led to such questionable notions as racial supe-

---

22. Quoted in Scoon, "Rise," p. 15.
23. S. F. Mason, "The Ideal of Progress and Theories of Evolution in Science," in S. Lilley, ed., *Essays on the Social History of Science* (Copenhagen: Ejnar Munksgaard, 1953), p. 103.
24. Quoted in Greene, "Biology," p. 431.

riority (and its corollary "super race"), Nietzsche's "master and slave morality," and his idea of the "superman." A graphic illustration of Social Darwinism at its worst is encountered in Walter Bagehot's *Physics and Politics, or Thoughts on the Application of the Principles of Natural Selection and Inheritance to Political Society* (1872). Bagehot proposes in this work that "the strongest nation has always been conquering the weaker," and thereby, "the best qualities wanted in elementary civilisation are propagated and preserved," mainly because "the most warlike qualities tend principally to the good."[25] Similar views were held by Karl Pearson, who in 1900 published *On national Life from the Standpoint of Science.* However, according to Binkley, the first application of political Darwinism occurred "in the slavery controversy in the United States, where the new theory arrived just in time to help to prove the inferiority of the Negro race, before the Civil War shifted the forum of decision."[26]

The parallel between the above relation of natural science and political philosophy, and the analogous relation of these two domains in the eighteenth (and seventeenth) centuries, is conspicuous. For Hobbes, Condillac, and Montesquieu are to Newton what Bagehot, Pearson, *et al.* are to Darwin. A similar parallel may here be noted between Spencer's unbounded faith in the progress of mankind, assured by evolutionary law, and the Enlightenment belief in man's perfectibility assured by Newton's "explanation" of the world in terms of simple mathematical formulas, formulas which were likewise allegedly discoverable and applicable in the human domain.

We turn now to the philosopher-economist Karl Marx. Although we are informed at the outset that Marx, like Hegel, developed a theory of social evolution apart from any biological considerations,[27] he nevertheless, according to Barzun, described the dialectical process of history in terms of "the germinating and growth of a plant from its seed—again the biological analogy—in which the germ is destroyed by its opposite, the plant; but is still in a sense part of it, in the same way that the new seed which the plant produces replaces its parent while continuing its form."[28] Hence Marx thought

25. Quoted in Mason, "Progress," p. 104.
26. Robert C. Binkley, *Realism and Nationalism, 1852–1871* (New York: Harper & Brothers, 1935; reprinted by Harper Torchbooks, 1963), p. 29.
27. Greene, *Darwin,* p. 92.
28. Jacques Barzun, *Darwin, Marx, Wagner: Critique of a Heritage,* 2d rev. ed. (Boston: Little, Brown & Company, 1941; reprinted by Doubleday & Company, Inc., Anchor Books, Garden City, N. Y., 1958), p. 12.

that history was going somewhere inexorably and that the historical process was ultimately redemptive of human nature. Social Science was the study of the laws of historical development. It explained why and how change took place and indicated man's duty and destiny.[29]

This again constitutes a striking contrast with the static, non-developmental Enlightenment view of history and the social order. Noting Marx's application of the "notion of development to the course of human life," Scoon quotes the general thesis of the *Critique of Political Economy* (1859), according to which "the Asiatic, ancient, feudal, and bourgeois modes of production" can be considered "as the progressive steps of the economic formation of society."

The impact of evolutionary biology on the philosophy of Bergson is more explicit. Rejecting both the Darwinian mechanistic and the Lamarckian teleological versions of evolution as inadequate, he postulates

> an intermediate position, which he calls creative evolution and which centers on a vital force (*élan vital*), whose characteristics in the main purport to be just those features of biological evolution which have actually appeared. But in the development of his theory the contrast between the biological and the mental (purposive) yields to a more fundamental contrast between both of them and the physical realm.[30]

The distinction between the physical and the living realm in Bergson's philosophy is described by Mead in the following manner:

> Bergson's philosophy arises out of a point of view of the world which is evolutionary as over against mechanical. And evolution as such is a process that is continually going on. Bergson's term for this process is an *élan vital*. Anything that is continually going on cannot be stated simply in terms of that which can be put into an instant. What evolution has done is to present to us the conditions out of which new forms can arise. It has given us those conditions; and our thought, our interpretation, of them implies constant appearance of new forms. If we turn back to a mechanical statement of the world, what we get is simply a distribution of physical particles now at one instant and now at another.[31]

Perhaps the profoundest philosophical consequences of biological natural science are to be encountered in the thought of Alfred North Whitehead. Whitehead bases his entire theory of

29. Greene, *Darwin*, p. 92.
30. Scoon, "Rise," pp. 12, 37.
31. Mead, *Movements*, p. 304.

nature and its attendant philosophy on what he terms "the ultimate concept of *organism*." However, *organism* is here not limited to the living domain alone, but extends also to the ultimate constituents ("events" as opposed to bits of matter) of mathematical physics. Thus electrons, atoms, and molecules are organisms whose properties change, so to speak, according to their context. An electron "within a living body," for example,

> is different from an electron outside it, by reason of the plan of the body. . . . It runs within the body in accordance with its character within the body . . . and this plan includes the mental state. But the principle of modification is perfectly general throughout nature, and represents no property peculiar to living bodies.

That "the gap between living and dead matter is . . . vague" and arbitrary on the level of atoms and molecules is further indicated by the emergence in the twentieth century of biophysics, which, Whitehead asserts, is ultimately the study of organisms.

> Science is taking on a new aspect which is neither purely physical, nor purely biological. It is becoming the study of organisms. Biology is the study of the larger organisms; whereas physics is the study of the smaller organisms. . . . The organisms of biology include as ingredients the smaller organisms of physics.[32]

Another vivid illustration of the frequently vague boundary between a living body and the nonliving external environment is presented by Whitehead in another work. Here he writes that "we cannot define where a body begins and when external nature ends." The human body is in fact "just as much part of nature as . . . a river, or a mountain, or a cloud." He continues,

> Consider one definite molecule. It is part of nature. It has moved about for millions of years. Perhaps it started from a distant nebula. It enters the body; it may be as a factor in some edible vegetable; or it passes into the lungs as part of the air. At what exact point as it enters the mouth, or as it is absorbed through the skin is it part of the body? Exactness is out of the question. It can only be obtained by some trivial convention.[33]

Without going further into the details of Whitehead's theory of nature, it is evident from what has been said that Whitehead, incorporating the content of twentieth-century physics and mathe-

32. Whitehead, *Science*, pp. 63, 76, 97.
33. A. N. Whitehead, *Modes of Thought* (New York: The Macmillan Company, 1938; reprinted by G. P. Putnam's Sons, Capricorn Books, New York, 1958), p. 30.

matics, formulates a holistic view of reality, a view which is equally consonant with biological phenomena and their evolution. The theory of evolution, in this context, is for him, "nothing else than the analysis of the conditions for the formation and survival of various types of organisms."[34]

The thinkers discussed in the preceding pages exemplify, to a greater or lesser extent, a protest against a world view which rested on ideas of fixity and immutability. Evolution, in opposition to those ideas, "pointed to . . . a continuous process of organic invention . . . , and a cosmological organization loose enough to permit a real freedom to human endeavor." Above all it was a protest, in the words of William James, against the "block-universe eternal and without a history."[35]

The ideas and modes of thought generated by the progressively emerging life sciences (and their attendant epistemology) during the late eighteenth and nineteenth centuries find their way just as readily into literature as they do into philosophy. A foretaste of the manner in which biologically derived metaphors of creativity, structure, and unity are applied to literary criticism and invention has been presented, in the first chapter above, where it was ascertained that Samuel Taylor Coleridge most clearly exhibited this tendency. Before proceeding with a more extensive analysis of the relation between literature and biology, the distinction between the content of biological science and its method should be reiterated. Both are palpably manifest in the literature of the period, but it is the predominantly empirical method of biology which is the more pervasive and less apparent element. This method deals chiefly with "facts" on the level of immediate sense experience.

The literary movement which reflects the new life-centered cosmology and its concomitant world of concrete phenomena, as opposed to the former view of reality derivative from the abstractions of mathematical physics, is known as Romanticism. That Romanticism is unintelligible apart from life and its manifold corollary ramifications can be easily documented. For example, Alexander Gode-von Aesch writes, "The study of Romanticism is a biological study." And further along,

Romantic thought is biocentric thought. In it the phenomenal world is viewed as a physiognomic representation of universal life. The last

34. *Ibid., Science,* p. 96.
35. Quoted in Scoon, "Rise," pp. 39–40.

chapter, on the romantic world poem, is thus preceded by a discussion of the romantic conception of physiognomics.[36]

And physiognomics, we are told by Webster, deals chiefly with "outward appearance" and "external aspect." A similar view is expressed by Barzun when he asserts that "the Romantic movement was a reassertion of the living principle in all things," and that the "Biological Revolution is simply . . . [the] recognition that the laws of life, rather than those of mathematics and astronomy, should serve as a pattern for thought."[37] Still another writer, M. H. Abrams, in his discussion of Coleridge's distinction between mechanical fancy and the organic imagination, refers to the application of "organism as aesthetic model" during the early period of Romanticism. And finally A. W. Schlegel, leader of the new romantic criticism in Germany, lecturing in Berlin between 1801 and 1804, affirmed the parallel properties of art and nature. He writes, art "creating autonomously like nature, . . . must form living works, which are first set in motion, not by an outside mechanism like a pendulum, but by an indwelling power like the solar system."[38] Implicit in this statement is a "vitalistic" conception of art and nature (animate and inanimate), a conception which repudiates the former notion of causal mechanism as an adequate means of explanation in all provinces of human thought.

Hence, a corollary of romantic biocentrism is a reaction against, and a rejection of, Newtonian cosmology, with its exclusive dependence on the Galilean and Lockean "primary qualities" as the sole instrument of knowledge. That this reaction was not an isolated phenomenon, but a movement of major proportions is attested to by Wellek.

> There are individual differences among the great romantic poets concerning the conception of nature. But all of them share a common objection to the mechanistic universe of the eighteenth century. . . . All romantic poets conceived of nature as an organic whole, on the analogue of man rather than a concourse of atoms.

A good example of this objection is Blake's statement, "May

36. Alexander Gode-von Aesch, *Natural Science in German Romanticism* (New York: Columbia University Press, 1941; reprinted by the AMS Press, New York, 1966), pp. 8, 13.

37. Barzun, *Darwin*, p. 47.

38. M. H. Abrams, *The Mirror and the Lamp: Romantic Theory and the Critical Tradition* (New York: Oxford University Press, 1953; reprinted by W. W. Norton & Co., New York, 1958), pp. 167, 212.

God us keep/ From Single Vision and Newton's sleep."[39] White-head, concerned chiefly with the poetry of Wordsworth, expresses essentially the same view:

> the romantic reaction started . . . with nature. We are here witnessing a conscious reaction against the whole tone of the eighteenth century. That century approached nature with the abstract analysis of science, whereas Wordsworth opposes to the scientific abstractions his full concrete experience.[40]

In other words, what the romantics valued above all were the "secondary qualities" of the appearance of reality; colors, sounds, odors, and so on, the very subjective and ever-changing elements of experience which Galileo, Descartes, and Newton rejected as being incapable of producing reliable knowledge of the external world.

Accordingly, it may be affirmed that the common denominator of Romanticism is an appeal to the phenomenal world of the senses (and feelings), i.e., to those elements in human experience which are given in their presentational immediacy. To repeat the words of Joseph Beach, "The extraordinary power of the 'Rime of the Ancient Mariner' " is chiefly due to "sensory appeal on the level of primary physical experience."[41] Elsewhere Beach writes with respect to Wordsworth's poems that "they indicate a disposition to take one's start with natural phenomena."[42] And again, we read that in the poetry of Wordsworth, "there must be no abstractions, no symbols, no myths, to stand between the mind and its true object."[43]

It is instructive to read what Wordsworth himself had to say about his poetry and the aims it was intended to achieve. In the Preface (1800) to the epochal *Lyrical Ballads* (1798), Words-words writes that "the principal object . . . proposed in these poems was to choose *incidents and situations from common life,* and to relate or describe them, throughout, as far as was possible in a selection of *language really used by men,* and, at the same time, to throw over them a certain coloring of imagination"

39. René Wellek, *Concepts of Criticism* (New Haven and London: Yale University Press, 1963), p. 182.

40. Whitehead, *Science,* p. 78.

41. Joseph Beach, *A Romantic View of Poetry* (Minneapolis: The University of Minnesota Press, 1944), pp. 8–9.

42. *Ibid., The Concept of Nature in Nineteenth-Century English Poetry* (New York: Pageant Book Co., 1956), p. 4.

43. Basil Willey, "On Wordsworth and the Locke Tradition," in M. H. Abrams, ed., *English Romantic Poets* (New York: Oxford University Press, 1960), p. 85.

[italics added]. The phrase "language really used by men" is significant in that it indicates a frank appeal to the empirical reality of spoken English as opposed to the "arbitrary and capricious habits of expression"[44] known as poetic diction which was prevalent in the previous era. And poetic diction, with its prescribed and formalized manner of expression, is the very antithesis of Wordsworth's blank verse. Likewise an antithesis to Wordsworth's reliance on the local and immediately available environment, "incidents and situations from common life," as he terms it, is Dr. Johnson's belief that

> the business of a poet is to examine, not the individual, but the species; to remark general properties and large appearances; he does not number the streaks of the tulip. He must write as the interpreter of nature and the legislator of mankind, and consider himself as presiding over the thoughts and manners of future generations, as a being superior to time and place.[45]

An even more revealing statement with respect to the primacy of sensory experience and its role in Wordsworth's poetry is found in the poet's Preface of 1815 to the first collected edition of his poems. Here he writes, "The appropriate business of poetry . . . her appropriate employment, her privilege and her *duty*, is to treat of things not as they *are*, but as they *appear*; not as they exist in themselves, but as they *seem* to exist to the *senses*, and to the passions" [Wordsworth's italics].[46] This arresting declaration, it will be noticed, with its radical empiricism and its modern phenomenological strain of thought, is the diametrical opposite of Samuel Johnson's conception of poetry as being concerned with the general, and "as being superior to time and place." It implicitly repudiates those features of the world which were of the utmost importance to the eighteenth-century mind.

Therefore, the two cardinal factors which enter into Wordsworth's philosophy of nature are 1) a reaction against the scientific abstractions of the eighteenth century and 2) an attendant predilection to view reality in its full concrete experience. A third factor has been proposed by Rader, who suggests that

44. William Wordsworth, *The Prelude and Other Poems, with Three Essays on the Art of Poetry,* ed. Carlos Baker (New York: Holt, Rinehart and Winston, 1965), pp. 3–4, 5.
45. Quoted by Donald A. Stauffer, "Poetic Diction," in *Dictionary of World Literature,* ed. Joseph T. Shipley (Paterson: Littlefield, Adams & Co., 1960), p. 100.
46. Wordsworth, *The Prelude,* p. 39.

Wordsworth's concern with things seen, heard, and felt are a continuation of traditional British empiricism. For example, in tracing Wordsworth's exposure to works which may have influenced him during his formative years at Cambridge, Rader writes, "we do know . . . that the Empirical tradition was strongly entrenched at Cambridge, and that Wordsworth must have been introduced to it during his student days."[47] Rader further quotes another author who asserts that doctrinally Wordsworth "appeals to Hartley, Locke, and the general tradition of English philosophy."[48] The probable connection between British empiricism and Wordsworth's interest in sense perception is likewise suggested by Basil Willey:

> [Locke's] doctrine which derived all our knowledge from sensation was capable of serving Wordsworth, who imbibed it through Hartley, as a philosophic sanction for his own deep-rooted instincts, and furnished him with at least a foundation for his conscious poetic theory. Wordsworth was working in the spirit and tradition of Locke when he rejected gaudy and inane phraseology and devoted his powers to the task of making verse "deal boldly with substantial things."[49]

A more recent study on Wordsworth by Heffernan also explores the likelihood that the central role of the senses in Wordsworth's poetry is traceable to the traditional empirical philosophy of such men as Locke, Hartley, and Godwin. Heffernan first observes that Coleridge, who was more of a "dreamer . . . comfortable in a realm of polar mists and oriental chasms," "censured Wordsworth for his 'matter-of-factness,' for his 'laborious minuteness and fidelity in the representation of objects.'" Thus, despite the fact that both of these poets shared common ground with respect to their dependence upon firsthand experience, and with respect to their mistrust for traditional scientific notions in their work, it was Wordsworth who was more of the radical empiricist.

> Wordsworth exploited his senses. . . . [He] was first of all an observer, a student of everything that he could see and hear. The sources of his hunger for sensory impressions may be debated. If we cast about for philosophical influences, we may strike immediately on the sensationalism of William Godwin, proximately on the associationism of David Hart-

47. Melvin Rader, *Wordsworth, a Philosophical Approach* (Oxford at the Clarendon Press, 1967), p. 41.
48. Arthur Beatty, *William Wordsworth: His Doctrine and Art in Their Historical Relations,* quoted in Rader, *Wordsworth,* p. 40.
49. Quoted in Rader, *Wordsworth,* p. 48.

ley, and ultimately on the empiricism of John Locke, who declared that all knowledge was compounded of sensation and reflection.[50]

The parallel between the radical empiricism of Wordsworth and the method of biological science, especially its so-called natural-history stage, should now be clearer. Both rest on the immediate experience of physical phenomena, approaching what Northrop designates as "pure fact," i.e., "that portion of our knowledge which remains when everything depending upon inference from the immediately apprehended is rejected."[51] Hence, Samuel Johnson's injunction against the individual and particular here-and-now properties of nature notwithstanding, the romantic poet does in fact number "the streaks of the tulip," just as the biologist scrutinizes the minutiae of his object of knowledge.

Another corollary of biology which manifests itself in romantic literature is the notion of change, growth, and transformation. This notion, it has already been disclosed, is basic to nineteenth-century philosophical thought. It is also fundamental in the scientific and literary work of Goethe. "Goethe's doctrine of metamorphosis attained its greatest clarity as an hypothesis of botany. Its importance, however, is not thus limited. It is of generally biotic significance and represents the key to all of Goethe's thought." The *Metamorphosis of Plants,* both in its scientific and poetic versions, may here be cited as an example. However, the idea of transformation, Alexander Gode-von Aesch continues, is not only a feature of Goethe's thought, but can be applied to his age as a whole, for Goethe is "the summary and fullest representative of his entire era." And if we can assert that his scientific activities "supply the key to all of his thought, then it follows that the problems of his age can be profitably approached from the standpoint of the natural sciences."[52]

According to Whitehead, change and transformation are conspicuous features of Shelley's poetry. First of all, notes Whitehead, "Shelley's nature is in its essence a nature of organisms, functioning with the full content of our perceptual experience." Yet it must be remembered that Whitehead's notion of organism extends beyond the traditional conception of life. We read further,

50. James A. W. Heffernan, *Wordsworth's Theory of Poetry: the Transforming Imagination* (Ithaca, New York: Cornell University Press, 1969), pp. 6, 7.
51. F. S. C. Northrop, *The Logic of the Sciences and the Humanities* (New York: The Macmillan Company, 1925; reprinted by The New American Library, Mentor Books, New York, 1959), p. 39.
52. Gode-von Aesch, *Natural Science,* pp. 3–4.

"Shelley thinks of nature as changing, dissolving, transforming. . . . The leaves fly before the West Wind 'Like ghosts from an enchanter fleeing.'" With regard to the poem entitled "The Cloud," Whitehead writes that here "it is the transformations of water which excite his [Shelley's] imagination. The subject of the poem is the endless, eternal, elusive change of things: 'I change but I cannot die.'" It is this aspect of nature, change and transformation, "not merely to be expressed by locomotion, but a change of inward character"[53] which constitutes Shelley's concept of nature.

The concept of transformation also plays an important role in Wordsworth's theory of artistic creation. In contrast to the older doctrine of art as imitation of nature, an essentially mechanical and static process requiring no great imaginative powers, Wordsworth, in the final book of *The Prelude* "defines a new kind of mimesis," whereby "the poet's imagination imitates, not the products of nature, but rather her creative action, especially her power to transform and to unify natural objects."[54] Goethe as a scientist and poet makes a similar transition, according to Cassirer, whereby "the previous *generic* view" was superseded by "the modern *genetic* view of organic nature," and whereby the "process of life" is comprehended in addition to its products.[55] It is relevant to note the great significance which was attached to the creative faculty of the imagination by Wordsworth and his fellow romantics. Dryden, the representative poet of the Age of Reason, in opposition to this, regarded imagination as "wild and lawless,"[56] and hence undesirable in poetic invention. On the other hand, Wordsworth considers the transforming imaginative powers of the mind as the core of the poet's creative process.

The ideas of growth, transformation, and evolution are perhaps most clearly disclosed in the poetry of Tennyson. Tennyson's life span (1809-92) is in the very center of the biological revolution, and he was very sensitive to the philosophical implications of science. "From his earliest manhood Tennyson breathed the atmosphere of scientific theory and discovery, and throughout his life his meditations were governed by the conceptions of law, process, development and evolution—the characteristic and ruling

53. Whitehead, *Science,* pp. 81, 82.
54. Heffernan, *Imagination,* p. 2.
55. Ernst Cassirer, *Rousseau, Kant and Goethe,* trans. James Gutman *et al.* (Princeton, N.J.: Princeton University Press, 1945; reprinted by Harper Torchbooks, New York, 1963), p. 69.
56. See above, chapter 3.

ideas of his century." According to Willey, the sciences which first interested Tennyson were astronomy, especially Laplace's nebular hypothesis, and embryology. It will be noticed that growth and gradual development are central to both sciences. As Willey points out, the poetic version of the nebular hypothesis and of organic evolution up to man are found in Tennyson's *The Princess* (1847), where we read,

> This world was once a fluid haze of light,
> Till toward the center set the starry tides,
> And eddied into suns, that wheeling cast
> The planets: then the monster, then the man.

However, evolutionary ideas are encountered even earlier in Tennyson's *The Palace of Art* (1832), where "we see not only the conception of biological evolution but supporting evidence for it taken from the new science of embryology, which taught that the brain of the foetus passed through all the previous phases of evolution, recapitulating in brief the whole history of the species." We are further informed that Tennyson was also influenced by geology, especially its evolutionary conception by Charles Lyell, whose *Principles of Geology* Tennyson read in 1837. What struck the poet about Lyell's uniformitarianism were the "immense tracts of time" which were responsible for the earth's evolution and the appearance and extinction of "species after species of living creatures,"[57] ideas which disturbed Tennyson's views of the divine and its role in the nature of things. We may conclude with William Rutland's statement that

> in the realm of thought the nineteenth century will probably always remain associated with the theory of Evolution. With the idea of Evolution Tennyson's mind was saturated. No poet of equal rank has ever been more dominated by an idea than was Tennyson by this, taking the word in its wider philosophical, and not merely its biological sense. . . . The conviction of human free will was not more fundamental to Milton's justification of the ways of God, than was the belief in an evolutionary Process necessary to Tennyson's whole conception of the nature and meaning of the Universe.[58]

No less apparent than ideas of process, growth, and develop-

---

57. Basil Willey, *More Nineteenth Century Studies: a Group of Honest Doubters* (New York: Columbia University Press, 1956; reprinted by Harper Torchbooks, 1966), pp. 82, 83, 84.

58. William R. Rutland, "Tennyson and the Theory of Evolution," in *Essays and Studies by Members of the English Association* 26 (Oxford: The Clarendon Press, 1941):7.

ment in romantic poetry, is the literal content of biological evolution in prose writing of the period. For example, seventeen years prior to the publication of Darwin's *Origin,* Balzac, evidently adopting a Lamarckian evolutionary conception, writes in the Foreword to his *Comédie Humaine* (1842),

> There exists but one animal. The Creator used only one pattern for all organized beings. An animal is an entity taking its shape . . . from the environment in which it develops. Zoological species are the result. . . . I saw that in these regards society resembled nature. . . . There have always existed and will always exist social species similar to zoological species.

A parody of organic evolution is encountered in Benjamin Disraeli's novel *Tancred; or, The New Crusade* (1847). In the following passage, Lady Constance, urging the hero, Tancred, to read *Revelations of Chaos,* says,

> You know, all is development—the principle is perpetually going on. First there was nothing; then there was something; then—I forget the next—I think there were shells; then fishes; then we came—let me see—did we come next? Never mind that; we came at last, and the next change will be something very superior to us, something with wings.

Turning once again to poetry, we find not only " 'Nature red in tooth and claw' of natural selection" in Tennyson's *In Memoriam* (begun in 1834, published in 1850), but also, according to Barzun, "man's kinship with the ape, the chain of beings, their development, and the consequences to religion and morals of the thorough-going naturalism of science."[59]

The predominantly nondeductive epistemology of biological science (and also the experimental method of chemistry) is most clearly evident in the latter nineteenth-century literary movement known as naturalism (also realism). Naturalism, in its technique and philosophy, clearly reflects the method and content of natural science, i.e., the natural science of biology, whose method is primarily inductive, as opposed to the equally "natural philosophy" of Galileo and Newton, who depended chiefly upon mathematical deduction. Naturalism also implies complete "scientific" objectivity, divorced from any value judgments or idealization. For example, we read, regarding Realism and Naturalism,

> Realism was . . . the novel's . . . pretense at the literal, historical truth of what it presents in terms of positivist science. With Naturalism

59. Quoted in Barzun, *Darwin,* pp. 23, 54, 55.

the process went further. In his *Le roman expérimental* (1880), Émile Zola codified the analogy of the novelist and the scientist: neither of them selects or creates; they merely study and report.[60]

The alliance of Naturalism with "positivist science" is made clear by Cowley's assertion that " 'Science' for naturalistic writers usually means laboratory science."[61] Another indication of this may be gathered by the fact that Zola, who was primarily influenced by positivist historian Taine (1828-93) and physiologist Claude Bernard (1813-78), "maintained that the novel should serve the same ends as scientific study," and that its "purpose was to study 'the human temperament and the deep modifications of the human organism under the pressures of environment and events.' "[62]

However, Naturalism, above all, appealed for its literary material to the evolutionary and hereditary doctrines of biology, deriving therefrom a relentless determinism whose iron necessity rendered man a mere "pawn on a chessboard."

> The naturalists were all determinists in that they believed in the omnipotence of natural forces. . . . They regarded the individual as merely "a pawn on a chessboard"; the phrase recurs time and again in their novels. . . . Man was, in Dreiser's words, "the victim of forces over which he has no control."

European, as well as American, Naturalism "was inspired by Darwin's theory of evolution and kept repeating the doctrine that men, being part of the animal kingdom, were subject to natural laws." Zola, accordingly, regarded himself as "a positivist, an evolutionist, a materialist," stating further that "what matters most to me is to be purely naturalistic, purely physiological. Instead of having principles (royalism, Catholicism) I shall have laws (heredity, atavism)." The law of heredity, in fact, was a central theme in Zola's work, serving to unify an entire succession of novels.

> The principal laws, for Zola, were those of heredity, which he assumed to be as universal and unchanging as the second law of thermodynamics.

60. Ian Watt, "Novel," *Encyclopaedia Britannica,* 1964, 16 : 578; see further Watt's *The Rise of the Novel* (Berkeley: University of California Press, 1957), pp. 9–35 and 290–301, *passim.*

61. Malcolm Cowley, "Naturalism in American Literature," in Stow Persons, ed., *Evolutionary Thought in America* (New Haven: Yale University Press, 1950), p. 328.

62. Pierre-Georges Castex, "French Literature," *Encyclopaedia Britannica* (1964), 9 : 899.

He fixed upon the hereditary weakness of the Rougon-Macquart family as a theme that would bind together his vast series of novels. Suicide, alcoholism, prostitution, and insanity were all to be explained as the result of the same hereditary taint. "Vice and virtue," he said, "are products like vitriol and sugar."[63]

Balzac likewise, in his *La Comédie Humaine*, "set out to be the scientific naturalist of the human species," while Flaubert believed that the purpose of the novelist "was to be a wholly objective recorder of 'reality.' "[64]

Such American naturalists as Stephen Crane, Theodore Dreiser, and Jack London also found in Darwinism principles which they imported into their work. A frequent theme in Crane's work, for example, is the inescapable force of the environment on the behavior of its victims. Writing about his short story *Maggie*, Crane observes, ". . . it tries to show that environment is a tremendous thing and often shapes lives regardlessly." Still, the most influential figure in American literature during the last four decades of the nineteenth century was Herbert Spencer. We are told by Cowley that "Spencer's American popularity during the last half of the nineteenth century is something without parallel in the history of philosophic writing. From 1860 to 1903 his books had a sale of 368,755 copies in the authorized editions, not counting the many editions that appeared without his consent." Dreiser writes that the reading of Spencer's *First Principles* "quite blew me, intellectually, to bits," and "I was completely thrown down in my conceptions or non-conceptions of life." Jack London's autobiographical hero, Martin Eden, hoping that Spencer's *First Principles* would act as a soporific, found himself reading the book through the night and through the following day. "To give up Spencer," he said, "would be equivalent to a navigator throwing the compass and chronometer overboard." Cowley, in commenting on the naturalists in general and London in particular, writes that

There was a tendency in almost all the naturalistic writers to identify social laws with biological . . . laws. For Jack London, the driving force behind human events was always biology—"I mean," says . . . Martin Eden, "the real interpretive biology, from the ground up, from the laboratory and the test tube . . . right up to the widest esthetic and social generalizations."[65]

63. Cowley, "Naturalism," pp. 313, 300, 314.
64. Watt, "Novel," p. 578.
65. Cowley, "Naturalism," pp. 315, 302, 303, 304, 316.

The concern for facts on "the level of primary physical experience," disclosed in nineteenth-century literature is equally evident in the art of painting of the period. The major movements here are Romanticism, Realism, and Impressionism, and in their essential features these movements correspond methodologically to the literary styles discussed in the previous section. In fact, art, even more so than literature, reflects the predominantly empirical epistemology of natural-history biology. Thus declares Barzun, with respect to the parallel between romantic poetry and romantic painting,

> What is true of the poets is, *a fortiori,* true of the painters. The romanticist revolution in painting was achieved by the simple means of stepping out of the studio and observing nature. From Constable rushing out of the room . . . to show his skeptical friends that grass is really greener than old varnish, to Gericault, . . . Turner, and Delacroix filling notebooks with effects of color, motion, and shadow under every conceivable light, the school—if it must be called one—was a realistic school.[66]

Again it must be emphasized that the term "realistic" refers to the literal, positivist apprehension of fact, as opposed to fact plus inferred knowledge. The visual experience of the romantic artist deals, accordingly, with "color, motion and shadow," as Barzun asserts, not with the largely postulated world of solid, three-dimensional objects. This is precisely the point of Goethe's remarkable passage from his *Theory of Colours* (1810):

> We now assert, extraordinary as it may in some degree appear, that the eye sees no form, inasmuch as light, shade and colour together constitute that which to our vision distinguishes object from object, and the parts of an object from each other. From these three, light, shade and colour, we construct the visible world, and thus, at the same time, make painting possible.[67]

The concern for what Northrop terms "pure fact," i.e., fact apart from inference, is likewise apparent in Ruskin's statement that everything we see around us "presents itself to your eyes only as an arrangement of patches of different colours variously shaded," and his further affirmation that "the perception of solid Form is entirely a matter of experience."[68]

---

66. Jacques Barzun, *Classic, Romantic and Modern* (Boston: Little, Brown & Co., 1963), p. 63.

67. Quoted in John Gage, *Color in Turner* (New York: Frederick A. Praeger, Publishers, 1969), p. 14.

68. Robert L. Herbert, ed., *The Art Criticism of John Ruskin* (Garden City, N. Y.: Doubleday & Company, Inc., Anchor Books, 1964), p. 46.

Color and subtle gradations of light intensity in conjunction with the attempt to record the ever-changing and mutable meteorological phenomena in landscape painting are the distinguishing features of William Turner (1775-1851) and John Constable (1776-1837). As a consequence of this aesthetic, detailed preparatory drawings were abandoned in favor of oil sketches rendered out of doors and executed quickly enough to preserve the spontaneity and uniqueness of the particular atmospheric conditions of a given day or season. Subsequently these sketches would be elaborated upon to produce the finished work. The fact that the artist went out of doors is of the greatest significance here, since only in such manner, by immediate sensory apprehension, and by a deliberate effort to exclude all cognitive elements not given in the immediate environment, could he hope to capture the phenomenal singularity of nature. It is for this reason that Turner, in *ca.* 1799, painted "out of doors on a large scale . . . in a group of watercolours of English Lakes and North Wales subjects,"[69] while Constable painted his oil sketches "on the spot under the direct inspiration of nature." These sketches, writes the annotator, "transmit a strong power of suggestion, because they have captured and preserved what were essentially passing manifestations of nature, and changing effects of light." Further along we read that Constable "painted quickly, . . . and his talent demanded a technique which would by-pass the slow process of studio painting."[70] The result was spontaneity, a certain unfinished quality, the absence of clearly defined objects, and, above all, the illusion of change, transformation, and mutation in actual process. This constitutes a striking contrast to Poussin's landscapes, where the "phenomenal 'disorder of nature' " was reduced to " 'the order of geometry' [and] where even 'trees and shrubs are made to approach the condition of architecture.' "[71] Hence, whereas Poussin's nature is rational, static, and fixed, Constable's nature is ever-changing, fluid, and hence irreducible to a rational system. The willful exclusion of all knowledge outside of bare sense data is illustrated by the fact that Constable, in his "observation of a specific moment in the day and the season . . . chose to forget that he had ever seen a picture."[72] Turner likewise exhibits this radical empiricism,

69. Gage, *Color,* p. 34.
70. John Baskett, *Constable Oil Sketches* (New York: Watson-Guptill Publications, 1966), p. 5.
71. See above, chapter 3.
72. Elizabeth G. Holt, ed., *From the Classicists to the Impressionists* (Garden City, N. Y.: Anchor Books, Doubleday & Co., 1966), p. 113.

and we are told that while "working out of doors, [he] omitted to draw the portholes of a ship in the distance though he knew full well they were there, answering to the objections of a naval officer that 'my business is to draw what I see, and not what I know is there.'" The following passage by Ruskin (1819-1900) expresses essentially the same methodological objectives.

> The whole technical power of painting depends on our recovery of what may be called the *innocence of the eye;* that is to say, a sort of childish perception of these flat stains of colour, merely as such, without consciousness of what they signify—as a blind man would see them if suddenly gifted with sight.[73]

The corollary of the primacy of vision was the primacy of color. For example, with respect to Turner, we read that his "practice as a colourist in his maturity was so startling to his public that critics were led to attribute it to an obsession with pigments for their own sakes."[74] After studying Goethe's *Theory of Colours* he even entitled one of his paintings, "Light and Colour (Goethe's Theory) . . ." (1843).[75] Constable, we learn, also "discarded the traditional color scheme of tonal gradations and divided a color into its components in order to intensify it."[76] Concerning Ruskin's writing on art, it is said that "regardless of the type of color Ruskin is discussing, he finds so much sheer release in its sensory power that he comes to love it for its own sake." Ruskin himself, writing of Turner, declares that "for the conventional colour he substituted a pure straight-forward rendering of fact, as far as was in his power."[77]

Turner, Constable, and Ruskin represent English thought on the subject of painting. Contemporaneously on the continent of Europe, we find that the conspicuous feature of romantic art is also the exploitation of color. Thus writes Delacroix in 1852, "painters who are not colorists produce illumination and not painting," and "the colorists, the men who unite all the phases of painting, . . . have to mass things in with color, even as the sculptor does with clay, marble or stone."[78] Elsewhere we learn that Delacroix once said that "color is painting," and that gray was its enemy. "Let us banish from our palette all earth colors

73. Herbert, *Ruskin*, pp. viii, 2.
74. Gage, *Color*, p. 18.
75. *Ibid.*, plate no. 52.
76. Holt, *Classicists*, p. 113.
77. Herbert, *Ruskin*, pp. xiv, 351.
78. Quoted in Holt, *Classicists*, p. 162.

. . . the greater the opposition in color, the greater the brilliance."[79] This amounts to a fully formulated basis of Impressionism, exactly twenty years before Monet's "Impressionism, Sunrise" was exhibited in Paris in 1872. The *plein air* techniques of Turner and Constable, in addition to their insistence on an optical realism divorced from any other form of knowledge, similarly constitute techniques which were more thoroughly implemented in Impressionism. It is clear that the painting of Turner, Constable, and Delacroix (all of these artists flourishing during the first half of the nineteenth century) was almost exclusively based on an aesthetic of color and the infinite variables of light and atmosphere, in contradistinction to former theories of art which rested chiefly on the relational, and hence more abstract, elements of line, composition, and design.

The desire to record visual fact apart from inference is intensified in Realism, and brought to a logical conclusion in Impressionism. With respect to the former style, the realist Courbet affirmed that "painting is essentially a *concrete art* which can exist only in the representation of *real* and *actual* things,"[80] while the impressionists went beyond this in attempting to paint not reality, but its appearance. "The artists that followed Courbet sought for even greater closeness to nature in order to develop an art based on immediacy of expression. . . . Optical realism was pursued to the point of separating visual experience from memory and avoiding any associations the mind normally calls into play." Accordingly, "impressionism was more the ultimate phase of realism than a new style itself."[81] The extent to which this process excluded nonempirical cognition is indicated by Venturi:

The grasping of appearance is a form of sensation as free from reasoning and will as it can possibly be. Thus impressionists were faithful to their sensations, that is to their impressions of nature, and found a form closer to the first impression of the appearance of nature than previous painters. And it was closer because of their vivid sensibility, whereby they understood the absolute value in art of the appearance of things, nor did they undervalue their impressions since their mind was sufficiently free from the traditional principles of abstract form.[82]

---

79. William Fleming, *Arts and Ideas*. 3rd ed. (New York: Holt, Rinehart and Winston, Inc., n.d.), pp. 455, 454.
80. Gerstle Mack, *Gustave Courbet* (New York: Alfred A. Knopf, 1951), p. 101.
81. Fleming, *Arts*, pp. 482, 483.
82. Quoted in Robert F. Davidson *et al., The Humanities in Contemporary Life* (New York: Holt, Rinehart and Winston, 1960), p. 294.

A more striking example of the effort to eliminate from painting all theoretically inferred knowledge is implicit in Monet's statement that "he wished he had been born blind and then had suddenly gained his sight so that he would have begun to paint without knowing what the objects were that he saw before him" (cf. Ruskin's similar view with respect to this, above). Maurice Grosser's assertion that "for the impressionist, the world he paints is the world of the eye's sensations,"[83] gives further corroboration of what has already been said. The *plein air* technique, initiated by Turner and Constable, and used by them primarily for preparatory studies, was extended by the impressionists to the point where a picture was initiated and completed out of doors, not in the studio. Once again, the purpose of this was absolute fidelity to the visual experience as it recorded the ever-changing atmospheric conditions of light, clouds, and water. This concern for the unique properties of atmosphere at a given time of the day or the year led Monet in the 1890s to the presentation on canvas of multiple versions of the same scene recorded on different occasions of the year ("Poplars," "Haystacks," and "Rouen Cathedral"). Monet thus approaches an epistemological state of pure empiricism which, according to Northrop, is tantamount to Oriental mysticism. "The pure empiricists are the mystics of the world, as the Orientals, who have tended to restrict knowledge to the immediately experienced, clearly illustrate." Northrop writes further, "Impressionism, therefore, may be defined as art which uses pure fact, i.e., immediately sensed qualities or impressions of the aesthetic continuum. . . . It is to be noted that classical Oriental art, especially Chinese landscape painting, is nearer Western impressionism than it is to the classical art of the West."[84]

In conclusion to this section, several remarks will be made with regard to the development of photography in the nineteenth century, and its possible connection with art. The first successful photograph was made in 1822, and the period from that year through the 1880s witnesses a progressive technological refinement of the photographic process. It might appear, on first thought, that the invention of photography was one of the primary causal agents of style in art, generating a demand for the depiction "of the smallest local minutiae,"[85] as Ruskin de-

---

83. Quoted in *ibid.,* pp. 307, 303.
84. Northrop, *Logic,* pp. 40, 52.
85. Quoted in Holt, *Classicists,* p. 121.

scribes the painting of Turner. Admittedly, there is strong plausibility in this argument; the converse sequence of cause and effect, however, has even greater explanatory power. This is the point of the following writer, who declares that

> the invention of photography did not . . . produce visual habits which the painters had not already begun to develop. One might almost argue that photography was invented to meet an existing demand for records of visual fact, rather than the other way round. There is little evidence that in its early days photography seriously influenced painting one way or another. Both camera and painter's eye were alike used to make all-inclusive visual records.[86]

The same line of argument can be applied to the predicament of nineteenth-century music. Here the increasing demands for a greater range and accuracy in the gradations of sonority, dynamics, and pitch production were largely responsible for such technical innovations as valved brass instruments and the modern pianoforte.[87] Of course, it must be admitted that the causal connection between technological advances and the demands for certain objectives in a given artistic domain is reciprocal.

The above survey illustrates once again that nineteenth-century art reflects more the predominantly empirical method of the life sciences than their literal content, although it may be argued that the demand for a "lifelike" depiction of natural phenomena, whether they be animate or inanimate, constitutes a closer link with life itself. That this happens to be the case is suggested by the fact that Rodin's statue of a youth entitled "The Bronze Age," exhibited at the Paris Salon in 1877, was criticized by the academicians as being "too lifelike." A similar case of censure occurred with respect to Gericault's painting "Raft of the Medusa" (1818-19). " 'This is not art,' cried the academicians, 'it is life.' "[88]

The increasing friction between the academician and the free artist of the nineteenth century ultimately symbolizes a conflict between an aesthetic based on a fixed and immutable universe, fostered by the very first Academy and its founder Plato, and an aesthetic which has as its source the infinite variety of the ever-changing phenomenal world.

---

86. Humphry House, "Man and Nature: Some Artists' Views," in *Ideas and Beliefs of the Victorians* (New York: E. P. Dutton & Co., Inc., 1966), pp. 224–25.
87. See further Thomas J. Anderson, "A Study of Correspondence Between Musical Style and Instrumental Technology" (Master's thesis, Florida State University, Tallahassee, 1967).
88. Fleming, *Arts*, pp. 489, 481.

We now turn to the domain of architecture. Although most nineteenth-century architecture is dominated by revivals of former styles (such as neo-Classical, neo-Gothic, neo-Renaissance and neo-Baroque), writer Donald Egbert finds that Horace Walpole's gothic revival villa "Strawberry Hill" (begun in 1750) reflects the newly emerging view of nature characterized by the emphasis on the phenomenon and consistent with the contemporaneously rising biological sciences and their equally "phenomenological" epistemology. "Strawberry Hill" is considered by Egbert to represent pantheistic Romanticism, according to which "the phenomenal world of nature is to be regarded as most real and most significant because in it God and man come together." Furthermore, the romanticist architectural aesthetic dictates that "only those buildings which similarly harmonize with the surrounding natural environment are natural and worth while." "Strawberry Hill" is thus "not only romantic because of the conscious harmony between the picturesque form of the architecture and the picturesque nature around it, . . . but also because of its intentional appeal to the emotion of the individual." In opposition to this we have the "formal and rationally conceived Palladian architecture then predominant in Georgian England under the influence of the Italian Renaissance." That Palladio's rationalism more clearly conforms to a Platonic fixed and permanent universality, as opposed to Walpole's dependence on the local and unique features of the environment, is implicit in the following passage:

> While the plans of Palladian buildings consist of simple geometric forms arrived at primarily by means of abstractly rational principles of design considered good for all time and thus independent of evolution, the plan of Strawberry Hill was determined very largely by the individualist whims of Horace Walpole himself. As the word "whim" suggests, Walpole designed Strawberry Hill by relying on his own emotions and intuition rather than on any kind of abstract logic.[89]

Thus here we have two antithetical (but not necessarily mutually exclusive) views of nature as applied to architecture: 1) Walpole's view of nature as a phenomenon, unique and always different according to locality, and 2), Palladio's view of nature as a law-bound system which is supra-local, uniform, and eternally

---

89. Donald Egbert, "The Idea of Organic Expression and American Architecture," in Stow Persons, ed., *Evolutionary Thought in America* (New Haven: Yale University Press, 1950), pp. 342, 343.

valid. "Natural architecture is [thus] an architecture according to Palladio"[90] in the Newtonian world view.

Perhaps the clearest expression of the life-centered nineteenth-century mentality occurs in the so-called "organic" architecture of Louis Sullivan (1856-1924), Frank Lloyd Wright (1869-1959), and, to a lesser extent, Walter Gropius (1883-1969). Sullivan's connection to evolutionary ideas of organic nature is immediately made explicit by his own assertion that "in Darwin he [Sullivan] found much food. The Theory of Evolution seemed stupendous."[91] In his *Kindergarten Chats,* the notion of organismic process—as a philosophy of architecture, as a creative aesthetic, and as an all-embracing cosmology—recurs time and again. Hence, we read, in language tinged with poetic expression and holistic vitalism,

> we, in our art, are to follow Nature's processes, Nature's rhythms, because those processes, those rhythms, are vital, organic, coherent, logical above all book-logic, and flow uninterruptedly from cause to effect. And that we, being greater than trees—at least we think we are—and possessed of heart, imagination, mind, . . . and above all, gifted with spiritual insight, should use those faculties to give to our art a power, a vital, a creative beauty, that shall make with Nature a harmony and not a discord.

The organic metaphor appears once more when Sullivan writes, "a great work, for us, must be an organism—that is, possessed of a life of its own." And elsewhere in the same book we read, "The architecture *we seek* shall be as a man active, alert, supple, strong, sane. A generative man."[92]

Frank L. Wright, a pupil of Sullivan, further developed, in philosophy and practice, the idea of an organic architecture. In his Princeton Lectures on *Modern Architecture,* Wright wrote, "The word [organic] applies to 'living structure—a structure or concept wherein features or parts are so organized in form and substance as to be, applied to purpose, *integral.* Everything that 'lives' is therefore organic." The organic metaphor appears once again in Wright's *Modern Architecture,* where he declares that "an organic form grows its structure out of conditions as a plant grows out of soil . . . both unfold similarly from within."

90. Nikolaus Pevsner, *An Outline of European Architecture* (Baltimore, Md.: Penguin Books, 1961), p. 227.

91. Quoted in Egbert, "Organic," p. 352.

92. Louis H. Sullivan, *Kindergarten Chats and Other Writings* (New York: George Wittenborn, Inc., 1965, pp. 119, 160, 49.

And further on we read, "An inner-life principle is a gift to every seed. An inner-life principle is also necessary for every idea of a good building." Finally, Gropius enunciated an organic philosophy of architecture when he wrote in *The Theory and Organization of the Bauhaus* (1923), "We want to create a clear organic architecture whose inner logic will be radiant and naked, unencumbered by lying façades and trickeries, . . . an architecture whose function is clearly recognizable in the relation of its forms."[93]

It is now appropriate to determine the meaning of the term *organic* as applied to architecture. Two distinct meanings actually make themselves apparent. In the first place *organic*, especially as used by Sullivan and Wright, refers to the harmony of a building with the phenomenal world of nature. According to this principle the natural environmental conditions of topography, climate, and native materials should play a key role in determining the character of a structure. "Kinship of building to ground"[94] is Wright's phrase describing this procedure.

A building should appear to grow easily from its site and be shaped to harmonize with its surroundings. . . . We of the Middle West are living on the prairie. The prairie has a beauty of its own and we should recognize and accentuate this natural beauty, its quiet level. Hence, gently sloping roofs, low proportions, quiet sky lines, suppressed heavy-set chimneys and sheltering overhangs, low terraces and out-reaching walls sequestering private gardens.

This principle of harmonizing the external environment of a particular site with a building is also extended to the same relation of a building to its internal components (furniture, appliances, decoration, color scheme), and to the individuality of the patron and of the architect. "There should be as many kinds (styles) of houses as there are kinds (styles) of people and as many differentiations as there are different individuals."[95] Egbert, noting the similarity of this organic principle to Walpole's aims, and the fact that both rest on a view of nature as a phenomenon, correctly identifies this portion of Wright's (and Sullivan's) organic aesthetic with Romanticism. Or better yet, it is a romantic naturalism which rests "on a belief that buildings should be in

---

93. Quoted in Egbert, "Organic," pp. 340, 353, 382.
94. Frank L. Wright, *Writings and Buildings,* selected by E. Kaufmann and Ben Raeburn (New York: Meridian Books, 1960), p. 305.
95. *The Architectural Record,* March 1908, as quoted in Davidson, *The Humanities,* p. 470.

harmony with the phenomena of the natural world . . . : and
since the forms of architecture are held to be so largely deter-
or even God—have been thought of as part of nature itself."
mined by natural environmental conditions, buildings—like man

The second meaning of the word *organic* is expressed by Sullivan's axiom, enunciated in 1896, "Form follows function." In
contrast to the first organic principle described above, whereby
a building is harmonious with its natural environment, the functionalist side of organic architecture depends more on a logical
analysis of form and the function it is supposed to perform.
Hence, the functionalist believes that "an ultimate order and
truth reside in the laws, mechanistic or biological, through which
nature operates" and that "the laws of nature discovered through
science must be made use of. . . . As a result, the scientifically
direct expression of function and structure is for him of first
importance."[96] The biological source of the principle "form
follows function," or Coleridge's "such as the life is, such is the
form," which Wright regarded as perhaps being an even more
appropriate formulation,[97] is clear from his assertion that "an
organic form grows its structure out of conditions as a plant
grows out of soil . . . both unfold similarly from within." Egbert thus observes,

> In this concept of growth as an unfolding from within, there is again
> a suggestion of vitalism that is further borne out by Wright's statement,
> "An inner life-principle is a gift to every seed. An inner life-principle
> is also necessary for every idea of a good building." And when this is
> combined with Wright's insistence that "form changes with changing
> conditions," a vitalistic kind of evolutionism is again clearly implied.[98]

Morrison, in his biography of Sullivan, likewise writes that the
axiom "form follows function" is a ". . . direct adaptation of
a great biological principle to the sphere of architecture."[99]

The two cardinal principles of organic architecture thus described are clearly manifest in Wright's building "Falling Water."
Here, according to Egbert, both the logical-functionalistic and
the phenomenal-romantic viewpoints are combined, as is often
the case, "in a naturalistic philosophy of architecture." This
organismic philosophy, in turn,

96. Egbert, "Organic," pp. 341–42, 346.
97. Wright, *Writings*, p. 314.
98. Quoted in Egbert, "Organic," p. 353.
99. Hugh Morrison, *Louis Sullivan: Prophet of Modern Architecture* (New
York: The Museum of Modern Art and W. W. Norton & Co., Inc., 1935), p. 251.

is likely to imply an interest in the processes of development or change in nature for their own sake, an interest also in the effects of environmental conditions on structure and form and so lends itself to belief in doctrines of evolution. It is primarily for this reason that both Wright and Sullivan have shown a considerable degree of direct and indirect sympathy with Darwinian and Spencerian thought.[100]

It is interesting and significant to note that, aside from the influence of Darwin and Spencer, Wright esteemed and occasionally quoted the works of Herder[101] and Coleridge,[102] while Goethe was included "in a list of Wright's favorite authors."[103] The crucial role of these three figures in the development of a biocentrically (or organismically) conceived cosmology has already been discussed in the initial chapter of this study.

In the light of Sullivan's and Wright's organic philosophy of architecture, it does not appear to be merely accidental that Wright detested the Palladian ideal of Renaissance architecture, on the grounds that its absolute rationalism, formalism, and abstractionism were no respecters of time and place. "This soulless thing, the Renaissance . . . ," he said, "has betrayed the artist. . . . Let us have done with it forever." And at another time he stated, "Instinctively, I think, I hated the empty pretentious shapes of the Renaissance."

Gropius's statement concerning his idea of organic architecture has already been cited. That this architectural philosophy was to a great extent inspired by the living world is made clear by his assertion that at the Bauhaus, "We did not base our teaching on any preconceived ideas of form, but sought the vital spark behind life's ever-changing forms."[104] However, it must be admitted that Gropius, Le Corbusier, and Mies van der Rohe are commonly associated (at least before 1930) with more rationalistic methods of architecture (standardization, prefabrication, and a severe, modular, cubist style) antithetical to Wright's insistence on the unity and uniqueness of house, site and dweller. On the contrary, their architecture derives more from the fact that man, despite his singular individuality, belongs to one species and that his needs, accordingly, are fairly uniform throughout the civilized world. It is thus suggested that the philosophical premises upon which Gropius, Mies van der Rohe, and Le Cor-

100. Egbert, "Organic," pp. 345, 347.
101. *Ibid.,* p. 370.
102. See above, chapter 6.
103. Egbert, "Organic," p. 371.
104. Quoted in *ibid.,* pp. 354, 350, 382.

busier (all Europeans) proceed belong more to the tradition of
Continental rationalism, while Sullivan and Wright, with their
emphasis on the phenomenal uniqueness of each structure, are
more consistent with the tradition of Anglo-American empiricism.

This section may be concluded with Egbert's observation that
organic architecture "usually implies that the ultimate reality lies
within nature itself as a single great organism," and that

> it has usually connoted some form of philosophical naturalism in archi-
> tecture as in other aspects of life. As a result of this belief in nature as
> fundamental, those who insist upon the necessity for organic expression
> in art have often been much interested in natural science. They have
> therefore often sought to take over the findings of the natural sciences,
> particularly those of paleontology, botany, and zoology, which, during
> the last two centuries, have given a new emphasis to the fact that the
> natural world is characterized by change, growth, and development—
> in short, by evolution.[105]

---

105. *Ibid.*, p. 341.

8

The Biological Metaphor in
Nineteenth-Century Musical Structure

The present chapter is devoted to an analysis of certain structural features in nineteenth-century music, a period commonly designated by the term Romanticism. Specifically, I hope to show that the principles of 1) cyclical form, 2) the metamorphosis of themes, and 3) the fusion of multi-movement works into one are products of a biocentrically oriented mentality. This chapter thus constitutes a counterpart to chapter 5, where it was demonstrated that eighteenth-century musical Classicism depends for its structural unity on principles more commensurate with the logocentrism of the Enlightenment. It will next be shown that the nineteenth-century concern with the phenomena of sound is an epistemological corollary of the chiefly empirical method relevant to natural-history biology.

That a great deal of nineteenth-century music is infused with the literal content of life itself may be gathered by such features as the

introduction of funeral marches . . . into certain of Beethoven's works. More generally, it is a commonplace of music history that the absolute music of the eighteenth century gave way to a romantic music where even symphonies and sonatas were apt to have descriptive titles, e.g., Beethoven's Opus 81a, where the three movements are respectively entitled *Les Adieux, L'Absence et Le Retour.* This self-evidently indicates a desire to make music more the expression of everyday life, as opposed to Bach's *Art of Fugue,* which can be related to "life" only on a most abstract, logocentric level.[1]

1. John F. Spratt, "Philosophical Implications of Modern Science as Reflected in the History of Music" (paper presented at Hiram College, Hiram, Ohio, November 1969), p. 8.

Furthermore, unlike music of the classical and all former style-periods, music of the Romantic era is frequently described in terms of organic and developmental metaphors. For example, we read that "every measure" in Beethoven's *"Hammerklavier* [Sonata] is a sprout growing from a few germinal motifs," while Franck's Sonata for Violin and Piano discloses the "application of the sonata form, in the sense of strictly organic development."[2] The cyclical unity of Schumann's Fourth Symphony is, in Alfred Einstein's words, "not merely an external feature, for all the movements are developed from melodic seeds that are given in the Introduction; they are blossoms of various colors springing from the same bush."[3]

More important, thematic transformation, in conjunction with the cyclical principle, is, according to Leichtentritt, "a particularly striking musical application of the dominant romantic idea of evolution. In his various 'symphonic poems,' his 'Faust' and 'Dante' symphonies, and his concertos, Liszt has brilliantly demonstrated the possibilities of this principle of organic structure." Leichtentritt adds further that the idea of evolution is central in "the romantic philosophy of Fichte, Hegel, Schelling, and Schopenhauer," and that

> this concept, which also dominated the science and literature of the nineteenth century, is carried over into music, and to it we owe the form of the sonata as Beethoven conceived and shaped it. Romantic music is not static, like Bach's music; it is no longer the exhaustive statement of a single idea, a single mood. Its very essence is dynamic.[4]

Gordon Epperson substantially concurs with Leichtentritt's observation when he writes that

> Schopenhauer and Nietzsche brought to the theory of music a new concept, articulated by each in different ways and in different terms but faithful to the same principle: *dynamism*. Each one espoused a world view in which the Newtonian framework appeared a fragile structure indeed.[5]

Even Donald J. Grout, who generally eschews the implications

2. Hugo Leichtentritt, *Musical Form* (Cambridge, Mass.: Harvard University Press, 1951), pp. 327, 346.

3. Alfred Einstein, *Music in the Romantic Era* (New York: W. W. Norton & Co., Inc., 1947), pp. 130–31.

4. Hugo Leichtentritt, *Music, History, and Ideas* (Cambridge, Mass.: Harvard University Press, 1964), pp. 225, 218.

5. Reprinted by permission from p. 53, *The Musical Symbol*, by Gordon Epperson, © 1967 by The Iowa State University Press, Ames, Iowa.

of science and philosophy on music, concedes that musical romanticism "was regarded as exemplifying the prevalent conception that the nineteenth century was an era of progress and evolution."[6] Thus, all of these writers suggest in various degrees that romantic music was conceived more on the analogue of the evolving organism undergoing a dynamic process of change and growth in contradistinction to the more statically conceived structural principles of the Baroque and Classical eras. That the same process occurred in such areas as literature, philosophy, art, and architecture need hardly be further emphasized.

Despite the predominance of cyclical form in the nineteenth century, and despite the conspicuous absence of this form in the Classical era ("the cyclic method . . . had been forgotten in the eighteenth century"),[7] the cyclical recurrence of themes is almost as old as Western polyphonic music itself. Smith, for example, cites two paired dances of the fourteenth century, the *Lamento di Tristano* and *La Manfredina* (no. 28 in Schering's *Geschichte der Musik in Beispielen*), "the second of which is a variation of the first."[8] A similar example, written *ca.* two hundred years later, is *Der Prinzen-Tanz* and *Proportz* (*Tanz* and *Nachtanz*), reproduced by Parrish and Ohl.[9] However, the most famous and the most frequently discussed example of cyclical thematic treatment in medieval music occurs in the Machaut Mass. Here the motif,

writes Armand Machabey, "may be regarded as the generating cell of this vast composition: not only does one encounter it in each of the sections, but in addition it gives rise to imitations, to fugal entries, to repetitions, to counter-melodies in long time values (Kyrie), well proving that Machaut made of it the basic material of his *Messe Notre-Dame.*"[10]

6. Donald J. Grout, *A History of Western Music* (New York: W. W. Norton & Co., 1960), p. 498.

7. Leichtentritt, *Ideas,* p. 225.

8. Warren S. Smith, "The Cyclic Principle in Musical Design, and the Use of it by Bruckner and Mahler," *Chord and Discord* 2, no. 9 (1960):3.

9. Carl Parrish and John F. Ohl, *Masterpieces of Music Before 1750* (New York: W. W. Norton & Co., 1940), no. 22.

10. Quoted in Gustave Reese, *Music in the Middle Ages* (New York: W. W. Norton & Co., 1940), pp. 356–57.

Another form of cyclical recurrence of themes occurred around the year 1400, when composers began to use the same head-motifs for paired Mass sections. For example, in the Old Hall MS. we find that "the Gloria and Credo . . . , attributable to Leonel Power, begin with similar initial motifs."[11] During the period of Dufay the cyclical treatment was intensified in the so-called *cantus firmus* Mass. Here the *cantus firmus* melody was repeated in every movement of the Mass, thus becoming the basis for polyphonic elaboration. A good example of this is Dufay's *Missa Se la face ay pale,* which also discloses the use of the recurrent head-motif.[12] The sixteenth-century parody Mass, a technique which incorporates the musical substance of a pre-existing composition into the fabric of the Mass, likewise exhibits the cyclical principle.

The cyclical treatment of themes in multi-movement compositions is also encountered in the Baroque period. However, this principle is in most cases confined to the *incipits* of the individual movements (a practice identical to the recurrent head-motifs of the Renaissance Mass). Some of the composers mentioned by Newman who employ this technique are Frescobaldi, Reinken, Corelli, Vitali, and Veracini, although the practice is common "throughout the era in all regions of the sonata and in other multisectional forms as well."[13] Bach's cantata "Christ Lag in Todesbanden" is perhaps the best known example of the cyclical treatment and polyphonic elaboration of a chorale *cantus firmus* in a manner reminiscent of the *cantus firmus* Mass. These examples of cyclical form notwithstanding, the predominance of late-Baroque music is noncyclical in nature. No evidence of this principle is found in Bach's "Brandenburg Concerti," in his Suites for Orchestra or for solo instruments, in his numerous solo concerti, or in the majority of his vast choral output. The same statement is generally applicable to the multi-movement works of Handel. In the case of each composer the unifying principle consists of the logical juxtaposition of contrasting sections rather than of the literal repetition of the same thematic material.

The paucity of works displaying the cyclical principle in the Classical era has already been noted. Admittedly, certain examples of cyclical form (conscious or unconscious) in the music of

11. *Ibid., Music in the Renaissance* (New York: W. W. Norton & Co., Inc., 1959), p. 39.
12. See further *ibid.,* pp. 71–72.
13. William S. Newman, *The Sonata in the Baroque Era* (Chapel Hill: The University of North Carolina Press, 1959), p. 78.

Mozart have been brought to attention by the musicologist Karl Marx (see above, chapter 5). Similar examples have been reported by Smith, who notes that the first two movements of Haydn's String Quartets op. 20, no. 4 and op. 76, no. 5 begin with the same four notes, although Smith likewise admits that the Classical period witnesses "a comparative dearth" of cyclical treatment.[14] Furthermore, cyclical form, in the examples cited above, and in similar examples of the period, consists primarily of a literal quotation of a previous theme as opposed to the thematic permeation of an entire composition, as is the case in most cyclical works of the nineteenth century. Therefore, it must be concluded that the bulk of classical music rests on the unifying principle of logical complementarity rather than on the cyclical recurrence of themes.

With Beethoven we witness a transition from Classicism to Romanticism. The latter style is vaguely characterized by most music historians as one which "seeks out the new, the curious, and the adventurous,"[15] as one which "cherishes freedom, movement, passion, and endless pursuit of the unattainable,"[16] and as one which displays a more "personal way of creation."[17] The validity of these assertions is not here disputed. I merely maintain that in the profoundest sense Beethoven constitutes a transition from the logocentrism of the eighteenth century to the biocentrism of the nineteenth. His music (especially after 1800) embodies the some ideational tendencies as those found in the thought of his exact contemporaries, Goethe, Herder, and Coleridge.

The literal reference to life in Beethoven's *Les Adieux* Sonata and in his introduction of funeral marches into his works (Sonata op. 26, *Eroica* Symphony) has been noted. Similar examples alluding to human events or feelings are the *Pathétique* Sonata, the *Pastoral* Symphony ("expression of feelings"), and the "Choral" Symphony (the Ninth), whose final movement is dedicated to the brotherhood of man by incorporating Schiller's "Ode to Joy." This connection of music with the direct experience of life is symptomatic of a trend which becomes increasingly removed from the more abstract conception of the classical symphony or sonata. Equally conspicuous features indicating the

14. Smith, "Cyclic Principle," p. 5.
15. Homer Ulrich and Paul A. Pisk, *A History of Music and Musical Style* (New York: Harcourt, Brace & World, Inc., 1963), p. 426.
16. Grout, *History*, p. 493.
17. Curt Sachs, *Our Musical Heritage* (Englewood Cliffs, N. J.: Prentice-Hall, Inc., 1955), p. 257.

same tendency are encountered in Beethoven's use of recitative-like passages in the Sonata op. 110, in the Ninth Symphony, and in the String Quartet op. 135, to mention the most obvious examples. Finally Beethoven's music begins to manifest what are here regarded as the most important biologically derived principles of structure, namely, cyclical form, the fusion of multi-movement works, and the metamorphosis of themes.

It is now appropriate to specify in what manner the above techniques involve a biological metaphor of unity and structure. First of all, the cyclical recurrence of a theme (or themes) involves a more literal principle of identity, i.e., a principle which does not require the degree of inference necessary to comprehend the unity produced by logical contrasts in the classical work. Hence, on an epistemological level, the literal repetition of a theme is more akin to the empirical method of biology, while the comprehension of unity by logically juxtaposed contrasting parameters is more analogous to rational processes of the physical sciences. This has been designated as the principle of "logical complementarity," which satisfactorily accounted for the manner in which disparate elements in music of the eighteenth century belong together (see chapter 5).

The biological metaphor inherent in the principle of metamorphosis of themes is more obvious. To begin with, the term "metamorphosis," we read, is chiefly applied to zoology and entails "a conspicuous change in shape and mode of life in an animal occurring in a comparatively short time."[18] This closely parallels the frequently drastic modifications a theme undergoes in the works of such nineteenth-century composers as Berlioz, Liszt, and Wagner. It is significant that in the entry "Metamorphosis," Willi Apel refers chiefly to composers of the Romantic era who employ this technique in strong contrast to former, "more 'technical,' methods of modification as, e.g., the augmentation and diminution of a fugal subject."[19] It will be noticed that augmentation and diminution customarily involve simple and hence predictable ratios characteristic of inanimate systems, while the proportional changes in thematic transformation are in most cases more complex and unpredictable, reflecting the less predictable nature of the animate world.

---

18. Ernest W. MacBride and Vincent B. Wigglesworth, "Metamorphosis," *Encyclopaedia Britannica* (1964), 15 : 323.

19. Willi Apel, *Harvard Dictionary of Music* (Cambridge: Harvard University Press, 1958), p. 442.

The elimination of the silent pause between the movements, leading to the gradual fusion of a four-movement work into one, likewise constitutes a self-evident attempt to conceive music more along organismic lines. It was noted previously that the silent pause between the movements of a classical symphony served to set off the logically contrasting character of the movements and to intensify their disparity. Ingarden went even further by suggesting that the silent pause itself was a positive structural parameter in that it presented to the listener the logical contrast between sound and silence.[20] The frequent elimination of this parameter from the romantic sonata and symphony, and the emphasis on one continuous, unbroken, tonal fabric, where the classical clarity of melodic, rhythmic, and harmonic distinctions is deliberately obscured, clearly suggests the indivisible nature of the organism. The breakdown of distinctions is acknowledged by Grout, who writes that "classical clarity [in Romantic music] is replaced by a certain intentional obscurity, definite statement by suggestion, allusion, or symbol."[21]

All three techniques—cyclical form, the metamorphosis of themes, and the elimination of the pause between movements—begin to manifest themselves in the music of Beethoven. The first example of cyclical recurrence cited by most writers is in the *Pathétique* Sonata (1799), where the second subject of the first movement strongly resembles the opening theme of the Finale.

(a)

(b)

It is uncertain whether this is a conscious or unconscious use of cyclical thematic recurrence. It is certain, however, that the inter-

20. Roman Ingarden, *Untersuchungen zur Ontologie der Kunst* (Tübingen: Max Niemeyer Verlag, 1962), p. 111.
21. Grout, *History*, p. 493.

polation of the Scherzo in the final movement of Beethoven's Fifth Symphony is a deliberate use of the cyclical principle. A more subtle form of this technique is the transformed recurrence of the four-note motif in movements one, three, and four.

Additional examples of this principle may be encountered in his Piano Sonata op. 110 (citation of slow movement in the middle of the fugue), and in the Ninth Symphony (citation of major themes at the beginning of the finale). With the exception of the transformed motif in the Fifth Symphony, these examples constitute the literal repetition of previously presented thematic material, a practice which is occasionally found before Beethoven in the Classical era (see for example Haydn's Symphony no. 46, where a portion of the minuet is interpolated toward the end of the Finale).

Numerous examples of pause elimination are found in Beethoven's music. Some of the best known are the transition from the Scherzo to the Finale in the Fifth Symphony, the transition from the second to the last movement of the *Emperor* and Violin Concertos, and the fusion of the final three movements in the *Pastoral* Symphony. Perhaps the earliest example of this practice presents itself in the *Sonata Quasi Una Fantasia,* op. 27, no. 1. Here each movement ends with the inscription *attaca subito,* thus weakening the finality of the full cadences at the end of movements one and two, while movement three tonally leads directly into movement four. Additional examples of movement connection in the works of Beethoven are in the *Waldstein* and *Apassionata* Sonatas, the Piano Sonatas ops. 81a, 101, and 110, the Violin Sonata op. 96, and the String Quartets op. 59, nos. 1 and 3, and op. 131, where all seven movements are interconnected. It will be noted here that the deviation, in the last-named work, from the standard four-movement plan, and the departure from the predictable character of each movement, in addition to the use of more remote tonal relations, further suggests a theory of nature consistent with the less predictable behavior of the organic world in contrast to the greater predictability of inanimate nature.

The principle of thematic metamorphosis, at least in its formative stage, is likewise discernible in the mature works of Beethoven. Here again the four-note motif from the Fifth Symphony may be cited as an example. The transformation is here principally rhythmic, although melodic modification is also present. The noteworthy feature in Beethoven's fugal technique of his final years may be regarded as involving thematic transformation, in contrast to the more static proportional methods use by J. S. Bach. Note the following rhythmic changes of the "Grosse Fuge" theme:

Similar thematic mutations occur in the *Fuga "con alcune licenze"* of the *Hammerklavier* Sonata. The inscription *"con alcune li-*

cenze" is further suggestive of free thematic growth rather than the strict contrapuntal methods of former periods. Beethoven's variation technique, in such works as the Sonatas ops. 109 and 111, the *Diabelli* Variations, and the String Quartet op. 131, is also more describable in terms of growth, mutation, and metamorphosis, in contrast to the former, more fixed, methods of his predecessors. Willi Apel's statement that Beethoven "replaced the more conventional methods . . . by a wealth of individual treatments and ideas which evades all attempts at summary description"[22] again brings to mind the complexity and indescribability of an organic process rather than the relative simplicity and fixity of inorganic processes.

Beethoven's late style is thus characterized by an increasing blurring of the clear and distinct lines of demarcation found in classical music. This occurs

> within a musical sentence by making cadential progressions terminate on a weak beat, by . . . placing the third or the fifth of the tonic chord in the upper voice at such a resolution, or by otherwise concealing the cadential effect . . . : within a movement, by interpenetration of Introduction and Allegro (first movements of Sonata Op. 109 and Quartets Opp. 127, 130, 132) . . . : even within a complete work, by interpenetration of movements (Adagio and Fuga in the Sonata Op. 110; recall of the first movement theme after the Adagio of Op. 101).[23]

What is implicit in Beethoven becomes explicit in the period following him. This is clear not only in the intensification of the above features, or in the wholesale adoption of cyclical form, the metamorphosis of themes, and the unification of movements (features increasingly encountered in Beethoven's late works), but also in the romantics' unbounded veneration for Beethoven and conversely, in their disinterested view of Haydn and Mozart. With respect to Beethoven we read that "the Romantic era . . . set Beethoven on a pedestal as its patron saint and emphasized his 'Romantic' traits."[24] Franz Liszt bears out Einstein's observation, writing to Wilhelm von Lenz,

> For us musicians, Beethoven's work is like the pillar of cloud and fire which guided the Israelites through the desert—a pillar of cloud to guide us by day, a pillar of fire to guide us by night, *"so that we may progress both day and night."* His obscurity and his light trace for us

---

22. Apel, *Dictionary,* p. 786.
23. Grout, *History,* pp. 487–88.
24. Alfred Einstein, *Romantic Era,* p. 79.

equally the path we have to follow; they are each of them a perpetual commandment, an infallible revelation.[25]

Liszt's reverence for Beethoven may be further inferred from the fact that he transcribed all of Beethoven's symphonies for the piano, and that all of Beethoven's "piano sonatas were in Liszt's repertory," sonatas, which we are told, "he used to play . . . to Berlioz in the dark."[26]

In contrast to the esteem accorded Beethoven by Liszt and other romantics, Haydn and Mozart received, at best, polite respect. Generally speaking,

> the Romantics felt for Haydn little more than a somewhat patronizing affection. His clarity, his strict mastery, his wit, his spirit—an 18th-century spirit—ran counter to the tendencies of the Romantic movement. For the so-called "neo-Romantics"—Berlioz, Liszt, Wagner—he seemed scarcely to exist at all.

This comment is clearly illustrated by Schumann's statement, made in 1841, "that one could not learn anything new from Haydn, that he was 'like an old friend of the family, who is always received with pleasure and respect'—but 'he is no longer highly interesting for the present day.' " Mozart fared little better. In him "the Romantics saw little more than the master, the polisher of formal elements, at best," and in Otto Jahn's words, " 'a master whose passions in their workings are not laid bare to view, but who offers us perfect beauty victorious over turbulence and impurity.' "[27] The same attitude is implicit in Liszt's mind when he praises Lenz's censure of a certain Mozart biographer "for having made of Mozart a sort of *Dalai-Lama,* beyond which there is nothing." Liszt's attitude to classical form is further disclosed in a letter to Louis Köhler dealing with Liszt's symphonic poems, which are "only . . . *Prolegomena* to the *Faust* and *Dante* Symphonies. . . . 'Away, away,' with Mazeppa's horse, regardless of the lazy hack that sticks in the mud of old patterns !"[28]

The pivotal work in the development of the biocentric musical aesthetic, an aesthetic which is based almost entirely on the principles of cyclical thematic recurrence, the metamorphosis of themes, and movement fusion, is Schubert's *Wanderer Fantasy.*

25. Franz Liszt, *Letters of Franz Liszt,* collected and ed. La Mara, trans. Constance Bache. 2 vols. (New York: Charles Scribner's Sons, 1894), vol. 1, p. 151.
26. Sacheverell Sitwell, *Liszt* (New York: Dover Publications, 1967), p. 27.
27. Alfred Einstein, *Romantic Era,* pp. 80, 79, 81.
28. Liszt, *Letters,* vol. 1, pp. 50, 271.

Written in 1822, this work clearly displays all three principles. The germ theme, or "thematic cell," as Paul Badura-Skoda refers to it, occurs at the beginning of the slow movement:

This motif is taken from Schubert's *lied* "Der Wanderer," and becomes here the basis for the thematic material of the entire composition. It is transformed as follows in the remaining three movements:

(a)

(b)

There are no pauses between the movements.

With regard to the influence of this work on the music of the era, Badura-Skoda writes, "the Wanderer-Fantasia points to the future in a manner scarcely equalled by any other work of the period and contains the seeds of the whole symphonic development of the 19th century." More specifically, the work had a direct influence on Franz Liszt, who not only transcribed it for piano and orchestra, but also was "one of the first to assemble material for a biography of Schubert."[29] Liszt himself refers to the work as "the splendid *Wanderer*-dithyramb."[30] The direct

29. Editor's Preface to Franz Schubert, *Fantasy in C Major* (Vienna: Universal Edition, 1965), p. ii.

30. Liszt, *Letters,* vol. 1, p. 165.

result of this influence was the symphonic poem which exemplifies most clearly cyclical form, thematic transformation, and the telescoping of all movements into one. These principles became an end in itself in all of Liszt's large-scale works, such as the B Minor Sonata, the two Piano Concertos, and the *Faust* Symphony.

The proliferation of these techniques is as conspicuous in the nineteenth century as their absence is notable in the eighteenth. Such composers as Mendelssohn, Schumann, and Brahms, Berlioz, Franck, and Saint-Saëns, Tchaikovsky and Dvořák, Bruckner, Mahler, and Strauss, at one time or another made use of these principles. Some of the notable examples are Mendelssohn's *Scotch* Symphony, Schumann's Second and Fourth Symphonies, as well as his Piano Quintet, op. 44; Brahms's Quartet op. 51, no. 1, his Violin Sonata op. 78, and the Piano Sonatas nos. 1 and 2; Berlioz's *Symphonie fantastique* and *Harold en Italie*, Franck's Symphony in D Minor, and Saint-Saëns's Third Symphony; Tchaikovsky's Fifth and Dvořák's Ninth Symphonies, and most of the symphonies of Bruckner and Mahler. The symphonic poem found its successors in such composers as Franck (*Le Chasseur maudit, Psyché*), Saint-Saëns (*Danse macabre, Le Rouet d'Omphale*), Tchaikovsky (*Fatum, Francesca da Rimini*), Dvořák (*The Midday Witch, The Golden Spinning Wheel*), and Strauss (*Don Juan, Till Eulenspiegel*).

It was suggested in chapter 5 above that the formal process in romantic music depends chiefly on the principle of compensatory change, while classical music is based more on the principle of logical complementarity. Compensatory change was then defined as modification of a given musical idea x by x', x'', x''', and so on, or, in Taylor's words, "change which compensates for completeness, sameness or homogeneity but does so through a more or less literal principle of identity."[31] It is here maintained that the principle of compensatory change is a dominant factor in most nineteenth-century music. First of all it should be noted that the metamorphosis of themes rests exclusively on this principle as opposed to the principle of logical complementarity, where unity is achieved by the complementary variables x, y, z. This may be seen in the musical examples already cited in this chapter, namely, the two themes of Beethoven's *Pathétique* Sonata, the recurrent motif from Beethoven's Fifth Symphony, the fugue theme of Beethoven's *Grosse Fuge,* and the germ theme of Schubert's

31. See above, chapter 5.

Wanderer Fantasy. Although structural unity in the Beethoven works (particularly in the *Pathétique* Sonata and Fifth Symphony) is still largely achieved by the union of logically juxtaposed disparate elements, we can already see here the incipient shift to a more empirical type of unity, i.e., unity based on the same recognizable musical idea. In the Schubert example, compensatory change, involving the recurrent use of the "Wanderer" motif, becomes the dominant mode of musical structuring, although the classical clarity of rhythm, melody, and formal design is still here apparent.

When we examine Liszt's symphonic poem *Les Préludes* (1849-50), we find compensatory change, in the form of thematic metamorphosis, carried to the point of almost totally excluding logically contrasting thematic material. Here the biological metaphor of a thematic cell giving rise to almost an entire composition becomes an end in itself. The work consists of 419 bars, 228 of which are devoted to motif *x* or its manifold permutations, while 131 bars are devoted to the subsidiary motif *y,* the only underived contrasting theme of the composition. Here is an example of motifs *x* and *y* as they are presented in their original versions and in their transformations:

x⁴

x⁵

x⁶

x⁷
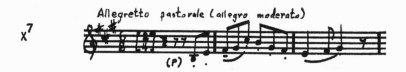

x⁸
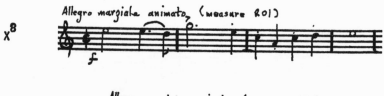

x⁹

Only versions X^5 and X^7 require some explanatory remarks. The two sixteenth-note patterns of X^5 appear to be derived from the same pattern in X^1, while the upward leap of a minor third seems to be a contraction of the upward fourth in X. This is further confirmed when in bars 164-66 the interval of a third in X^5 is expanded to a fourth:

The eighth-note pattern of X^7 appears to be a freely transformed version of the corresponding pattern in X, while the long-short-long rhythm of X^7 directly reflects a similar rhythm of the first three notes of X.

That this method of composition is essentially weak, artificial, and susceptible of producing tedium is acknowledged by most music critics. For example, Norman Demuth, here writing of Franck's application of this method, asserts that "the strongest point against the form is that it tends to monotony and inevitability."[32] Cecil Gray is more emphatic when he implies that Liszt's aspiration to produce a more organic form by means of a more literal principle of identity produced the opposite result. According to him, Liszt is not a great master of form because "his form is often, perhaps generally, too mechanical, . . . logical, and symmetrical, lacking in the living, spontaneous, organic quality which is characteristic of the highest achievements in musical form."[33] Demuth's use of the word *logical* can be understood here on only the lowest level of abstraction. For it is precisely the relative absence of the more abstract, logically contrasting complementary variables which renders cyclical form and the metamorphosis of themes ineffectual as a means of achieving high-grade structural unity. Demuth's observation that Liszt's form lacks "living, spontaneous, organic quality" further suggests that true "organic" form must partake of a logical process in the sense of an "organizing" principle. Liszt and the romantics in general, on the other hand, tended to exclude logic from their conception of musical form.

The blurring of clear outlines in Beethoven's late works, noted earlier, is also intensified in Liszt's music. Notice for example the rhythmic ambiguity in the opening measures of *Les Préludes*.

The opening half rest, the two pizzicato quarter notes falling on the third beat, and the beginning of the principal theme on the second beat, all produce anything but a clear and distinct feeling of common time. This sort of rhythmic unpredictability and rhythmic displacement is distinctive of the whole period.

What has been said about Liszt with respect to formal processes involving compensatory change (metamorphosis of themes), and involving a more literal (more empirical) principle of the-

32. *César Franck* (London: Dennis Dobson, Ltd., 1949), p. 57.
33. *Contingencies and Other Essays* (New York: Oxford University Press, 1947), p. 87.

matic identity (cyclical form), can also generally be said about such composers as Berlioz, Franck, Wagner, Debussy, and, to a lesser extent, Mendelssohn, Schumann, Tchaikovsky, Dvořák, and so forth. That compensatory change of a given musical idea (x', x'', x''') as opposed to uniting disparate musical entities by complementary variables (x, y, z), is a dominant mode of structuring nineteenth-century music is further indicated by the popularity of the variation form in the Romantic era. We read with respect to this,

> The exceptional attachment evinced by Romantic composers for repeated motives and *maqam* methods of thought seems to be bound up with the practice of variation, which during the 19th century had such a decisive role to play. The melody is responsible for shaping the whole form, and hence for renewing it as well. From the time of Beethoven's last works, the Romantics laid ever greater stress on the principle of construction by means of the single theme, even applying it to the building of large forms. . . . And what is more natural than that a unified melodic texture should imply a unified structural scheme, that a work built round a single theme should try to turn into a work in one movement, a single giant span?[34]

Szabolcsi's use of the term *maqam* (an Arabic melody-type similar to the Hindu *raga*) to describe the romantic propensity for varying a melody implies that compensatory change, as a principle for patterning music, is more characteristic of non-Western cultures. This has been conclusively confirmed by Taylor's study which shows that African, Hindu, and Chinese music depends primarily on this principle. Complementary variables, on the other hand, appear to be the almost exclusive property of Western culture, "because no culture outside the Western (and especially the Western since the Renaissance) elevates to as high a status the type of logical relationship—or the higher order completeness with which it is associated—which constitutes the nature of that factor."[35] That the Orient in general is dominated by the radically empirical component of knowledge, in contrast to the primacy of logical postulation in the Occident, has been further demonstrated by Northrop's monumental study, *The Meeting of East and West*. Hence, compensatory change, combined with the romantic concern for sonority *per se*, is chiefly

34. Bence Szabolcsi, *A History of Melody*, trans. Cynthia Jolly and Sara Karig (New York: St. Martin's Press, 1965), p. 170.
35. See further Gene F. Taylor, "Culturally Transcendent Factors in Musical Perception" (Ph.D. diss., The Florida State University, Tallahassee, 1969), pp. 124–67, 151.

an Eastern trait, a trait which came to an end with the decline of Impressionism.

We will now consider the position of Brahms in view of what has been said about Romanticism and its dominant tendency. To begin with, Brahms has frequently been described as the classical romanticist or the romantic classicist. The reasons for this are clear: Brahms, unlike such romantics as Berlioz, Liszt, and Wagner, maintained the classical clarity of his predecessors Beethoven, Haydn, and even Bach. "Clear and unbroken outlines were infinitely more important to him than musical color."[36] However, in a profounder sense, Brahms's classicism resides in the fact that complementary variables still play a dominant role in his music. This is clearly reflected in Brahms's attitude to the methods of composition adopted by Liszt *et al.*, namely cyclical form, the metamorphosis of themes, and the telescoping of all movements into one.

In his early years Brahms was visibly affected by these methods, and most of his biographers note this influence.[37] An examination of his early works discloses these Lisztian features. For example, in the C Major Piano Sonata, op. 1 (1852-53), composed when Brahms was barely twenty, the final three measures of the Andante anticipate the opening theme of the Scherzo. More important, there is an obvious thematic relationship between the opening themes of the first and last movements of this work:

(a)

(b)

---

36. Karl Geiringer, *Brahms: His Life and Works* (London: George Allen and Unwin, Ltd., 1936), p. 341.

37. See E. Markham Lee, *Brahms: the Man and His Music* (London: Sampson Low, Marston & Co., Ltd., 1916), p. 85; J. A. Fuller-Maitland, *Brahms* (London: Methuen & Co., Ltd., 1911), pp. 72–73; Peter Latham, *Brahms* (New York: Pellegrini and Cudahy, Inc., 1949), pp. 112–13.

An even clearer example of thematic transformation and cyclical recurrence occurs in the Second Piano Sonata, op. 2 (1852). Here the principal theme of the Andante becomes the principal theme of the Scherzo:

(a)

(b)

Liszt, who met Brahms in Weimar in 1853, was greatly impressed with these works and saw in Brahms a musical ally with similar aesthetic ideals. Regardless of whether the episode concerning Liszt's catching Brahms dozing while playing his B Minor Sonata is true or not,[38] it is quite clear that Brahms quickly became disaffected with Liszt's methods of composition. Brahms's "instinct for form . . . made him acutely conscious of the flimsiness of Liszt's compositions, of the woeful lack of consecutive thought and constructive power which no amount of bright colouring and superficial brilliance could hide."[39] Thus Brahms's sudden departure from Weimar was symbolic of a musical parting of the ways which was to last until Brahms's death.

38. According to Latham this was a fabrication of Reményi; see his *Brahms,* pp. 11–12.
39. *Ibid.*

Predictably, only rarely does one encounter these principles of composition, which rely chiefly on compensatory change, in the mature works of Brahms. Those which do come readily to mind are the Third Symphony, where the opening theme is quoted in the closing bars of the work, the String Quartet op. 67, where the principal subject of the first movement is contrapuntally combined with the main theme of the Finale, and the Violin Sonata in G Major, op. 78, where the repeated-note motif recurs with subtle modifications in each of the three movements. There are other works in which some form of cyclical recurrence and/or thematic metamorphosis occur: the Clarinet Quintet, op. 115, the String Quartet in C Minor, op. 51, no. 1, and the Horn Trio, op. 40. However, it is clear from Brahms's musical corpus that these are minority cases, wherein these techniques are used with the greatest discretion. The overwhelming majority of the symphonies, concertos, and chamber works depend on principles set forth in conjunction with Mozart and with musical Classicism. "Although successful in some cases, the principles of Liszt, with his metamorphosis of themes, and his contraction of cyclic works into one movement, have rarely been applied by Brahms."[40] The same opinion is expressed by Fuller-Maitland: "It is fairly clear that Brahms' adoption of the one invention claimed by the new school was never very whole-hearted."[41]

It is instructive to read Brahms's own view with respect to Liszt and his methods. In a letter to Clara Schumann, he wrote in 1857, "I feel uneasy about anything that smacks of Liszt" (*"ich habe eine wahre Angst vor allem, was nach Liszt riecht"*). In another letter to Clara, dated 1854, he refers to a "wild" (*"schwärmerisch"*) article on Liszt's Piano Sonata in the *Neue Zeitschrift für Musik*, which seems to have been evoked by "magnetic experiments" (*"durch magnetische Experimente hervorgerufen"*).[42] These letters were written when Brahms was twenty-four and twenty-one years old, respectively. Despite the fundamental differences between Brahms's and Liszt's philosophy of music, Brahms in his later years was able to take a more considered view of Liszt's achievement and significance. In a letter to his friend Theodor Billroth he wrote in 1886 (he was then fifty-three), "I am looking forward to his [Hanslick's] article

40. Lee, *Brahms,* pp. 84–85.
41. *Brahms,* pp. 72–73.
42. Berthold Litzmann, ed., *Clara Schumann Johannes Brahms: Briefe aus den Jahren 1853–1896.* 2 vols. (Leipzig: Breitkopf & Härtel, 1927), vol. 2, pp. 210, 19.

on Liszt, although one article is nothing for that man and his story."[43]

A corollary of the greater empiricism inherent in the principles under consideration is an intensified interest in sonority for its own sake. Here the romanticist concern for what Einstein terms "sheer sound" parallels the emphasis on color in the painting of the period.

> In the development of music, sheer sound has always played a role . . . but . . . never the significant one that it did in the Romantic period of the 19th century. . . . With the first Romantics, sound took on a new meaning. It was a stronger factor in the body of the music than it had ever been before; it won a higher value purely in and for itself.

Perhaps in this realm is the change from a more abstract conception of music in the previous era to the preoccupation with the phenomena of sound in the nineteenth century most clear. Bach's *Art of Fugue* has no specified instrumentation, while numerous of his concerti were readily transcribed from one medium to another. This relative indifference to performance medium and its associated sonority is characteristic of a mentality which regards music as something beyond mere sound, music as an ordered microcosm reflecting the order of the cosmos at large. Even in the works of Haydn, Mozart, and Beethoven, this implicit view of music persists. Thus instrumentation in musical Classicism was still something which was fairly uniform and conventional. Moreover, we are reminded, "there was no 'textbook of orchestration' in the 18th century." This state of affairs is unimaginable by the time of Berlioz and such works as his *Symphonie Fantastique* (1830). The symbol of the romantic approach to sonority was this composer's *Traité d'Instrumentation* (1844), "the bible of the new orchestral sonority."[44] Elsewhere we read,

> To Berlioz the orchestral setting of his music was no mere secondary matter. In his musical organism . . . instrumental effect occupied a position of great importance; so much so, that it is almost impossible to avoid the impression that he sometimes built up music in order to show off a particular pre-conceived orchestral effect.[45]

---

43. Hans Barkan, ed. and trans., *Johannes Brahms and Theodor Billroth: Letters from a Musical Friendship* (Norman, Okla.: University of Oklahoma Press, 1957), p. 170.

44. *Romantic Era*, pp. 7–8.

45. Adam Carse, *The History of Orchestration* (New York: Dover Publications, Inc., 1964), p. 255.

In this domain also, what can be said about Berlioz is applicable more or less to all composers of the era. "The unifying principle that links all the composers from Weber and Schubert to the end of the neo-Romantic movement and brings together such seemingly antipodal composers as Wagner and Brahms is this: their relationship to the most direct and perceptible element of music, its sound."[46] The symphony orchestra of such composers as Liszt, Wagner, and Strauss, in connection with this, reaches unprecedented levels of sheer power and coloristic range. The extreme form of this development may be noted in Mahler's Eighth Symphony (1906-7), which is scored for the following mammoth complement of instruments: piccolo, four flutes, four oboes, English horn, E-flat clarinet, three B-flat clarinets, bass clarinet, four bassoons, contrabassoon; eight horns, four trumpets, four trombones, tuba, timpani, bass drum, cymbals, tam-tam, triangle, chimes, glockenspiel, celesta; piano, harmonium, organ, two harps, mandolin; four trumpets and three trombones as a fanfare group; first and second soprano, first and second alto, tenor, baritone, and bass soloists, two mixed choruses, boys' choir; first violins, second violins, violas, violoncellos, and double-basses.

Although moving in a different direction from Mahler, Debussy and musical Impressionism constitute the final stage in this development. In Impressionism the abstract-relational components of music, such as formal pattern, thematic development, and harmonic structure, are almost totally superseded by a succession of tonal colors, atmospheric effects, and subtle gradations in tonal intensity. The expression "orchestral palette," according to Apel,[47] has been frequently applied to describe this technique.

In Debussy's hand the orchestra became a super-sensitive instrument. In *Pélleas and Mélisande* (score 1902) it murmurs dreamily to itself, speaks or suggests in veiled tones, swells up for a moment and again subsides or dwindles down almost to disappearance. The outspoken clearness, the well-defined outlines and transparent intentions of his native predecessors were of less use to Debussy than their delicacy and their tentative experiments in impressionistic tone-painting.[48]

This radically empirical approach to music has its counterpart, as has been noted, in painting, literature, philosophy, and even in science. That the epistemological limit of this method had

46. Einstein, *Romantic Era*, p. 8.
47. *Dictionary*, p. 521.
48. Carse, *Orchestration*, p. 325.

been reached during the final decades of the nineteenth century is well illustrated by the rapidly growing reassertion of the *logos* in Western mentality during succeeding years. Neoclassicism in music, analytical cubism in painting, logic in philosophy, and a more abstract foundation in physical science are all manifestations of this reversal.

Indeed, the twentieth century may be characterized, to a large extent, by a synthesis of eighteenth-century logocentrism and nineteenth-century biocentrism. The contemporary science of biophysics is indicative of this synthesis, and further suggests a more holistic approach to the description of nature. This is evident in the work of such eminent thinkers as Niels Bohr, Walter M. Elsasser, and Werner Heisenberg. Bohr, for example,[49] dwells on the wholeness and irreducibility of atomic processes on the quantum level, and on a parallel wholeness and irreducibility of living organisms, both being limiting cases. In addition to this, the principle of complementarity as a means of understanding inhomogeneous processes in organic and inorganic nature plays a central role in Bohr's thought. A similar synthesis is apparent in the work of Elsasser,[50] who extends physics in such manner as to incorporate the uniquely complex properties of life. Finally, the introduction of the uncertainty principle by Heisenberg,[51] with its attendant weaker causality, has enlarged our view of nature to the extent of reintroducing the ancient Greek speculative component into knowledge. That this principle, combined with the influence of Oriental philosophy, has had wide cultural repercussions during the past twenty years or so, is witnessed by the introduction of random elements in all sectors of the creative arts.[52]

We have surveyed three centuries of Western culture. Analysis of the evidence introduced from the major areas of the creative arts has revealed that cultural change, beginning with the Renaissance-Modern world, is intimately linked with change in theories of nature and their attendant epistemologies. It has been disclosed that the cosmological development which began with Copernicus

---

49. *Atomic Physics and Human Knowledge* (New York: Science Editions, Inc., 1961), pp. 5–101, *passim*.

50. *Atom and Organism: A New Approach to Theoretical Biology* (Princeton, N. J.: Princeton University Press, 1966).

51. Werner Heisenberg, *Physics and Philosophy* (New York: Harper & Brothers, 1958; reprinted by Harper Torchbooks, 1962).

52. See further Joseph Blass, "Indeterminacy as a Factor in Scientific and Artistic Attitudes of the Twentieth Century" (Ph.D. diss., Florida State University, Tallahassee, 1968).

and culminated with Newton infected the intellectual environment of the civilized world, and concretely affected man's conception of the universe, himself, and his creative products. It has also been disclosed that the cosmological change which began *ca.* 1750, and which came to a climax with Darwin, was largely due to the emergence and influence of the life sciences and their unique methodology. The consequences of this change were likewise palpably felt in all provinces of human thought and creativity. This study thus illustrates the proposition that civilizations are what they are by virtue of their view of nature.

Bibliography

Books

Abrams, M. H., ed. *English Romantic Poets*. New York: Oxford University Press, 1960.

————. *The Mirror and the Lamp: Romantic Theory and the Critical Tradition*. New York: Oxford University Press, 1953. Reprinted by W. W. Norton & Co., Inc., 1958.

Aiken, Henry. *The Age of Ideology: The 19th Century Philosophers*. Selected, with an Introduction and Interpretive Commentary by Henry Aiken. New York: The New American Library (Mentor Books), 1956.

Allen, Warren D. *Philosophies of Music History*. New York: Dover Publications, Inc., 1962.

Andrade, E. N. da C. *Sir Isaac Newton*. New York: The Macmillan Company, 1954. Reprinted by Doubleday & Company, Inc. (Anchor Books), Garden City, N.Y., n.d.

Apel, Willi. *Harvard Dictionary of Music*. Cambridge, Mass.: Harvard University Press, 1947.

Aristotle. *Physics. Great Books of the Western World*, vol. 8. Chicago: Encyclopaedia Britannica, Inc., 1952.

Baker, James V. *The Sacred River: Coleridge's Theory of the Imagination*. Baton Rouge, La.: Louisiana State University Press, 1957.

Barkan, Hans, ed. and translator. *Johannes Brahms and Theodor Billroth: Letters from a Musical Friendship*. Norman, Okla.: University of Oklahoma Press, 1957.

Barzun, Jacques. *Classic, Romantic and Modern*. Boston: Little, Brown & Co., 1963.

————. *Darwin, Marx, Wagner: Critique of a Heritage*. 2d. rev. ed. Boston: Little, Brown & Company, Inc., 1941. Reprinted by Doubleday & Company, Inc. (Anchor Books), Garden City, N.Y., 1958.

————. *Science: The Glorious Entertainment*. New York: Harper & Row, Publishers, 1964.

Baskett, John. *Constable Oil Sketches.* New York: Watson-Guptill Publications, 1966.

Bate, Walter Jackson. *From Classic to Romantic: Premises of Taste in Eighteenth-Century England.* New York: Harper & Row, 1946. Reprinted by Harper Torchbooks, 1961.

Beach, Joseph W. *The Concept of Nature in Nineteenth-Century English Poetry.* New York: Pageant Book Co., 1956.

———. *A Romantic View of Poetry.* Minneapolis: The University of Minnesota Press, 1944.

Beardsley, Monroe C. *Aesthetics: Problems in the Philosophy of Criticism.* New York: Harcourt, Brace & Co., 1958.

Beck, William S. *Modern Science and the Nature of Life.* New York: Harcourt, Brace and Company, 1957. Reprinted by Doubleday & Company, Inc. (Anchor Books), Garden City, N.Y., in cooperation with The American Museum of Natural History, 1961.

Berlin, Isaiah. *The Age of Enlightenment: the 18th Century Philosophers.* Selected, with Introduction and Interpretive Commentary by Isaiah Berlin. New York: The New American Library (Mentor Books), 1956.

Binkley, Robert C. *Realism and Nationalism, 1852–1871.* New York: Harper & Brothers, 1935. Reprinted by Harper Torchbooks, 1963.

Blackburn, Robert T., ed. *Interrelations: The Biological and Physical Sciences.* Chicago: Scott, Foresman & Co., 1966.

Blume, Friedrich, ed. *Die Musik in Geschichte und Gegenwart.* Kassel und Basel: Bärenreiter-Verlag, 1949–68.

Bohr, Niels. *Atomic Physics and Human Knowledge.* New York: Science Editions, Inc., 1961.

Bowle, John and Willey, Basil. "Origins and Development of the Idea of Progress," in *Ideas and Beliefs of the Victorians.* New York: E. P. Dutton & Co., Inc., 1966.

Brewster, Sir David. *Memoirs of the Life, Writings, and Discoveries of Sir Isaac Newton.* The Sources of Science, vol. 2, no. 14. New York and London: Johnson Reprint Corporation, 1965.

Bridgman, P. W. *The Way Things Are.* Cambridge, Mass.: Harvard University Press, 1959. Reprinted by The Viking Press, New York, 1961.

Brown, K. C. *Hobbes Studies.* Oxford: Basil Blackwell, 1965.

Bukofzer, Manfred F. *Music in the Baroque Era.* New York: W. W. Norton & Co., 1947.

Burney, Charles. *A General History of Music.* 2 vols. New York: Harcourt, Brace and Company, n.d.

Bury, J. B. *The Idea of Progress.* London: Macmillan and Co., Limited, 1920.

Butterfield, H. *The Origins of Modern Science.* New York: The Macmillan Company, 1951.

Calder, Ritchie. *Man and the Cosmos: the Nature of Science Today.* New York: Frederick A. Praeger, Publishers, 1968.

Cannon, Beekman C.; Johnson, Alvin H.; and Waite, William G. *The Art of Music.* New York: Thomas Y. Crowell Company, 1960.

Carse, Adam. *The History of Orchestration.* New York: Dover Publications, Inc., 1964.

Cassirer, Ernst. *The Philosophy of the Enlightenment.* Translated by Fritz C. A. Koelln and James P. Pettegrove. Princeton, N.J.: Princeton University Press, 1951. Reprinted by the Beacon Press, Boston, 1964.

————. *Rousseau, Kant and Goethe.* Translated by James Gutmann *et al.* Princeton, N.J.: Princeton University Press, 1945. Reprinted by Harper & Row, New York, 1963.

Cassirer, Fritz. *Beethoven und die Gestalt.* Stuttgart: Deutsche Verlags-Anstalt, 1925.

Caullery, Maurice. *A History of Biology.* New York: Walker and Co., 1966.

Chipp, Herschel B., ed. *Theories of Modern Art: A Source Book by Artists and Critics.* Berkeley: University of California Press, 1968.

Clagett, Marshall, ed. *Critical Problems in the History of Science.* Madison, Wis.: The University of Wisconsin Press, 1959.

Coleridge, Samuel Taylor. *Biographia Literaria.* Edited by John Calvin Metcalf. New York: The Macmillan Co., 1926.

Collingwood, R. G. *The Idea of History.* New York: Oxford University Press, 1946. Reprinted by Oxford Galaxy Books, 1959.

————. *The Idea of Nature.* New York: Oxford University Press, 1945. Reprinted by Oxford Galaxy Books, 1960.

Commoner, Barry. *Science and Survival.* New York: The Viking Press, 1966.

Cook, Theodore A. *The Curves of Life.* New York: Henry Holt and Co., 1914.

Crocker, Richard L. *A History of Musical Style.* New York: McGraw-Hill, 1966.

Dampier, Sir William C. *A History of Science and Its Relations with Philosophy and Religion.* New York: The Macmillan Co., 1943.

————. *A Shorter History of Science.* New York: The Macmillan Co., 1944.

Dantzig, Tobias. *Number: the Language of Science.* New York: The Macmillan Company, 1930. Reprinted by Doubleday and Company, Inc. (Anchor Books), Garden City, N.Y., 1954.

Davidson, Robert F., *et al. The Humanities in Contemporary Life.* New York: Holt, Rinehart and Winston, 1960.

Demuth, Norman. *César Franck.* London: Dennis Dobson Ltd., 1949.

Descartes, René. *Discourse on Method.* Translated with an Introduction by Arthur Wollaston. Baltimore: Penguin Books, 1960.

————. *Discourse on Method*. Translated by Elizabeth S. Haldane and G. R. T. Ross. *Great Books of the Western World*. vol. 31. Chicago: Encyclopaedia Britannica, Inc., 1952.

D'Indy, Vincent. *Beethoven*. Translated by Th. Baker. Boston: The Boston Music Co., 1911.

————. *César Franck*. Translated by Rosa Newmarch. London: John Lane the Bodley Head, Ltd., 1909.

Driesch, Hans. *The Science and Philosophy of the Organism*. London: A. & C. Black, Ltd., 1929.

Drinker, Henry S., Jr. *The Chamber Music of Johannes Brahms*. Philadelphia: Elkan-Vogel Co., 1932.

Durant, Will and Ariel. *The Story of Civilization*. Part 10. *Rousseau and Revolution*. New York: Simon and Schuster, 1967.

Einstein, Albert. *Essays in Science*. New York: The Wisdom Library, a Division of Philosophical Library, n.d.

————. *Ideas and Opinions*. Edited by Carl Seelig. New York: Crown Publishers, Inc., 1954.

Einstein, Alfred. *Music in the Romantic Era*. New York: W. W. Norton & Co., 1947.

Eiseley, Loren. *Darwin's Century: Evolution and the Men Who Discovered It*. New York: Doubleday Anchor Books, 1958.

Elsasser, Walter M. *Atom and Organism: A New Approach to Theoretical Biology*. Princeton, N.J.: Princeton University Press, 1966.

————. *The Physical Foundation of Biology: An Analytical Study*. New York: Pergamon Press, 1958.

Epperson, Gordon. *The Musical Symbol*. Ames, Iowa: Iowa State University Press, 1967.

Fleming, William. *Arts and Ideas*. 3rd. ed. New York: Holt, Rinehart and Winston, Inc., n.d.

Ford, Boris, ed. *From Dryden to Johnson*. Baltimore: Penguin Books, 1963.

Fuller-Maitland, J. A. *Brahms*. London: Methuen & Co., Ltd., 1911.

Gage, John. *Color in Turner*. New York: Frederick A. Praeger, Publishers, 1969.

Galilei, Galileo. *Discoveries and Opinions of Galileo*. Translated by Stillman Drake. Garden City, N.Y.: Doubleday Anchor Books, 1957.

Gasking, Elizabeth B. *Investigations into Generation 1651–1828*. Baltimore: The Johns Hopkins Press, n.d.

Geiringer, Karl. *Brahms: His Life and Work*. London: George Allen and Unwin, Ltd., 1936.

————. *Haydn, a Creative Life in Music*. New York: W. W. Norton & Co., 1946.

Giedion, Siegfried. *Space, Time and Architecture: The Growth of a New Tradition*. Cambridge, Mass.: Harvard University Press, 1963.

Gode-von Aesch, Alexander. *Natural Science in German Romanticism*. No. 11 of the Columbia University Germanic Studies. Edited by

Robert Herndon Fife. New Series. New York: Columbia University Press, 1941. Reprinted by the AMS Press, New York, 1966.

Goethe, John Wolfgang von. *Faust.* Part I. Translated by Bayard Taylor. New York: Appleton-Century-Crofts, Inc., 1946.

Gray, Cecil. *Contingencies and Other Essays.* New York: Oxford University Press, 1947.

————. *The History of Music.* London: Kegan Paul, Trench, Trubner & Co., Ltd., 1947.

Greene, John C. *Darwin and the Modern World View.* Baton Rouge, La.: Louisiana State University Press, 1961.

————. *The Death of Adam: Evolution and Its Impact on Western Thought.* Ames, Iowa: Iowa State University Press, 1959. Reprinted by The New American Library (Mentor Books), New York, 1961.

Grout, Donald J. *A History of Western Music.* New York: W. W. Norton & Co., 1960.

Hambidge, Jay. *The Elements of Dynamic Symmetry.* New Haven: Yale University Press, 1959.

Hampshire, Stuart. *The Age of Reason: the 17th Century Philosophers.* Selected, with Introduction and Commentary by Stuart Hampshire. New York: The New American Library (Mentor Books), 1956.

Heffernan, James A. W. *Wordsworth's Theory of Poetry: The Transforming Imagination.* Ithaca, N.Y.: Cornell University Press, 1969.

Heisenberg, Werner. *Physics and Philosophy: The Revolution in Modern Science.* New York: Harper & Brothers, 1958. Reprinted by Harper Torchbooks, 1962.

Herbert, Robert L., ed. *The Art Criticism of John Ruskin.* Garden City, N.Y.: Doubleday & Company, Inc. (Anchor Books), 1964.

Hobbes, Thomas. *Body, Man and Citizen.* Edited by Richard S. Peters. New York: Collier Books, 1962.

Höffding, Harald. *A History of Modern Philosophy.* New York: Dover Publications, Inc., 1955.

Hogarth, William. *The Analysis of Beauty.* Edited with an Introduction by Joseph Burke. Oxford: The Clarendon Press, 1955.

Holt, Elizabeth, ed. *Literary Sources of Art History: An Anthology of Texts from Theophilus to Goethe.* Princeton, N.J.: Princeton University Press, 1947.

————, ed. *From the Classicists to the Impressionists: A Documentary History of Art and Architecture in the Nineteenth Century.* Garden City, N.Y.: Doubleday & Co., Inc. (Anchor Books), 1966.

Hull, Lewis W. H. *History and Philosophy of Science.* London: Longmans, Green and Co., 1959.

Hume, David. *A Treatise of Human Nature.* Book I: *Of the Understanding.* Edited with an Introduction by D. G. C. Macnabb. Cleveland and New York: The World Publishing Company (Meridian Books), 1962.

Ingarden, Roman. *Untersuchungen zur Ontologie der Kunst.* Tübingen: Max Niemeyer Verlag, 1962.

Kline, Morris. *Mathematics in Western Culture.* New York: Oxford University Press, 1964.

Kuhn, Thomas S. *The Structure of Scientific Revolutions. International Encyclopedia of Unified Science,* vol. 2, no. 2. Chicago: The University of Chicago Press, 1962.

Lang, Paul H. *Music in Western Civilization.* New York: W. W. Norton & Co., 1941.

Landon, H. C. Robbins and Mitchell, Donald, eds. *The Mozart Companion.* New York: Oxford University Press, 1956.

Langer, Suzanne K. *Feeling and Form: A Theory of Art.* New York: Charles Scribner's Sons, 1953.

Latham, Peter. *Brahms.* New York: Pellegrini and Cudahy, Inc., 1949.

Lee, E. Markham. *Brahms the Man and His Music.* London: Sampson Low, Marston & Co., Ltd., 1916.

Leichtentritt, Hugo. *Musical Form.* Cambridge, Mass.: Harvard University Press, 1951.

————. *Music, History, and Ideas.* Cambridge, Mass.: Harvard University Press, 1964.

Levey, Michael. *Rococo to Revolution: Major Trends in Eighteenth-Century Painting.* New York: Frederick A. Praeger, Publishers, 1966.

Lilley, S., ed. *Essays on the Social History of Science.* Copenhagen: Ejnar Munksgaard, 1953.

Liszt, Franz, Letters of. Collected and edited by La Mara, translated by Constance Bache. 2 vols. New York: Charles Scribner's Sons, 1894.

Litzmann, Berthold, ed. *Clara Schumann Johannes Brahms, Briefe aus den Jahren 1853–1896.* 2 vols. Breitkopf & Härtel, 1927.

Loeb, Jacques. *The Mechanistic Conception of Life.* Edited with an Introduction by Donald Fleming. Cambridge, Mass.: The Belknap Press of Harvard University Press, 1964.

Lovejoy, Arthur O. *The Great Chain of Being; a Study in the History of an Idea.* Cambridge, Mass.: Harvard University Press, 1936.

Mack, Gerstle. *Gustave Courbet.* New York: Alfred A. Knopf, 1951.

Magnus, Rudolf. *Goethe as a Scientist.* New York: H. Schuman, 1949.

Marrou, Henri-Irénée. *The Meaning of History.* Translated by Robert J. Olsen. Baltimore and Dublin: Helicon Press, Inc., 1966.

Mason, Stephen F. *A History of the Sciences.* New York: Crowell-Collier Publishing Company, 1962. Previously published as *Main Currents of Scientific Thought,* by Abelard-Schuman Limited, New York, 1956.

Mead, George H. *Movements of Thought in the Nineteenth Century.* Chicago: The University of Chicago Press, 1936.

Meessen, H. J., ed. *Goethe Bicentennial Studies,* by Members of the Faculty of Indiana University. Bloomington, Ind.: Indiana University Press, 1950.

Mellers, Wilfrid. *Romanticism and the 20th Century*. Fair Lawn, N.J.: Essential Books, Inc., 1957.

Melsen, Andrew G. van. *Evolution and Philosophy*. Pittsburgh, Pa.: Duquesne University Press, 1965.

Merz, John T. *A History of European Thought in the Nineteenth Century*. 4 vols. New York: Dover Publications, Inc., 1965.

Meyer, Leonard B. *Emotion and Meaning in Music*. Chicago: The University of Chicago Press, 1965.

Morrison, Hugh. *Louis Sullivan: Prophet of Modern Architecture*. New York: The Museum of Modern Art and W. W. Norton & Co., Inc., 1935.

Murray, Peter and Linda. *Dictionary of Art and Artists*. Baltimore: Penguin Books, 1963.

Nallin, Walter. *The Musical Idea*. New York: The Macmillan Co., 1968.

Newman, William S. *The Sonata in the Baroque Era*. Chapel Hill: The University of North Carolina Press, 1959.

———. *The Sonata in the Classical Era*. Chapel Hill: The University of North Carolina Press, 1963.

———. *Understanding Music*. New York: Harper & Row, 1961.

Niemann, Walter. *Brahms*. New York: Alfred A. Knopf, Inc., 1929.

Northrop, F. S. C., ed. *Ideological Differences and World Order*. New Haven: Yale University Press, 1949.

Northrop, F. S. C. *The Logic of the Sciences and the Humanities*. New York: The Macmillan Company, 1947. Reprinted by The World Publishing Company (Meridian Books), New York, 1959.

———. *Man, Nature and God*. New York: Pocket Books, Inc., 1963.

———. *The Meeting of East and West*. New York: The Macmillan Co., 1946.

Parrish, Carl and Ohl, John F. *Masterpieces of Music Before 1750*. New York: W. W. Norton & Co., 1940.

Pauly, Reinhard G. *Music in the Classic Period*. Englewood Cliffs, N.J.: Prentice-Hall, Inc., 1965.

Persons, Stow, ed. *Evolutionary Thought in America*. New Haven: Yale University Press, 1950.

Pevsner, Nikolaus. *An Outline of European Architecture*. Baltimore: Penguin Books, 1961.

Plato. *The Dialogues of Plato*. Translated by Benjamin Jowett; vol. 7 of *Great Books of the Western World*. Chicago: Encyclopaedia Britannica, Inc., 1952.

———. *Great Dialogues of Plato*. Translated by W. H. D. Rouse. Edited by Eric H. Warmington and Philip G. Rouse. New York: The New American Library (Mentor Books), 1956.

Polanyi, Michael. *The Tacit Dimension*. Garden City, N.Y.: Doubleday & Company, Inc. (Anchor Books), 1967.

Rader, Melvin. *Wordsworth: A Philosophical Approach.* Oxford at the Clarendon Press, 1967.

Rameau, Jean-Philippe. *Complete Theoretical Writings.* vol. 1. *Traité de l'harmonie réduite à ses principes naturels.* Edited by Erwin R. Jacobi. N.p.: American Institute of Musicology, 1967.

Randall, John Herman, Jr. *The Making of the Modern Mind.* New York: Houghton Mifflin Co., 1926.

Reese, Gustave. *Music in the Middle Ages.* New York: W. W. Norton & Co., 1940.

————. *Music in the Renaissance.* New York: W. W. Norton & Co., 1954.

Reti, Rudolph. *Thematic Patterns in the Sonatas of Beethoven.* New York: Macmillan Co., 1968.

————. *The Thematic Process in Music.* London: Faber & Faber, 1961.

Reynolds, Sir Joshua. *Discourses on Art.* Edited with an Introduction by Robert R. Clark. San Marino, Calif.: Huntington Library, 1959.

Richards, J. M. *An Introduction to Modern Architecture.* Harmondsworth, Middlesex: Penguin Books, Ltd., 1940.

Rosen, Robert. *Optimality Principles in Biology.* London: Butterworths, 1967.

Rozental, S., ed. *Niels Bohr: His Life and Work as Seen by His Friends and Colleagues.* New York: John Wiley & Sons, Inc., 1967.

Rufer, Josef. *Composition with Twelve Tones.* London: Rockliff, 1954.

————. *Das Werk Arnold Schönbergs.* Kassel: Bärenreiter-Verlag, 1959.

Ruskin, John. *The Criticism of John Ruskin.* Selected, edited and with an Introduction by Robert L. Herbert. New York: Doubleday & Company, Inc. (Anchor Books), 1964.

Russell, Bertrand. *A History of Philosophy.* New York: Simon & Schuster, Inc., 1965.

Rutland, William R. "Tennyson and the Theory of Evolution." *Essays and Studies by Members of the English Association,* vol. 26. Oxford: The Clarendon Press, 1940.

Sachs, Curt. *Our Musical Heritage.* Englewood Cliffs, N.J.: Prentice-Hall, Inc., 1955.

Sarton, George. *The Life of Science: Essays in the History of Civilization.* New York: Henry Schuman, Inc., 1948.

Schauffler, Robert H. *Franz Schubert: The Ariel of Music.* New York: G. P. Putnam's Sons, 1949.

Schenker, Heinrich. *Harmony.* Translated by Elizabeth Mann Borgese and edited by Oswald Jonas. Chicago: The University of Chicago Press, 1954.

Schilpp, Paul, ed. *Albert Einstein: Philosopher—Scientist.* vol. 1. New York: Tudor Publishing Company and the Library of Living Philosophers, Inc., 1949. Reprinted by Harper & Brothers (Harper Torchbooks), 1959.

Schoenberg, Arnold. *Style and Idea*. New York: Philosophical Library, 1950.

Schrödinger, Erwin. *What is Life? and Other Scientific Essays*. Garden City, N.Y.: Doubleday & Company, Inc. (Anchor Books), 1956.

Sherrington, Sir Charles S. *Goethe on Nature and on Science*. Cambridge, Eng.: The University Press, 1949.

Shipley, Joseph T., ed. *Dictionary of World Literature*. Paterson, N.J.: Littlefield, Adams & Co., 1960.

Shirlaw, Matthew. *The Theory and Nature of Harmony*. Box 91-C, RR #1, Sarasota, Fla. 33577, Dr. Birchard Coar, 1970.

Sitwell, Sacheverell. *Liszt*. New York: Dover Publications, Inc., 1967.

Sullivan, Louis H. *Kindergarten Chats and Other Writings. The Documents of Modern Art*. Director, Robert Motherwell. New York: George Wittenborn, Inc., 1965.

Szabolcsi, Bence. *A History of Melody*. Translated by Cynthia Jolly and Sára Karig. New York: St. Martin's Press, 1965.

Taton, René, ed. *History of Science. The Beginnings of Modern Science From 1450 to 1800,* vol. 2. *Science in the Nineteenth Century,* vol. 3. New York: Basic Books, Inc., 1964, 1965.

Thompson, D'Arcy W. *On Growth and Form*. New York: The Macmillan Company, 1943.

Tovey, Donald F. *Essays in Musical Analysis,* vols. 1–7. London: Oxford University Press, 1935–44.

————. *Musical Articles from the Encyclopaedia Britannica*. New York: Oxford University Press, 1944. Reprinted by The World Publishing Company (Meridian Books), New York, as *The Forms of Music,* 1956.

————. *Essays and Lectures on Music*. New York: Oxford University Press, 1949. Reprinted by The World Publishing Company (Meridian Books), New York, as *The Main Stream of Music and Other Essays,* 1959.

Toynbee, Arnold. *A Study of History*. 2 vol. abridgement by D. C. Somervell. New York: Oxford University Press, 1946.

Ulrich, Homer. *Chamber Music: The Growth and Practice of an Intimate Art*. New York: Columbia University Press, 1948.

Ulrich, Homer and Pisk, Paul A. *A History of Music and Musical Style*. New York: Harcourt, Brace & World, Inc., 1963.

Ulrich, Homer. *Symphonic Music: Its Evolution Since the Renaissance*. New York: Columbia University Press, 1952.

Ungar, Frederick. *Goethe's World View*. New York: Frederick Ungar Publishing Co., 1963.

Veinus, Abraham. *The Concerto*. New York: Doubleday, Doran & Co., Inc., 1945.

Watt, Ian. *The Rise of the Novel*. Berkeley: University of California Press, 1957.

Webern, Anton von. *The Path to the New Music*. Edited by Willi Reich and translated by Leo Black. Bryn Mawr, Pa.: T. Presser Co., 1963.

Wellek, René. *Concepts of Criticism.* New Haven and London: Yale University Press, 1963.

――――. *A History of Modern Criticism: 1750–1950.* 4 vols. New Haven: Yale University Press, 1955.

Whitehead, A. N. *Adventures of Ideas.* New York: The Macmillan Company, 1933. Reprinted by The New American Library (Mentor Books), 1955.

――――. *Modes of Thought.* New York: The Macmillan Company, 1938. Reprinted by G. P. Putnam's Sons (Capricorn Books), New York, 1958.

――――. *Science and the Modern World.* New York: The Macmillan Company, 1925. Reprinted by the New American Library (Mentor Books), New York, 1959.

Wiener, Norbert. *The Human Use of Human Beings: Cybernetics and Society.* New York: Houghton Mifflin Company, 1952. Reprinted by Avon Books, New York, 1967.

Wiener, Philip P. and Noland, Aaron, eds. *Roots of Scientific Thought; a Cultural Perspective.* New York: Basic Books, Inc., 1957.

Willey, Basil. *The Eighteenth Century Background: Studies on the Idea of Nature in the Thought of the Period.* New York: Columbia University Press, 1940. Reprinted by The Beacon Press, Boston, 1961.

――――. "How the Scientific Revolution of the Seventeenth Century Affected Other Branches of Thought." *A Short History of Science.* Garden City, N.Y.: Doubleday Anchor Books, 1959.

――――. *More Nineteenth Century Studies; A Group of Honest Doubters.* New York: Columbia University Press, 1956. Reprinted by Harper Torchbooks, New York, 1966.

Wilshire, Bruce, ed. *Romanticism and Evolution: The Nineteenth Century.* New York: G. P. Putnam's Sons, 1968.

Windelband, Wilhelm. *A History of Philosophy.* vol. 2. New York: Harper & Brothers, 1958.

Wordsworth, William. *The Prelude with Other Poems, and Three Essays on the Art of Poetry.* Edited by Carlos Baker. New York: Holt, Rinehart and Winston, 1965.

Wright, Frank Lloyd. *Writings and Buildings.* Selected by Edgar Kaufmann and Ben Raeburn. New York: Meridian Books, Inc., 1960.

Articles

Aiken, Henry D. "The Aesthetic Relevance of Belief." *Journal of Aesthetics* 9 (1950): 301–15.

Benziger, James. "Organic Unity: Leibniz to Coleridge." *Publications of the Modern Language Association of America* 66 (March 1951): 24–48.

Castex, Pierre-George. "French Literature." *Encyclopaedia Britannica* 9 (1964): 894–900.

David, Hans. "Principles of Form in Use from the Middle Ages to the Present Day." *Bulletin of the American Musicological Society,* nos. 9–10 (June 1947), pp. 9–10.

House, Humphry. "Man and Nature: Some Artists' Views," in *Ideas and Beliefs of the Victorians.* New York: E. P. Dutton & Co., Inc., 1966.

Jacobi, Erwin R. "Rameau, Jean-Phillipe." *Die Musik in Geschichte und Gegenwart.* Kassel und Basel: Bärenreiter-Verlag, 1962, vol. 10. cols. 1898–1907.

Keller, Hans. "K503: The Unity of Contrasting Themes and Movements." *The Music Review* 17 (February–May 1956) : 48–58 and 120–29.

Kitson, Michael W. L. "Poussin, Nicolas." *Encyclopaedia Britannica* 18 (1964) : 383–84.

Locke, Arthur W. "Descartes and Seventeenth-Century Music." *The Musical Quarterly* 21 (1935) : 423–31.

Lowinsky, Edward E. "The Concepts of Physical and Musicological Space in the Renaissance." *Papers of the American Musicological Society— 1941* (1946).

MacBride, Ernest W. and Wigglesworth, Vincent B. "Metamorphosis." *Encyclopaedia Britannica* 15 (1964) : 323.

Marx, Karl. *"Über die Zyklische Sonatenform"* *("Zu dem Aufsatz von Günther von Noé").* *Neue Zeitschrift für Musik* 125, no. 4 (1964) : 142–46.

Nordmark, Jan. "New Theories of Form and the Problem of Thematic Identities." *Journal of Music Theory* 4 (November 1960) : 210–17.

Noé, Günther von. *"Der Strukturwandel der Zyklischen Sonatenform."* *Neue Zeitschrift für Musik* 125, no. 2 (1964) : 55–62.

Northrop, F. S. C. "The History of Modern Physics in its Bearing Upon Biology and Medicine." *Yale Journal of Biology and Medicine* 10 (1937–38) : 209–32.

————. "Toward a General Theory of the Arts." *The Journal of Value Inquiry* 1, no. 2 (Fall 1967) : 96–116.

Smith, Warren S. "The Cyclic Principle in Musical Design, and the Use of It by Bruckner and Mahler." *Chord and Discord* 2, no. 9 (1960) : 3–35.

Stephan, Rudolf. "Descartes, René." *Die Musik in Geschichte und Gegenwart.* Kassel und Basel: Bärenreiter-Verlag, 1954, vol. 3, cols. 209–11.

Supičić, Ivo. "Science on Music and Values in Music." *The Journal of Aesthetics and Art Criticism* 28 (Fall 1969) : 71–77.

Treitler, Leo. "On Historical Criticism." *The Musical Quarterly* 53 (April 1967) : 188–205.

Watt, Ian. "Novel." *Encyclopaedia Britannica* 16 (1964) : 511–81.

Wilkinson, Elizabeth M. "Goethe, Johann Wolfgang von." *Encyclopaedia Britannica* 10 (1964) :522–29.

Wolf, Robert Erich. "The Aesthetic Problem of the Renaissance." *Revue belge de musicologie* 9, nos. 3–4 (1955).

Miscellaneous

Badura-Skoda, Paul. Preface to Franz Schubert's Fantasy in C Minor. Vienna: Universal Edition, 1965.

Bauman, Alvin. Review of the *Thematic Process in Music* by Rudolph Reti, *Journal of the American Musicological Society* 5 (Summer 1952) : 140–41.

Blom, Eric. Review of *The Mozart Companion*. *Music and Letters* 37 (July 1956) : 287.

Northrop, F. S. C. "The Relationally Analytic and the Impressionistically Concrete Components of Classical Western Music." Essay based on the speech delivered to the Tanglewood Symposium of "Music in American Society" sponsored by the Music Educators National Conference, July 24, 1967, Heaton Hall, Stockbridge, Massachusetts.

Ringer, Alexander, Stevens, Denis, and Buelow, George J. "Guidelines for The Doctor of Philosophy Degree in Musicology." Prepared by the Committee on Curriculum and Accreditation of the American Musicological Society. 1st ed. December 1969.

Unpublished

Anderson, Thomas J. "A Study of Correspondence between Musical Style and Instrumental Technology." Master's thesis, Florida State University, Tallahassee, 1967.

Blass, Joseph. "Indeterminacy as a Factor in Scientific and Artistic Attitudes of the Twentieth Century." Ph.D. diss., Florida State University, Tallahassee, 1968.

Camp, Jane Perry. "Temporal Proportion: A Study of Sonata Forms in the Piano Sonatas of Mozart." Ph.D. diss., School of Music, Florida State University, Tallahassee, 1968.

Carter, Roy E. "Barock, by Friedrich Blume: a Translation." Master's thesis, School of Music, Florida State University, Tallahassee, 1961.

Eddins, John M. "A Study of Cartesian Musical Thought, with a Complete Translation of the *Compendium musicae*." Master's thesis, School of Music, Florida State University, Tallahassee, 1959.

Kliewer, Vernon I. "The Concept of Organic Unity in Music Criticism and Analysis." Ph.D. diss., Indiana University, 1961.

Opper, Jacob. "'Klassik' by Friedrich Blume: a Translation." Master's thesis, School of Music, Florida State University, Tallahassee, 1965.

Singleton, Ira C. "The Rationality of 18th Century Musical Classicism." Ph.D. diss., New York University, 1954.

Spratt, John F. "Philosophical Implications of Modern Science as Reflected in the History of Music." Paper presented at Hiram College, Hiram, Ohio, November 1969.

———. "The Speculative Content of Schoenberg's *Harmonielehre*." Paper presented at the American Musicological Society Convention, South Central Chapter, March 1968.

————. "The Unity of Baroque Culture." Paper presented at Brunswick Junior College, Brunswick, Georgia, January 1967.

Taylor, Gene Fred. "Culturally Transcendent Factors in Musical Perception." Ph.D. diss., Florida State University, 1969.

Wilcox, James H. "The Symphonies of A. Bruckner." Ph.D. diss., Florida State University, 1956.

Index

Abrams, M. H., 158
Abstract deduction, 126
Abstraction, of mathematical physics, 33; Newton's postulates, 45
Addison, Joseph, 64, 65
Adler, 98
Adventures of Ideas (Whitehead), 14
Aesthetics, 60, 61, 62
Affectenlehre, 71, 72, 88
Age of Prose, 63
Age of Reason, 62, 75, 89
Aiken, Henry D., 111–12, 150
American Musicological Society: "Guidelines for the Doctor of Philosophy Degree in Musicology," 12
Animism, 150
Anthropomorphism, 150
Apassionata Sonata (Beethoven), 187
Apel, Willi, 185, 189
Application, period of, 45, 51, 79
Arabic *maqam,* 192
Architecture: Greek and Roman, 83; nineteenth-century, 174–79; organic, 176–79
Aristotle: cosmology, 47; forms by privation, 91, 115; inductive epistemology, 46; organismic concept of nature, 42
Art: Descartes's theory, 50; eighteenth-century law, 62; and nature, parallel properties, 158; nineteenth-century, 173; vitalistic concept, 42
Art of Fugue (Bach), 76, 77, 86, 180, 201
Arts, visual, 68
Aubignac, François d', 61

Bach, Johann Sebastian: *Art of Fugue,* 76, 77, 86, 180, 201; *Brandenburg Concerti,* 86; cyclical treatment, 183; Fugue in C sharp minor, 120; *Gold-*

berg Variations, 76; law of contrast, 92; *logos* of Western music, 86; mathematical uniformity, 86; *Orgelbüchlein,* 72; Passacaglia in C minor, 85; polyphony, 110; rational method of composition, 77; regulated church music, 77; suprasensory scheme, 77; synthesis of Baroque, 75, 87; *Well-Tempered Clavier,* 75
Bacon, Francis, 34, 54, 55
Badura-Skoda, Paul, 191
Baer, Ernst von, 140
Bagehot, Walter, 154
Balzac, 165, 167
Baroque music, 71, 75, 84, 183
Barzun, Jacques, 56, 154, 158, 168
"Basic shape," 105
Batteux, Charles, 60, 62
Bauman, Alvin, 98
Beach, Joseph W., 43, 159
Beardsley, Monroe C., 108
Beethoven, Ludwig van; adding or exchanging movements, 88; *Apassionata* Sonata, 187; classicism, 88; contact with Goethe, 39; cyclical themes, 105; *Eroica* Symphony, 90; Fifth Symphony, 187; fugal technique, 188; funeral marches, 180; late style, 189–90; *Les Adieux* Sonata, 184; metamorphosis of themes, 39; Ninth Symphony, 187; Opus 81 A, 180, 181; *Pastoral* Symphony, 184; *Pathétique* Sonata, 184; progenitor of Brahms, Berlioz, Liszt, and Wagner, 39; recitative-like passages, 185; Romanticism, 184; Sonata Op. 10, No. 1, 104; Sonata Op. 14, No. 2, 95; Violin Sonata in A Major, 96; *Waldstein* Sonata, 187
Bentham, Jeremy, 63, 67